BOBBY MOORE

BOBBY MOORE

The Life and Times of a Sporting Hero

Jeff Powell

ROBSON BOOKS

Dedicated to the lasting memory of a
great friend

This edition published in Great Britain in 2002 by Robson Books,
64 Blenheim Court, London N7 9NT

A member of Chrysalis Books plc

Copyright © 1993, 2002 Jeff Powell

The right of Jeff Powell to be identified as author of this work has been asserted
by him in accordance with the Copyright, Designs and Patent Act 1988

British Library Cataloguing in Publication Data
A catalogue record for this title is available from the British Library

ISBN 1 86105 511 0

Printed in Great Britain by Creative Print & Design (Wales), Ebbw Vale

Contents

Acknowledgements

The author wishes to record his perpetual appreciation to Bobby Moore for more than a quarter of a century of valued friendship and shared confidences. This relationship was fundamental to the preparation of his authorised biographies.

His thanks also to Stephanie Moore for telling the moving story of their years together, to Tina, Roberta and Dean Moore for their loving memories, to the *Daily Mail* for its invaluable support, to John Moynihan for his caring research and, most especially, to his own wife, Maria, for all her loyalty, love and understanding.

BOBBY MOORE

1

The Impact

It was 6.36 a.m. on the morning of February 24 1993 and the news which was to have such a profound impact on the people of Britain, provoke such an extraordinary outpouring of human emotion, inspire such an unprecedented sense of national loss and be borne around the globe with such sadness, was to remain a private matter for a little longer.

Robert Frederick Chelsea Moore, the public's last hero but an essentially private man, still belonged to his family.

The first fingers of dawn were tugging at the curtains of the charming corner residence cloistered behind electronic gates among other homes of taste and substance high on Putney Heath. It was quiet for the moment but what his wife and children knew from experience was that the instant word of his passing filtered to the outside world there would be no peace. And there would be more than a new day tapping at the window.

The revelation that Bobby Moore was seriously ill had been made only ten days earlier. It had been withheld until an accumulation of small changes in his commanding appearance had begun prompting inquiries as to his health. It had been delayed to defer speculation as to his prospects for survival.

Although the family had known for almost two years, since major intestinal surgery in April 1991, that his cancer was terminal, they had helped him maintain for as long as humanly possible – super-humanly in truth – the gallant and convincing facade that, as he put it in one of his familiar phrases, 'all is well'.

It seemed too soon. There was no reason, yet, for the media at large to be gathered in waiting at Lynden Gate.

Softly, one by one, Stephanie notified his uncles and aunts, cousins, nephews and nieces. The boyhood loss of his father and the recent burial of his mother had tied the most famous Moore son closely to this thoroughly decent, disarmingly old-fashioned family the like of which used to be the salt of London's East End community.

Stephanie called her own mother and father, of whom Bobby had grown increasingly fond. And she telephoned me to help prepare the formal statement. This would not be released until Roberta and Dean had waited for the sun to rise over the east coast of the United States before waking their mother, Tina, at her new home in Florida. Nor until their father had been removed in continuing peace to the premises of a funeral director who had been sworn to secrecy.

Unofficially, the word was spreading. But the dam held long enough to serve its purpose. When it broke it released a tidal wave of admiration, a flood of tributes, an ocean of nostalgia and a river of tears.

All were of such overwhelming magnitude that our society found itself challenged to accept the real significance of this footballer of humble birth and simple origin but princely integrity and regal aspirations, challenged to realise his importance to a succession of generations, challenged to assess his influence over the English way of life both now and in the future.

It came swelling up, as he would have wished, not from the privileged socialites who had sought briefly to bask in his reflected glory but then turned their backs on him, not from the self-important football institutions which had failed him in later life, but from the vast body of ordinary people.

Suddenly, as if guilty at having failed sufficiently to acknowledge its debt to this heroic defender of forgotten virtues and collapsing standards, England recognised the loss of something pure, something honest, something good, something intangible but something impossible to replace.

The national mourning ran – runs yet and maybe always will run – at least as deep as if a member of the Royal Family had died. Perhaps much deeper, given the House of Windsor's fall from grace during the months through which the most gracious of England's sporting captains rose so nobly above the ravages of cancer.

Bobby Moore was the Sixties icon. His was the decade in which the trapdoor of opportunity opened so that talent irrespective of background could come thrusting into the light. Moore, the representative supreme of the working man's game, became the symbol of hope to so many. Here was majestic, living proof that we could all make good.

The East End war baby with his fresh-faced universal appeal and his upright bearing in defiance of the class system transcended all the barriers to become the champion not just of the working class but of all the people. He had the style, the charm and the intelligence to walk with kings. He retained his compassion for others and an attachment to his roots to remain one of the common people. And proud of it.

Everyman was born.

The day Everyman died he touched the raw nerve of the Nineties to comparably dramatic and influential effect.

Britain's descent from a civilised society respected around the world into a primitive underworld of criminal violence, mob savagery, terrifying aggression, unemployed psychopathy and, by the very least of its manifestations, uncouth manners, was accelerating.

In the short time between the making public of Moore's illness and the morning of his passing the unspoken fears of the silent majority became tragically and intensely focused by the abduction of an innocent two-year-old child from a shopping precinct in Liverpool and his ghastly murder by the side of a railway track.

The brutal termination of this little boy's life compelled this country to address not merely the burgeoning issue of juvenile crime but also the chronic incidence of child abuse and molestation of the aged, statistics so rampantly high as to shame Britain in the eyes of the world.

When Bobby Moore went soon after it was likened to the dying of the light. It occurred so abruptly to so many anxious citizens that their last hope had died with him. Harnessed to his comparative youth – he was 47 days short of his 52nd birthday – that acute sense of loss then became transformed into a mighty force which swept the length and breadth of the land.

No life, young or old, was left untouched by his passing. He became enshrined as the symbol of how civilised life ought to be lived. He represented hope and good. Donations poured in to his chosen charity as the country simply refused to let his example perish.

Since it seemed there was no one else left to pick up the flag for all that is honest, responsible and worthwhile, Moore's spirit carried it beyond the grave.

Yes, he was my friend. No, this evaluation is not far-fetched. Newspapers are also the litmus paper of the population. Sometimes they dictate the colour of public thinking but in matters this close to the heart they know the wisdom of taking the nation's temperature, not trying to raise it.

In all the millions of sentences expended across endless miles of newsprint – as well as spoken on television and radio – there was not one critical word.

Jeffrey Richards, professor of cultural history at Lancaster University, lamented Moore's passing when he wrote in the *Daily Mail*: 'The new Englishman is increasingly being seen as a brutish and leering figure with little or no right to respect. He combines the thuggishness of Vinny Jones with the oafishness of Gazza, the brutishness of Johnny Rotten with the boorishness of Bernard Manning.'

Keith Waterhouse, the people's playwright, completed the philosophical equation in his complementary column: 'No wonder Bobby Moore's death leaves us with such a sense of loss.'

In its way the uncompromising, down-to-earth respect for Moore was manna from heaven for the media. Yet while his memory was milked it did no harm. Not to his family, not to his friends, not to his followers, not to that memory itself.

Those tribute acres were his proper due. Sadly, they came too late for the man himself to see and hear how deeply he was loved in his own country. Whenever and wherever he travelled abroad Bobby was greeted with a respect and affection verging on awe.

Even America, the land of baseball to which soccer is an alien game, identified Moore's social significance. *The New York Times* devoted more than a full column of its front page to an explanation of how his death was acting as a re-unifying force within an ageing nation threatened by violent division, the breakdown of law and order and the collapse of its moral society.

At home his own genuine modesty and the inbred restraint of his countrymen when it comes to expressing emotion had combined to separate Bobby from England's latent admiration.

As a nation, we took our hero for granted. Although not quite to the very end. In those few days after his illness became a matter of public sorrow the surge of appreciation began and he remained lucid and able to read the first of what mushroomed into countless triumphant reviews of his own life.

Those columns were no more than a foretaste of the patriotic volumes of praise which were to follow, but he enjoyed them just the same. Just as he would have smiled, on the morning after his funeral, at the final paragraph of one leading article. All the more so since it appeared in one of the brasher tabloids of which he was somewhat wary. This is how it read:

God can tell Heaven's Eleven to start getting changed. The captain has arrived.

2

The Lap of Honour

Obituaries are never easy.

By a reversal of normal fortunes, so far as what used to be called Fleet Street is concerned, they come even tougher when you have to write one about a subject you know well.

While a little knowledge can lend the appearance of informed objectivity to the black border section of the newspaper, too much intimate detail can lead the author into a literary minefield booby-trapped with excessive fragments of potential trivia.

There is also the danger of submerging clarity in a wash of sentiment. Which makes it all the harder when you love the person who has died.

And I loved Bobby Moore.

I loved him, if not like the brother neither he nor I ever had then the way one single child can relate to another ... finding good companionship, sharing good times, exchanging confidences, being there in a crisis, helping out in times of need, leaning on someone reliable when the problem is on the other shoulder, picking up the phone on a whim, debating sport as well as our life and times and being happy to get together either by chance or design.

Our friendship started slowly, gathered strength through the maturing years of his playing career, then became firmly cemented by a host of shared experiences culminating when we helped each other to the altar. A couple of older – but please never wiser – chaps smitten with two younger – and thank you beautiful – women.

Bobby did not come easy, either. It took time and loyalty to win his trust but we came to be as relaxed in each other's company as only good friends can be . . . and only when their wives approve.

We could pick up where we left off no matter how long the interval. So when we each returned from separate trips to America this fateful February and the first message was one to call him urgently the alarm bells began ringing even before the telephone.

When he had undergone his major operation at the London Clinic we had been concerned by the implications. Although he rallied impressively, recovered his age-defying physical condition and quickly re-engaged us in life on the golf links and the tennis court, in the bar and the restaurant, at his home or ours, we wondered if all really was as well as he insisted.

With characteristic lack of concern for himself he had been shielding his friends from the tragic reality. For a few hours longer he continued to do so:

'Hello, Bobby. How are you?'

'Tremendous holiday.'

'What's happening?'

'How about a drink?'

'Great.'

'See you lunchtime tomorrow at the Royal Garden.'

It was light conversation as normal. With Bobby it was hard to tell if something serious lay beneath the easy surface. And at first it did not occur to me that he had chosen this particular hotel not for its convenience of location in Kensington but because it was the very one in which he and his England colleagues had celebrated the night they won World Cup.

Bobby Moore was setting out on his last lap of honour.

It was Friday, February 12 and it was a miracle he was still able to do so. Unbeknown to all outside his family, unconfirmed by superficial observation of the fine figure of a man the world had always known, that insidious, indiscriminate cancer had spread from his colon to his liver and he had been fighting mightily for his life.

When he walked tall into the bar at the Royal Garden it was an imperceptible fraction more slowly than usual. There was a faint discoloration of the features of the kind which attends jaundice and when he ordered no more than a glass of water, a touch unusual for Bobby, I knew there were grounds for concern.

But in my heart I knew before he told me: 'We've got to get a statement out soon. One or two people have started asking questions. I have got cancer. Only Stephanie and the close family know. I am sorry to have to break it to you first. I don't want a paper chase so let's keep it correct and as pleasant as possible. No unseemly scramble. My illness is nobody's exclusive. How shall we do it?'

The details were simple. A news agency advisory statement issued early enough on Sunday evening to give all elements of the media a chance to react. An embargo on publication or broadcast – broken only by Sky News – until shortly after 11 p.m. so that Bobby and Stephanie could be in bed, telephone switched to automatic, safe from intrusion at least until morning.

The dismay was the problem. Hand on his arm. Got to ask: 'What's the diagnosis? What do the doctors say?'

Bobby always could communicate more with a single gesture than most men with a thousand words. Ask his World Cup teammates. So he smiled. Just slightly.

And he thought for a moment before drawing attention to his coat.

I had ribbed him about it on arrival. It was cut full-length from soft leather dyed deep red and it sported a multi-coloured silk lining. It was a hint more obvious than his usual, classic mode of attire and he used it cleverly to convey the truth: 'You remember when we were in Sweden last summer at the European Championships and I went shopping with Stephanie? Well, it was in the shop on the corner. It was something different. And it was lovely quality and at £600 I thought it was good value.

'I thought if I didn't buy it then I might never have something like it. But I never wore it. Not until now. If I don't wear it today . . .'

The sentence tailed into silence. I knew then he was on that farewell tour of his best-remembered places.

We cleared our throats and talked of old times, good days, long nights. We walked slowly to the revolving door and stood for a time on the steps from which he had reached out that summer's evening long ago to embrace a jubilant multitude.

We held each other's shoulders and we parted with a hug. We checked that we were both going to Wembley on Wednesday, him to offer his last words of wisdom as a commentator for Capital Radio, me for the *Mail*.

So we did and I stood by him while he chatted and joked with fellow members of the media about the modern England's World Cup difficulties against San Marino, the kind of team his England would have swamped. And I couldn't help but chuckle when I heard how he had stepped out of his car later to direct the traffic through Wembley's post-match congestion and all the drivers had jump-started to his command.

God knows how he even made it to Wembley, but somehow he did and he carried it off in style. He hoped to pay his last respects to West Ham four days later but that proved to be one match too far. We spoke on the telephone that Sunday afternoon and he just said: 'Bit too tired today, old son. But might see you later in the week. How's the family?'

Not once had he complained. Not once had he asked, 'Why me?'

That was our last conversation but we had said our goodbyes on those hotel steps. The statement we agreed that day quoted him as saying he had a battle to fight. That was enough to satisfy a curious world but in truth he had already fought the good fight and brave for almost two years.

Still it was hard to accept. Still I couldn't bring myself to start putting his life into words until the call came from the woman he loved.

Obituaries are never easy. This one seemed impossible. But I wrote it and I walked away from the office and next day people were generous enough to say it told them about the Bobby Moore they knew and about the Bobby Moore they wanted to know about.

And the family were kind enough to say they would like it to be kept in these pages for anyone someday who might like to read about the footballer who changed our lives and times.

So this, also by way of introduction to the chronicle of the rich, full life which follows, is what the six million readers of the *Daily Mail* read on the stunned morning of February 25 1993:

PERFECTIONIST TO THE FINAL WHISTLE

The manner of his leaving was in keeping with the man's way of living. No commotion, no complaint, no thought for himself and, most typically of all, no loose ends.

Bobby Moore was not only the world's most imperial defender but also the most immaculate footballer ever to grace the vast theatres of the people's game.

The meticulous attention to detail, the scrupulous care with appearance, the exact precision of time-keeping, the constant observation of manners which maketh a gentleman out of a hero, all were with him to the premature end.

A perfectionist to the last, right down to the uncanny antici-pation and instinctive sense of occasion which were the essence of his sporting genius. With only days to spare, Moore paid his farewell visits to the places where he had savoured the richest vintage of his fame.

The last public appearance was at Wembley, the nostalgic stadium he made his personal domain, and since it followed the announcement of his cancer the great man's presence at the radio microphone stirred warmer interest than England's World Cup fumblings against San Marino.

A lot of arms went round those still straight-back shoulders that night, a final, collective embrace from the family of football in all its generations.

No loose ends.

Our last personal reunion took place at the Royal Garden, the Kensington hotel at which England celebrated its only winning of the World Cup. We stood on the steps from which he had reached out to touch hands with the throng which stopped the mighty roar of London's traffic and replaced it with full-throated acclaim for the captain and his boys of '66.

Moore smiled as he remembered that heady, midsummer's evening more than a quarter of a century ago: 'You know, old son, we had the world at our feet that night.'

No loose ends.

Beneath his feet, as he spoke, lay a time capsule lodged in the foundation stone of the building, crammed with data on the twentieth century, waiting to be opened by some future life form.

The exact contents are a secret, but for sure the story of how a working-class boy came to take delivery from his Queen of the most prized piece of silverware on the planet, has been used to explain how the human species wove so many strands of its very existence into a round-ball game.

Robert Frederick Chelsea Moore – Chelsea after a paternal uncle, not the football club or the fashionable London borough – was born on April 12, 1941 in Barking, a rough-and-tumble border town on the cusp of Essex and East London.

From childhood he was painstakingly neat and clean, scrubbed spotless, school socks pulled up straight, a crease in his short pants, his books on their shelves, toys in their box and never a hair out of place, forget about dandruff on his lapels.

No detail was minute enough to be ignored and it was this unflagging characteristic which was the bedrock of his career. Not the most naturally gifted athlete – slow, weak left foot, less than commanding in the air – he applied remorseless practice and rare intelligence to perfecting his strengths and playing to them.

Ron Greenwood, West Ham's believer in the beautiful game, was the making of Moore and Alf Ramsey, England's tactical pragmatist, used him to fulfilment. Between them those two managers charted Moore's halcyon years.

The Sixties was the decade in which English society lifted the class barriers and patronised lads with more talent than breeding. The Cockney photographer, the Gorbals actor, the Yorkshire painter and, led by Moore, the heart-throb footballer stepped over from the wrong side of the tracks into the most polite drawing rooms. No dinner party was complete without one, not once the World Cup was won.

Moore prepared for football's ultimate moment by leading West Ham to the 1964 FA Cup and, also at Wembley, the 1965 European Cup Winners' Cup. Add all the faultless games there for England and he knew the hallowed turf like the carpet in his house on stockbroker row, could find his way up the Royal Box staircase blindfold.

The 1966 tournament was overflowing with supreme foot-ballers – Pele, Eusebio, a promising young West German called Beckenbauer ranged against the host nation in the Final itself –

as well as household English names like Banks and Stiles, Charlton and Ball, Hurst and Peters. But by the time Moore came to climb those steps once more, to espy Her Majesty's white lace gloves and so wipe his muddied hands on the velvet balustrade before reaching out for the Jules Rimet Trophy, there was only one Player of the Championship.

The captain's overwhelming composure, calculated suppression of emotion and self-possessed resistance to pressure, imbued Moore with an aura of haughty, almost arrogant superiority in the estimation of most of the international media.

Nevertheless, their vote for the ice-man was as near to unanimous as made no difference.

It was sealed in the closing moments of extra time against the Germans. With England leading 3–2 by courtesy of a Russian linesman he laid claim to the ball amid the pandemonium of his own penalty area, ignored Big Jack's bellowing entreaties to kick it over the twin towers, stepped calmly around two lunging opponents and floated out the inch-perfect pass which launched Geoff Hurst towards his historic hat-trick and commentator Ken Wolstenholme into his unforgettable line: 'They think it's all over, it is now.'

No loose ends.

Pele and Beckenbauer, Eusebio and his own team-mates are in mourning for him now. They knew the real Bobby Moore behind the chilling professional mask and the tackle like a vice, the lovable, loyal man devoid of ego who could laugh and cry with the best of them. They jousted with him through a golden age when not even the loftiest rivals ever lost respect for each other.

They recall not only Wembley '66 but Mexico '70, the World Cup year of Moore's sternest trial and England's strongest team but their mutual disappointment.

The ice-man hurried into the Finals from house arrest in Bogota, where the Colombian authorities had held him on a preposterous charge of stealing an emerald bracelet. He played majestically, as if nothing but football had ever been on his mind. At the conclusion of an epic duel in Brazil's group, Pele trotted past all other supplicants among his English opponents to exchange shirts with the man he calls: 'The finest and most honourable defender I ever played against.'

They would surely have met again in the final had Ramsey, by then Sir Alf, not substituted Bobby Charlton at two up against Germany in the quarter final and thereby invited the full-grown Franz Beckenbauer to run rampant. Extra-time revisited, but reversed.

So Bobby came home to mutterings about a bracelet instead of carrying another World Cup medal. He maintained a stoic, understated defence, privately and steadfastly protecting the one witness who could have silenced the whispers forever. Once, late at night, he swore me to secrecy and confided that one of the younger lads in the squad might have done 'something foolish, a prank with unfortunate consequences.'

No name was forthcoming and he took the culprit's identity with him to the grave.

No loose ends.

Here was loyalty of the highest order from a man who led not by word but by deed and example. When his first marriage, to Tina his boyhood sweetheart, broke up and he set up home with his beloved Stephanie, he shouldered all the blame. No complaint. Suffice it to say now that there are two sides to every divorce.

It was not always loyalty repaid, not even by the game he dignified.

Sir Alf dropped him for his only notable blunder in more than a hundred appearances for his country, a second managerial misjudgement punished when Norman Hunter committed a carbon copy in the return game with Poland which knocked England out of the 1974 World Cup and began the end of the Ramsey era.

Moore the human computer would never have repeated that error had he won another 108 caps, still a record for an outfield player. Only goalkeepers go on forever.

His country gave him the OBE but his game gave him the elbow. Ramsey described him as 'my general on the field who translates our strategy into reality.' His game was built on intelligence and, when still a teenager, he became the youngest holder of the Football Association's full coaching badge.

Yet while his alter-ego Beckenbauer led Germany to another World Cup as head coach, Moore's best offer in management was a mission impossible at Southend. While his great rival Pele became FIFA's ambassador to the world, the FA chose to ignore his treasure chest of knowledge, even though a succession of England teams were crying out for help.

His radio audience learned that 'you can't defend on your backside' while his successors down there on the Wembley pitch kept sliding into difficulty. Greenwood watched and listened with a smile: 'Bobby would stroll across to the near post and catch most of the crosses they put in these days on his chest. In fact he did it so often at West Ham we used to say he would end up with a hole in his chest.'

But it was the hole in his stomach which beat him in the end, that and the perforations of his liver. Still no complaint. 'Can't blame it on the old liver,' he said at our last meeting. 'Did us proud down the years.'

I went home and replayed some of the tapes recorded when we had gathered up all his memories for his biography. The recollections are interrupted by the frequent hiss of lager cans being opened. Never mind football, you didn't take on Bobby at drinking.

'A car needs petrol,' he used to say. Especially a high performance job like Bobby Moore. So when the fuel finally ran out you remembered the night in Turin after he had played against Italy and passed the other Bobby's record number of England caps. It was turned 6 a.m. when we wandered back to the hotel and he said: 'Back down at seven.' The rest of us complied, looking like death. He reappeared showered and spruce, all in the cause of seeing a team of amateur footballers from England on to their tour bus with a crate of champagne.

Last out of the bar, first in for training. That was Bobby Moore, the arch defender, the scourge of the Scots, the envy of the football world. It seemed he was indestructible.

As recently as September 1992 he turned out at a charity golf tournament, hit the ball out of sight, then sat down to lunch next to the Barnado boy who caddied for him. Until December he still looked as if he should be playing for England and thousands despairing of some of the new generation of defenders wished he would.

Yet long before recognition of his gaunt appearance prompted his admission of his illness, he knew his days were numbered. When they operated on his colon in April 1991 the specialists told Bobby his condition was terminal. He, in turn, told only the closest of his family and set about defying the odds.

Moore's in-built strength of will and physique drove him back into training and he held off even the customary ravages of chemotherapy. He treated death with all the respect he gave a dangerous forward, denying his opponent space in which to advance, cutting off his avenues of penetration, diverting him into areas where he could do least damage, always keeping his feet.

Thus he bought himself two years of extra-time, played and lived to the full, free from curious intrusion and spared the gush of sentiment he would have found embarrassing. He enjoyed friends unburdened by confirmation of his plight and he worked on, tidying his affairs as he went. His father died years ago and he buried his mother in 1992.

No loose ends.

Although fated never to succeed in business, he was lucky in love. Stephanie, the bright and cultured British Airways girl who had stabilised his life, became his pillar of support in death.

They married in December 1991, in time, in private, with myself and my wife as witnesses-in-chief and delighted to be so, I couldn't remember ever seeing him so happy, an honest man making certain he would be leaving an honest woman.

No loose ends.

When he knew he wasn't going to make his fifty-second birthday, when the time came to say goodbye, he looked me in the eye and said: 'It's cancer. That's nothing to be ashamed of, is it?'

Ashamed? Not only England, the whole of Britain is proud of him. The style with which he captained his country and the dignity with which he conducted himself remain a monument as to how football should be played and footballers should behave.

A more tangible memorial would not be out of place at Wembley: The Bobby Moore Steps. Because he died as he lived, the first and only Englishman to walk up them and raise the World Cup aloft.

The loss is ours. England has lost a distinguished ambassador, the world of football has lost a giant, Mrs. Moore has lost a loving husband. Roberta and Dean have lost a devoted father, little Poppy has lost a grandfather far too young and I have lost a friend who, when the mood and the after-dinner wine took him, imagined he could sing like Frank Sinatra.

We'll be seeing him in all the old familiar places . . .

3

Under the Influences

Bobby Moore was 17 the night he nerved himself to walk into West Ham's first team across the debris of Malcolm Allison's broken dreams.

The anguish behind the eyes of Allison's bold handshake was the image burned deepest into Moore's memory of that autumn evening in 1958 when the roar of a huge crowd first prickled his spine, when he first sniffed the addictive aroma of stardom.

It was not the new boy's thrill of playing the Manchester United legend off Upton Park which fidgeted with Moore's mind during his long, insomniac nights.

Through solitary hours spent counting shadows on bedroom ceilings, Moore still nursed the faint sense of guilt that his own precocious arrival on the central stage of English Soccer denied Allison the fulfilment of his own playing career. In the moment of Moore's accession to the No. 6 shirt, Allison lost his forlorn chance of playing just once in the First Division for West Ham United.

Allison, the man who taught Moore all he knew. Allison, his idol. Allison, friend. Allison, inspirational fighter against the gasping corrosion of tuberculosis. Allison, having put young Bobby on the road from West Ham's worst apprentice to England's most-capped international, turned from his protegee to walk heavily from the dressing room.

For that one night only, Big Mal was a beaten man. Yet of everything he gave Moore, that unwilling sacrifice was the most important. Bobby watched him go through a confusion of emotions, elation at his own imminent debut bruised by pity for the man whose teaching had made it possible. His own future was at the mercy of his feelings.

Many an adolescent might have collapsed under the weight of the guilt. Instead, Moore's boyhood went out into the corridor with Allison. As the door closed, Bobby shut out his feelings, locked away in some hidden corner of his private self all the dangerous turmoil of excitement, fear, passion and compassion.

Before he even kicked a ball, he was being forged into the haughty captain of England. The immaculate Bobby Moore was conceived out of Allison's most grievous disappointment.

He went out and wowed them.

West Ham, newcomers to the First Division, beat Manchester United 3–2. The press telephones chattered acclaim for a new young master of the defensive arts.

Moore smiled at that 'I just hit a couple of balls straight. Nothing really.'

The Allison connection could only be dredged up from the bottom of a long, long glass. Even then, Moore probed gingerly at the memory:

'Malcolm had been battling for months to recover from tuberculosis. I'd even seen him the day he got the news of his illness. I was a groundstaff boy and I'd gone to Upton Park to collect my wages. I saw Malcolm standing on his own on the balcony at the back of the stand. Tears in his eyes. Big Mal actually crying.

'He'd been coaching me and coaching me and coaching me but I still didn't feel I knew him well enough to go up and ask what was wrong.

'When I came out of the office I looked up again and Noel Cantwell was standing with his arm round Malcolm. He'd just been told he'd got T.B.

'It wasn't like Malcolm to give up. By the start of that '58 season we were battling away together in the reserves, Malcolm proving he could still play, me proving I might be able to play one day.

'West Ham had just come up. They went to Portsmouth and won. They beat Wolves at home in their second game. After three or four matches they were top of the First Division, due to play Manchester United on the Monday night, and they had run out of left halves. Billy Lansdowne, Andy Nelson, all of them were unfit. It's got to be me or Malcolm.

'I'd been a professional for two and a half months and Malcolm had taught me everything I knew. For all the money in the world I wanted to play. For all the money in the world I wanted Malcolm to play because he'd worked like a bastard for this one game in the First Division.

'It would have meant the world to him. Just one more game, just one minute in that game. I knew that on the day Malcolm with all his experience would probably do a better job than me. But maybe I'm one for the future.

'It somehow had to be that when I walked into the dressing room and found out I was playing, Malcolm was the first person I saw. I was embarrassed to look at him. He said "Well done. I hope you do well." I knew he meant it but I knew how he felt. For a moment I wanted to push the shirt at him and say "Go on, Malcolm. It's yours. Have your game. I can't stop you. Go on, Malcolm. My time will come."

'But he walked out and I thought maybe my time wouldn't come again. Maybe this would be my only chance. I thought: you've got to be lucky to get the chance, and when the chance comes you've got to be good enough to take it.

'I went out and played the way Malcolm had always told me to play. Afterwards I looked for him back in the dressing room. Couldn't find him.'

It went very quiet over Moore's big house when he told the story. He sat surrounded by the plush rewards of all the football years which followed, right hand holding a lager up to the light of a crystal chandelier, left forefinger tracing patterns in condensation on the expensive glass.

It was the sort of silence you are afraid to break with a cough.

Moore shattered the rare and brittle moment himself, snapping the top off another beer. He gulped down the merest hint of embarrassment. This man was accustomed to betraying as much emotion as the Post Office Tower.

Allison taught him that 'Be in control of yourself. Take control of everything around you. Look big. Think big. Tell people what to do.'

The words hummed in Moore's schoolboy ears. He said: 'I was

a boy, training at West Ham on Tuesday and Thursday evenings. Malcolm was in charge, always the commanding figure. For me it was an adventure. Malcolm was the hero.

'Now I see that for him I was the first of a long line of players who he looked upon as his own creations. Malcolm's always had one special player close to him.

'What a challenge it was for him to take an older player like Tony Book up from Bath and Plymouth to Manchester City. Then there was Mike Summerbee, then Colin Bell. He bought Rodney Marsh for City to be like a son he could adore. At Crystal Palace he had Don Rogers and then Peter Taylor. Malcolm has to have one.

'Well I was the first, when Malcolm was coaching schoolboys. He took a liking to me when I don't think anyone else at West Ham saw anything special in me. Just for that, I would have done anything for him. Every house needs a foundation and Malcolm gave me mine.

'It went beyond that. He was the be-all and end-all for me. I looked up to the man. It's not too strong to say I loved him.'

Behind that rush of sentiment lay Moore's undying gratitude for the simple philosophy which was the basis for his reputation as a player of vision, as the best reader of a football match in the world.

Moore's capacity for detecting the subtlest shifts and eddies of the highest quality play was the priceless gift handed down to him in one sentence by Allison.

Moore explained: 'Malcolm said one simple thing which was to stay in my life forever. We sometimes used to get the same bus from the ground and we were sitting upstairs one day when Malcolm said very quietly: "Keep forever asking yourself: If I get the ball now, who will I give it to?" He told me that was di Stefano's secret at Real Madrid.

'So simple. So real. So easy. I carried that with me into the middle of Wembley, Maracana, Hampden Park, every great stadium.

'Wherever it was, I would always know that maybe the left back was free, the right winger running, the inside left dropping off his man into space for me.

'There's nothing complicated about vision. It's pictures in your mind, put there purely and simply by looking around yourself. It's good because it's so simple. The bad players are the players who make the game difficult. I passed that piece of Malcolm on down to one or two players I believed could benefit. I'll always be in Malcolm's debt for that insight. It was like suddenly looking into the sunshine.'

The vision, however, did not blind Moore to the imperfections in Allison's life style. Bobby swallowed Malcolm's football philosophy, ran in many of the same social circles, but always held back something of himself, refusing to dive headfirst into the whirlpool of self-indulgence.

In his later years as captain of West Ham and England, Moore was probably more aloof from the majority of his fellow players than was Allison as manager of Manchester City and Crystal Palace.

Far from curbing the social habits of his players, Allison more often led them gaily into the night clubs and up to the bars. There was a swagger about such behaviour. It has style. It has dash. But it has dangers, and not only in Manchester's Piccadilly or London's Park Lane.

Even in the sunshine of a 1973 Summer in South Africa, Allison caught a cold. In a country where sport and the social life are the white man's haven from political criticism, Malcolm's high octane mixture of the two brought trouble to his touring team.

Moore said: 'Malcolm had a great life but he left some question marks behind him *en route*. As a manager I would have wanted to be part of my players. But only up to a point. I wouldn't have thought about taking them out to night clubs. I would like to feel that after a game I could go round to the local pub and have a drink with them.

'Come seven o'clock I would say "I'm going home." I might be going out somewhere later myself. But not with the lads. How else could you discipline people? I would have told Mike Summerbee he had it in him to be the greatest winger in the world and to go out and prove it to me every game. If he failed, he would have to get in the reserves and prove he was still in good physical condition. I don't know if Malcolm left himself the right to do that.

'Look at South Africa. I went there, had a marvellous time.

Malcolm went there with a team of great players: Rodney Marsh, Frank McLintock, Don Rogers.

'Yet they got diabolical publicity and I asked myself why? Why do it, Malcolm? He's no different from me in that whatever he does is going to get blown up by the publicity. We know that, and it happened to me once or twice, yet I've managed to stay clear of day-to-day troubles.

'Malcolm should have conquered South Africa but the truth is that he has a streak in him which made him abuse people or a situation. I appreciate life and don't want to spoil it for myself. If people put themselves out for me I won't abuse them.

'That's the difference between us and that difference is why I can't support Malcolm blindly in everything he does. Much as I love him as a man, much as I respect his knowledge of football, I still have to question him in my mind.'

That process of clinical reappraisal was digging to the very roots of Allison's teaching 15 years later, in Bobby's last season at West Ham.

Like a reliable computer, Moore's mind sifted its input of information absolutely on merit, aloof from the apparent importance of the source.

Hence the impact of one Lenny Heppell, ballroom dancer and night club proprietor who strictly belongs no closer to football than a distant relative. He is father-in-law to Bryan 'Pop' Robson, once a regular scorer of goals with Newcastle, West Ham and Sunderland.

Heppell had been loosely involved with West Ham for the best part of a year before he secured a firm introduction to Bobby Moore.

He moved south from Durham in the wake of his son-in-law's transfer from Sunderland and began to work with a handful of West Ham players on their balance and timing. Moore remembered thinking: 'What the hell's he doing? I can't believe in that nonsense.'

For months they exchanged no more than a good morning nod. The more appearances Heppell made at Upton Park, the more remote England's captain seemed. Moore had no problem presenting a forbidding exterior when he sensed someone fidgeting to get into his company.

Heppell got no further than 'hullo' until one day in February 1974 Moore went into a local steak house for lunch and found a spare chair at a table with Robson, Trevor Brooking and Lenny Heppell. Moore admitted he had enjoyed a lager or two after a hard morning's training and sat relaxed and easy in his chair.

Heppell looked across and said: 'I'm glad you're sitting like that.' Moore, on the defensive said: 'What do you mean?'

'I'm glad to see you relaxed and round shouldered. I never thought you could relax.'

'You don't know me. Maybe it's because I've had a lager.'

It was not the friendliest start to a relationship. Yet the seeds of interest were sown.

Moore said: 'I had a few sessions with him after that and he made simple common sense. He made me question the very first thing Malcolm ever told me: Stand big.

'Lenny told me I ran like a coat hanger. Upright. I looked at myself on television and saw he was right. It was what Malcolm had told me 15 years earlier. It made me look big alright but it made my running harder and slower. Lenny talked me into rolling my shoulders but not my body.

'West Ham went to play up at Newcastle and I knew Lenny was watching so I ran out the way he wanted. We lost, so it sounds crazy to say it, but it worked. I made one long run, the sort of run that would have had me blowing hard a few weeks earlier, and this time I was fresh and ready to go again.

'I watched myself on TV the next day, the Sunday. I looked terrific. It made me want to get out there and play, the way watching Tom Mix at the Saturday morning pictures made you want to go out and play Cowboys and Indians.

'Lenny got on at me then about turning. He told me to turn like the ballroom dancers – head first. It was logic when he made you think about it. He told me to turn my head and my body would follow. He made me notice that when I crossed the road I leaned forward head first. My feet followed. I started throwing my head and instead of falling flat on my face, my feet would follow.

'Simple? To me it was magic. It was something I wished I had heard years before. My turning and speed of movement had improved one hundred per cent. It was a bit late for me. But Lenny was helping the others. He told Trevor Brooking exactly the opposite to me. Trevor was too relaxed. Easy-ohsy, flopping here, flopping there. Lenny tensed him up. Put some oomph in him. Next thing Trevor's in the England team.

'Makes you realise that too many people in football think they know everything and don't want to listen to people outside the game.'

Nevertheless, Moore still needed a conscious effort to resist Allison's indoctrination. Unthinking, he stood erect at his private bar dispensing the drinks. Shoulders back.

The house was named with head-high pride: Morlands. In some distant corner the au pair was putting the children to bed. The latest in a succession of fast cars sat crouched and ready in the drive.

By road, it was perhaps ten miles from the chimneys of indust-rial Barking to the charm of stockbroker Chigwell. Essex is a county of sharp contrasts. Materially, Moore's progress could scarcely be measured. Mentally, he had also come a long way; able to turn a wry phrase around his origins.

'Ordinary street, ordinary people, ordinary home, a few ordi-nary factories in the back garden.'

Robert Frederick Chelsea Moore, only son of Robert and Doris Moore. Born in Upney Hospital on April 12, 1941. Bred in the whimsically mis-named Waverley Gardens, a terraced tributary of Barking's lorry-laden River Road. As destiny would have it, reared no more than a loud cheer from Alf Ramsey's native Dagenham.

Unlike Ramsey, unlike in fact so many local boys made good, Moore showed no desire to cut the umbilical cord which links us all to our heritage. Stretch the ties, yes. Sever them, never.

The voice remained unmistakably working-class-London as Moore recalled: 'I lost my first cup final 3–1 at the age of 12. I couldn't get home fast enough. To my Mum and Dad. To cry my eyes out. They made me see it wasn't the end of the world.

'I thought it was. I thought I was a failure. Deep down I had wanted to play for England way back, when I was a baby in the Barking Primary School team.

'When I passed the 11-plus I went to Tom Hood Grammar School in Leyton. The first two months were murder. I was the only boy from my district. Up at seven a.m., on my own on the bus from home to Barking station, train to Wanstead, trolleybus to Leyton, long walk to the school. I was sick with it. I went to the doctor pining for any sort of school in Barking and got a certificate for a transfer on the grounds of travel sickness.

'The same week, though, I got picked for the district at football. Played for them. Got into that first cup final but didn't realise I'd been spotted.'

The West Ham ground became thick with people willing to claim first sighting of Moore's talent. Between them, they talked Bobby into training at Upton Park.

It was a significant pointer to his personality that he remembered being overawed more vividly than he recalled most of his early triumphs.

'I was,' he said, 'the 13th player on the groundstaff. I was ordinary. I was lucky to be there. And every time I looked at one of the other lads I knew it.

'Every one of them had played for Essex or London, and at least been for trials with England Schoolboys. I had nothing. All around me were players with unbelievable ability. They were the same age as me and I was looking up at them and wishing I was that good, that skilful.

'The first time I got a representative game I played for Essex over-15s because they needed a makeshift centre forward. I kept lumbering down the middle until our keeper hit a big up-and-under clearance which their keeper caught as I bundled him into the net. Very classy.

'The referee was weak – there's a familiar thought – and gave the goal for Essex. Everyone knew it was a joke. Most of all, the lads who knew they were better than me.'

Inferiority was not a complex Moore enjoyed. The longer it lasted, however, the more it became a spur to improvement. 'The best quality I had was wanting to succeed.'

For a time, Moore was a better cricketer than footballer. As a young batsman with a quick eye and characteristic willingness to stand in the line of fire, he captained South of England Schoolboys against the North.

'Colin Milburn was their skipper but I won the toss, we batted, I opened. I'd just reached double figures when I got an edge and Ollie caught me in the slips.

'He said "On your way, Mooro." I was sick. But half an hour later it rained. The match was abandoned. At least I got my innings.'

Essex wanted Moore to take a lot more knocks for them. The County Cricket Club were interested in several other West Ham boys, Geoff Hurst and Martin Peters among them. They knew in which sport the real money was to be made.

Bobby was still a long way from being a perceptive footballer, but he was already a penetrating student of the game. The giants of England football in the early Fifties will be somewhat less than delighted to learn what the young Moore thought of them as he peered down from the terraces.

'When I first started playing, the England team was full of legends. Billy Wright. Stan Matthews. But there was no one, not one player in the England team I idolised.

'It seemed to me to be full of the wrong players. I used to go to Charlton Athletic a lot when they were in the First Division and they always seemed to be playing West Bromwich Albion in front of 70,000 people.

'West Brom, a magic side. Ronnie Allen, Johnny Nicol, Frank Dudley. Above all, Ray Barlow. He was my idol, a great left half. So calm, played it so easy, just knocked it about.

'Don't talk to me about Wright and Matthews. How often did Ray Barlow play for England?'

The answer: Just once, a token cap against Northern Ireland in the 1955 Home Championship. 'Diabolical,' said Moore. Barlow never met Bobby and had no clue to the profound influence he had on young Moore's career. Unsolicited and unexpected, Moore's words came as an overdue tribute to an underrated craftsman of the cloth cap age.

Not until Manchester United's young Duncan Edwards emerged as the brightest of all the Busby Babes for a brief and brutally truncated international career did Moore identify with a hero in the England team:

'I played truant from school to watch Duncan play at White Hart Lane. He put two past Tottenham. He was the Rock of Gibraltar at the back, dynamite coming forward.

'There will never be another player like him. Duncan's death was the greatest tragedy of the United plane crash. I cried when

I heard. I was visiting Malcolm at the time. I'd just been signed on by West Ham and I'd gone down to the T.B. convalescence home at Midhurst in Surrey with Noel. We all sat there crying. Two grown men and me.'

The exact passes of Johnny Haynes wiped away the tears. Never beginning to presume that one day they would be close friends, Moore stood and watched Fulham and England as Haynes gave a never-ending exhibition of how to hit the right pass, at the right moment, with just the right weight on the ball.

'Once you got used to watching that perfection, you realised the rest of the secret. John was always available, always hungry for the ball, always wanting to play. He was the master. I loved watching the player and later I learned to love the man.

'The two go together. I could never feel that close to anyone I did not respect.'

The economy of Barlow, the majesty of Edwards, the artistry of Haynes. The fragments of influence were coming together, waiting to be given their final push into place by Malcolm Allison and his own best friend at West Ham, Noel Cantwell.

'When Malcolm was looking finished as a player I looked to Noel on the pitch. That first year West Ham were back in the First Division, before my game against United, I went to Tottenham to watch them play.

'Noel Cantwell was left back, Noel Dwyer in goal. It was the best display of defending and goalkeeping I'd ever seen. They drew 2–2 but without the two Noels it would have been Spurs by a distance.' By then, West Ham manager Ted Fenton was convinced Bobby was ready. The debut against United was giddy confirmation. The first, sobering fall was already on its way.

'Three days later, on the Saturday, we went up to Nottingham Forest. They were a good team. They'd been to the Cup Final and just then were running third in the League.

'I should have been warned but I was full of myself. I thought it was a doddle. I got the roasting of my life. I've never since been turned over like that.

'A little Scots feller called Johnny Quigley did everything to me. Turned me inside out. There was a big crowd – crowds were big then – and as we came back up the tunnel for the second half they were all shouting "Play on the left half, that's the weak link".

'I thought: "What the hell am I doing here?" We lost 4–0 and the way Quigley took me apart it could have been forty. Embarrassment.

'That night I was having my first date with Tina. I had the paper in my pocket saying how I got roasted. I ripped it up. If I'd had the money I'd have bought every evening paper in London and torn them all up.

'I got dropped. Dropped? I was lucky to ever play again.'

For the rest of that season, Bobby's romance with Tina made better progress than his career. By the summer he had played only a handful of first team games but was holidaying in the South of France with his Ilford girl friend and her family.

On leaving their beach in St Aygulf, he was required to join West Ham's tour in Austria. 'I got the train to Nice where I was to catch a plane to Austria. How did I know where they kept the airport? For hours I walked up and down the seafront there. The Promenade des Anglais. Like an idiot. Suitcase on my head. I didn't have a penny on me. Finally, someone took pity and directed me down the coast road to the airport.'

Like coming up against Johnny Quigley, it was an instructive experience. 'I vowed I'd never let myself get in such a state again. I found it unbelievable that so many senior players couldn't get themselves through customs unless the club secretary was there with the tickets and passports.'

A few hours later, Moore was vowing never to go abroad again. 'I thought club tours were supposed to be glamorous. When I got to Baden Baden we were in an antique hotel and every time a door creaked open an old boy came through it in a wheelchair. They were all there to be cured by the waters.

'Ted Fenton said If I didn't like it I needn't bother to go on another trip.' Moore could smile at the memory countless years, thousands of flying hours and endless miles later. At that point, however, he was still a long way from first team regularity. He doubted he would ever have broken through had West Ham not sold John Smith to Tottenham.

Smith was the white hope of West Ham. Moore was one of the players-in-waiting when Smith considered Tottenham's money worth the risk of fighting Dave Mackay and Danny Blanchflower for a first team place at White Hart Lane.

Moore emerged from the shadows. Smith went into the sort of frustrating decline Bobby felt might have been his own destiny. He said: 'You've got to be lucky even if you know you're good enough to take the chance if it comes. If John hadn't gone to Spurs I might have been a reserve footballer who threw in the towel, gave up the game.'

Moore was pushing 20 when he finally began a full season in the West Ham team. In 1960, that was still young. But for Bobby it had been a long wait.

That season was something less than a riotous success.

'We went to Wolves in the first game, Noel Cantwell at left half and me at left back. We were playing the way the players wanted ... 4–2–4 with plenty of good football. We played well and lost 4–2.

'It went that way for a few games. Playing well but no breaks. Then the manager had his say. He wanted us to hit long through balls from the half way line. We became the world's best hitters of long through balls to nobody from the half way line. We seemed to lose every match 4–0.'

Moore's basic education was complete. That flash of contempt for Ted Fenton was the beginning of an irreverence for most managers.

It bred an artificial relationship with Alf Ramsey, made him fret for transfers to Bill Nicholson at Spurs, Brian Clough at Derby and Malcolm Allison at Crystal Palace, and finally pushed him into the unlikely arms of Alec Stock at Fulham.

Above all it fostered ten years of mutual but uneasy admiration between Moore and one comparably complex, influential and private person.

Ron Greenwood.

4

The Gospel According to St Ron

The end of the 747's heavy climb out of Heathrow was sig-
nalled by the snapping release of three seat belts. Bobby Moore,
Jimmy Greaves and Freddie Harrison were first up the stairs,
racing for the sanctuary of the bar which used to be housed
high in the dome of the Jumbo. The only way to travel to New
York.

The winter of 1970, although meteorologically unremarkable,
blew hard through the littered streets of Upton Park. It seemed
one more cold blast would be enough to dump the local First
Division football team in the gutter with the rest of the garbage.
By way of escapism, watching West Ham that season was as
much a relief from the Cockney working week as cementing the
back yards.

Moore's team were in retreat, momentarily forsaking the
trauma of the relegation struggle for the tinsel of a prestige
friendly against Pele's team, Santos of Brazil.

Yet Moore and Greaves were still very much names to impress
the American public. Harrison, who lurched from the East End
into business on his own wits and the coat-tails of Moore's reputation, was staying close to his partner. Moore: 'By the end of the
runway we were in the bar. Totting.'

Down in the body of the aircraft, as befitted the older-God-
fearing man, Ron Greenwood sat through the formalities, the
nasal blandishments of the air hostess, the permission to loosen
the seat belt. He is invariably unobtrusive. That day he was
an even quieter study in distant thought. Arguably England's

foremost authority on Soccer, Ron Greenwood was now manager of the most tattered team in the First Division.

That Saturday, West Ham had lost 4–1 at Newcastle United, again travelling as badly as Romanian claret. Greenwood had hoped that game would be their salvation. Instead, the result reeked of relegation.

If ever a non-drinker needed a drink . . .

But that was not Greenwood's way. Especially not near his players. He went forward and upward in search of nothing stronger than a throat-cooling Coke.

Harrison obliged. And kept obliging – lacing Greenwood's innocuous order with Bacardi, loosening the worried tongue with rum. Moore enjoyed what he knew to be a juvenile joke. He and Greenwood had arrived at a temporary point of restrained animosity.

Within an hour the spiked drinks put Greenwood where Moore had wanted him. He savoured the moment still. 'I knew the pressure was on him. West Ham were struggling again. The Newcastle result looked a killer. Freddie kept slipping him the Bacardis and he opened up somewhere over the Atlantic.

'He just blurted it out: "I'm going to resign." And he looked at me.' Moore sensed he might have crushed Greenwood then. One savage sentence would have applied the final push. The respect of his most famous player would have been publicly torn away.

Moore, playing the godhead, twirled his glass and said: 'No, Ron. Be bigger than resigning.'

Thus he repaid to Greenwood some of the debt for their early association. In those days he had lapped up all the knowledge the man had to offer and begged for more.

The young Bobby first fell under Greenwood's persuasive influence as an impressionable sixteen-year-old. In October 1957 Moore was recruited to the England Youth Team where Greenwood, then earning his living as assistant manager of Arsenal, was flexing the more progressive of his ideas.

Greenwood briefed the boy on how to handle Holland in Amsterdam's daunting Olympic Stadium and Moore's representative career began with a 3–2 away win. He said: 'I was magic that first night and I loved Ron for helping me. Coming home on the plane I grabbed the seat next to him and cross-questioned him wicked about football, football, football.

'For a long time it was the same. I followed him around like a puppy, being a pest to him. Picking his brains. It went on when he was manager of the England under-23 team and then when he came to West Ham to take over from Ted Fenton.'

Moore always glowed at the memory of the compliment Greenwood paid him at that time: 'Ron told me one of his major reasons for coming to West Ham was that he knew he had me there to start building his team around.'

The metaphorical flirtation during those meetings for junior international matches moved to a close and regularised club footing. As in many a marriage, the first rows were about money. 'There was a time,' said Moore, 'when we were having what is politely called a dispute over £2 a week. God knows I needed it, I couldn't believe Ron when he said the club couldn't afford it.'

'That was the start. All through I didn't earn good money at West Ham. I wasn't badly off, but I was not the monster money-earner everyone seems to think. All over the First Division, footballers were always earning more than I got at West Ham.

'I thought at the time that Ron resented the benefits I did get as a young man coming into the game as they were abolishing the maximum wage. Yet playing in some of the teams he put out for West Ham I had to earn every penny. I was lucky other things happened for me in football.'

The relationship between Moore and Greenwood was at its best when kept within the narrow confines of pure football strategy and technique.

Moore was learning that every worthwhile relationship entails disappointment. 'Not long after he came to Upton Park we had to play Arsenal, Ron's old team. I knew how much it meant to him for us to do well but we were paralysed. Lost 4–0. Yet it was one of the best games I ever played for West Ham. He knew I'd done everything for him and I needed him to swallow his own disappointment and thank me. He just whispered: "Well played." I wanted him to say I was magnificent. I wanted him to tell the world that he didn't know what we would have done without Mooro. Then I could have slept that night.'

Still at that time, West Ham were on the upswing and the depth of Greenwood's knowledge was the overpowering consideration.

Moore was impressed by the way Greenwood had used him and Johnny Byrne in a prophetic partnership to dominate an under-23 international match. In May of 1961, Young England went to Tottenham's White Hart Lane ground to face West Germany amid the chaotic administration which seemed to be the order of the day for representative teams at that time.

Greenwood was advised late by the Football Association staff that he was short of players and even had to call Mike Harrison away from the end of a full day's training at Chelsea to play on the wing. Yet the Germans were thrashed 4–1. Moore said: 'Budgie [Johnny Byrne] must have had 100 touches of the ball, 75 of them from my passes, most of that one-touch, all down to Ron's organisation.

'I couldn't deny his brilliance. The man is the encyclopedia of football. At international level, with international players, he was fantastic. In his prime without question he would have made a tremendous England manager. Perhaps an even better manager of England than Alf Ramsey.

'Even when his chance came late, giving England stability after Don Revie went off to the desert, he was in his element. He lost Kevin Keegan and Trevor Brooking and still came home from the 1982 World Cup Finals in Spain undefeated. On a World Cup level every player in the squad understood him and benefited from him. Ron has been involved in every FIFA report and analysis that has mattered. He sees things in football which are beyond the comprehension of many players and coaches in the game.

'That was one of his problems at West Ham. Ron talked about the game at such a high level that sometimes it went straight over the head of the average player.'

That realisation dawned on Moore one Saturday in the early Sixties when he glanced around the West Ham dressing room during a Greenwood team talk and saw ten other heads nodding agreement, but eight pairs of eyes glazed over. He said: 'Some days I believe there were only a couple of us who understood a word he was on about. He never seemed to realise that he should have been talking down to more than half the team. I was the one who was always being falsely accused of not adjusting to the need to play bread-and-butter club football. Yet really Ron was the one who needed to work with the best, the elite players.'

The irony of that will not have been lost on Greenwood, who more than once summarised Moore's apparent disdain for the more humdrum matches by saying: 'Bobby should play every game at Wembley.'

Greenwood mirrored professional respect by saying: 'Bobby was one of the few truly great players who could make the game look simple. For a long time I rated him the best player in the world.' He also reflected: 'Ask me to tell you about Bobby Moore the footballer and I will talk for days. Ask me about Bobby Moore the man and I will dry up in a minute.'

Moore said: 'I know very little of Ron as a man. We are different. I have a lot of enjoyment outside the game but I don't know if Ron has much of a life outside football.'

There was the essence of the contrast. Moore's character and life style assumed its own, more flamboyant proportions as he emerged from the professional shadow of Greenwood, a church-going man dedicated to the sanctity of his family life and purity in football.

Moore and Byrne became almost as good at cracking bottles as at splitting opposing defences. The pair became very much the hub of a social whirl involving most of West Ham's most successful team. Jim Standen, John Bond, Ken Brown, Eddie Bovington, Alan Sealey, Geoff Hurst, Peter Brabrook, and later Martin Peters. Only Jack Burkett and John Sissons were on the fringe.

What Moore regarded as an engaging life style which promoted an irresistible team spirit, Greenwood suspected to be a social problem rooted in drink and compounded by hangers-on. By way of illustration, there is Moore's recollection of the train journey home from Hillsborough in 1964 in the wake of what he believed was the finest performance in West Ham's history, the F.A. Cup semi-final victory over Manchester United.

'It was the only time I ever knew Ron to be emotional. The train was packed, a madhouse. Singing, sinking a few beers. Ron was upset, just sitting at a table in the dining car. Budgie and I went and asked him what was up. He said: "We've got this far without all these hangers-on. We don't need these people."

'I said: "Ron, please God we've got these people for the next five years. They used to hang on to Tottenham. Now they're hanging on to us. As long as they're with us, we know we're winning something."

'He said:"We don't need them," and he wanted the punters out of the bar.'

Moore's divergence of opinion with West Ham went well beyond the manager, and manifested itself before they reached Wembley.

The Members of the Football Writers' Association elected Bobby to the elite company of Footballers of the Year, which required his attendance at the presentation banquet on the Thursday evening before the Cup Final. The winner of the award is traditionally supported at that annual gathering of soccer people by all those close to him at his club. At 23, Bobby also had the distinction of being the youngest ever Footballer of the Year. Greenwood regarded the function as too close to Wembley for the players to attend, but Moore could not comprehend the attitude of the club. He said: 'I made my way over from our hotel alone. Yet even though Ron had refused to let the lads come I couldn't believe the club wouldn't support me. I looked round the Café Royal and I couldn't see a soul from West Ham. Not a single face. Not even a director. Did the directors think *they* were playing on Saturday? That hurt, deep down. I still left early enough to help win the bloody Final for them.'

Two days later Moore made what he regarded as a conciliatory gesture: 'We were a bit lucky against Preston in that Final but when we won I felt it was lovely for Ron most of all, achieving something by sticking to his principles. I went to cuddle him at the end but he didn't really want that from me.

'Ron felt deeply about people without showing it on the outside. I knew then that although he respected me, he didn't like me. I believe he had every reason to respect me and no reason to dislike me. But there it was.'

Thereafter even the Soccer discussions grew less frequent. 'Ron asked me why I didn't go to him any more, to ask about the game. He took it as a sign that I was turning against him.'

Moore still listened as intently as ever in team talks but made less effort to encourage concentration by the others, appearing distant: 'Once Ron called me to his office and said: "I know you take in what I'm saying, but will you please also look as if you're listening. How else can I make the rest pay attention?" Yet it wasn't my intention to undermine him.'

Greenwood was now experiencing almost as much trouble as everyone else in getting through to his captain. Moore insisted he did not consciously erect barriers but admitted to recognising the effect of his instinctive and somewhat aloof withdrawal from the herd. It was an indication of the awe in which he was held within the game that Moore told this anecdote, without a hint of surprise that he should have been the focal point of the story: 'Alan Ball highlighted to me how people had trouble getting close to me. The first time he got picked for England he went back to Everton, his club at the time, and all the players there asked him what Bobby Moore was like. He told them: "Just like the rest of you." They said: "Don't believe you."

'Once you're put on a pedestal where no one thinks you're touchable then you can't convince people you're the same sort of person as themselves.

'I noticed that people sometimes seemed nervous about coming up to me and talking to me but I couldn't believe that was the problem for Ron. I think, instead, he wanted me to go to him as his captain. Perhaps I was at fault, but that was not my way.

'Perhaps I should have been a go-between. Perhaps it would have helped when things started to go wrong. But I looked on myself as one of thirty professionals, one of the chaps. I didn't want the people I had to play with thinking I was one of THEM, picking the team. Budgie was much closer to Ron, always in and out of his office. But he had a bubbling personality and could get away with it. Nobody would accuse Budgie of getting them dropped.'

That aloof position – a shade superior to many of the team, deliberately distant from the management – was maintained by Moore until West Ham's cup-winning years of 1964 and 1965 paled into the long depression of relegation strife and humiliating failure in the knock-out competitions.

Moore felt he knew the answer to the problem and went to press his solution on Greenwood. He urged the manager to buy Maurice Setters, the one-time Manchester United and Coventry defender whose subsequent battles were fought in the courtroom over his dismissal as manager of Fourth Division Doncaster Rovers, then helping Jack Charlton turn the Republic of Ireland into an international force to be reckoned with.

Moore: 'I begged Ron to sign Maurice. He was tough and could play a bit and we needed to be harder at the back. Ron said: "No, he's a rebel. A problem."

'I said: "With Maurice we can win the world. Don't let it all go."

'He said: "Don't worry, I've got one for us. A nice boy. Been to college. Got a long body and short legs."

Moore walked out. A few days later John Cushley walked in from Celtic. 'John's strength when he came was that he was a hard Scottish boy,' said Moore. 'Ron knew in his heart that we needed someone to do some kicking. He knew I was professional enough to do it, even though I'm not a physical person. I've hammered people on a very few occasions when it's been absolutely necessary.

'Ron tried to close his eyes to it. In John Cushley he was buying a compromise which satisfied his conscience. A nice lad who could get stuck in. But he couldn't expect everyone to be like me and win by intelligence ... or by deciding when to kick people.

'Ron was in a right quandary. He'd bought someone to put some stick about but couldn't bear watching. One of John's first games was a friendly in Germany in 1967. We were playing against Dortmund and Siggi Held, their old World Cup forward, started making runs everywhere. John had the answer to that: whack, whack, whack. Everywhere Siggi ran John put him flat on his face. In the end Siggi ran up the white flag. Surrendered.

'We were all saying "Nice one Cush. You'll do for us." But when we got in at half time Ron pulled him to one side and said: "John, I've bought you to be tough but sometimes you've got to take it easy."

'As we walked out for the second half John came up to me looking puzzled and said: "I'm playing it too hard. The manager doesn't like me." John Cushley never made another tackle for West Ham.

'The same thing happened after he bought Alan Stephenson from Crystal Palace. After a game or two I heard Ron saying to Stevo: "Alan, you can't get stuck in like that all the time. Sometimes you've got to read it, hold off, use your brain." Ron was looking for perfection, but it was another centre half spoiled.'

Greenwood, however, was encouraged by the team's development. Cushley's arrival came at a time of much shuffling of the playing staff and in that same 1967, West Ham undertook one of their periodic jaunts to America. Moore said: 'Ron and I were talking in one hotel room about how pleased he was to have got rid of what he called the nasty characters in the team. He was worried about the nasty people. He was telling me even though I'm sure he wondered whether I was one of them, a dodge-pot. The difference with me and Budgie was that we could kick the ball in the right direction.

'Ron said he felt we were getting a team of nice lads together. I sat and wondered who the hell had ever won anything in football with eleven nice people. But in the next room John Cushley and John Charles, two of the nice boys, were falling off their beds drunk at three in the afternoon.'

Moore realised he could never influence a change in Greenwood and later grew to appreciate the honesty of his convictions. That belief was rooted in one early conversation in which Greenwood had recounted an incident from his own playing career to illustrate the importance of staying true to one's principles. Moore recalled: 'Ron was talking about playing centre half for Chelsea against Matt Busby's great old Manchester United team and I asked how he had coped with that terrific centre forward of theirs, Tommy Taylor.

'Taylor was tremendous in the air but Ron said he went into the match believing he could beat him in an honest jump for the headers. The first cross came in and he got a clear sight of the ball and went up expecting to head it away. Taylor timed his jump in front of him and got the touch and United nearly scored. A few minutes later the same thing happened and Taylor scored from the header.

'So it went on through the game. Ron never changed his tactics, never tried to block Taylor's run or nudge him off his jump, not even when Taylor stuck in United's third with his head. He believed he was doing the right thing and when the last high ball of the game came into Chelsea's penalty area he went up just the same. Still trying to win his first header of the afternoon, fair and square.'

Those principles guided Greenwood through his coaching and management and won him the respect and admiration of hundreds of people deeply involved in the game. The flowing, open football which Greenwood's beliefs demanded of West Ham also earned him the gratitude of tens of thousands of football-loving spectators who relished watching his team.

At times West Ham stood alone against the violence, brutality and intimidation which, in the late Sixties and early Seventies, threatened to bludgeon all the enchantment out of English football. When the tide turned again towards skill, Soccer was in many ways in Greenwood's debt. There were not enough men like him when aggression returned to dominate football in the late Eighties and early Nineties.

That became consolation for Moore, who had felt the years slipping by with no club honours to reward his individual genius. He made few bones about it: 'What annoyed me was that I was not that successful at club level. When we won the two cups Ron had a good team because he had a majority of good players. We could have gone on to dominate the game for a period, the way Leeds did later.

'I never won a League Championship medal. It wasn't just this business of not enough so-called steel. I could see through Ron and I knew he was hurt when we lost another bad cup tie to another poor team. I was hurt. A lot of us were hurt. He should have let himself show it. The lads would come in the dressing room with their heads down and he would say we would talk about it on Monday. Why wait? Tell me what I did wrong. Tell another one he can't bloody play. Tell that player he bottled it. He knew, alright. No man never saw so much in a game as Ron Greenwood. But motivation was not his strength.

'Some games I would love to have done it. Perhaps he wanted me to. But I didn't see it as my job. Not even as captain. It wasn't up to me to slag another player, and God knows I played with enough who weren't good enough.

'At Fulham, for example, they had to make do with what they'd got. But Ron kept on buying for West Ham. One or two buys came off for him. They won the cup again and a lot of his unsuccessful buys were forgotten.

'His best buy was Pop Robson. And he should never have let him go. After Pop got twenty-eight goals one season he should have told him he was the greatest in the world and sent him out to get even more next season. That was all Pop needed. A boost. Ron never said a thing to him. You didn't go to Ron for inspiration.'

Yet the paradox remained that if Moore needed counsel on a football problem, Greenwood was the man to whom he turned. 'It's true I felt cut off if I badly needed advice on something about football and could not go to Ron. No one in the world knows more about the game.'

It remained, then, the difference in life style, rather than any lack of professional respect, which put strain on a relationship which both parties were at pains to present to the outside world as untroubled.

Once, when they were discussing the social whirl, Greenwood counselled him: 'If the individual takes care of himself, the whole will of the team puts itself together.'

Yet the day still came when Bobby Moore was one of several individuals caught in an indiscretion which seemed to the public to have undermined the West Ham team.

That was in a northern seaside resort which has lured many footballers into the quicksands of scandal.

5

Blackpool

(Or how our hero stopped worrying and learned to love the booze)

Blackpool lights up a stub of coastline with the stuff impoverished dreams are made of: candyfloss and carousels, fish and chips, one-arm bandits and bingo, brittle rock and hard drinking, slap and tickle, day trippers and daft hats, two weeks and to hell with the cost.

Above all, there are the illuminations.

Lancashire textile workers and Yorkshire miners come up for sea air and flutter moth-like around that neon Tower. Blackpool is as sophisticated as pie and peas. Which is precisely why, in what might loosely be termed The Northern Season, its population multiples beyond the bursting limits of its boarding houses.

Bobby Moore would have chosen Blackpool for a holiday after almost anywhere from Benidorm to Barbados. Yet he made the most of the place, knowing that the Soccer season, unlike the holiday season, makes no allowances for such quirks of personal preference.

Blackpool also had a football team, which tended to hover optimistically between the old Second and First Divisions. West Ham were drawn away to Blackpool in the third round of the F.A. Cup. Irrevocably. The tie was to be played on January 2, 1971.

Even in deep winter, even with seas and collars up in unison, Blackpool holds on to an element of unreality. Some of the lights never go out. Those survivors are reinforced at Christmas by a festive flicker of the main switch.

New Year's Day is no easy day to take a professional team to

Blackpool in the hope of doing a professional job. Bobby Moore acknowledged that. 'Let's face it, no matter what you tell them, most footballers will go out somewhere to celebrate New Year's Eve. That year was no different but everyone felt up to light training on the Friday morning.

'Then we had that long and tedious train journey to Blackpool. We arrived about five o'clock and dinner was at 7.30 and even in that time we heard plenty of people suggesting the next day's game would be off because the pitch was iced up. The boredom was bad enough even without thinking we may have wasted the trip.'

Before dinner a group of West Ham players drank a lager each as they sat watching children swim in the heated indoor pool of the Imperial Hotel. Moore later sipped two glasses of wine during dinner and then, *en route* to an intended early night, stopped in the foyer 'just to sit for half an hour and watch the families who were up for the Christmas holiday.'

Moore sat in the company of Jimmy Greaves, Brian Dear and Clyde Best. They were joined by two members of a television crew come to Blackpool to film the match. Talk and time slipped by until 11 p.m. when the T.V. men upped and said they were off to take in another of the Blackpool sights: Brian London.

London, he of the lantern jaw and looping punches, had retired from heavyweight prizefighting into the equally colourful business of night club proprietorship. He was happily installed in the 007 Club, an archetypal rendezvous for those nocturnal beings among us who have trouble surviving the small hours without the help of a drink, a few friends and some background music.

Two taxis arrived at the hotel entrance, one for the television crew, the other ordered in error and therefore left vacant, waiting, available. The trap was laid and baited.

In some such moments Moore had as much resistance to the heat of temptation as an ice-cream in an oven: 'I couldn't even tell you the names of the television people but I'd met Brian London on many occasions and thought it would be nice to look him up. The transport was there. We just joined them. On the spur of the moment.'

Even at the peak of his career, Greaves never saw anything wrong in a beer or two before a match. Dear never needed his arm twisting to go for a drink. Best, the big young Bermudian, was swept along by the senior players towards an hour's devilment which was to mushroom into the biggest disciplinary incident Ron Greenwood had to handle.

The four of them were in London's club for little more than an hour. Moore, Greaves and Dear drank about four bottles of lager each. Best sat with them at the bar but did not drink, making his own compromise between personal friendship and professional discipline. They were back in the hotel foyer a few minutes before 1 a.m. . . . ordering coffee and sandwiches.

Moore said: 'I suppose we all realised at the time that we were leaving ourselves vulnerable. People will throw up their hands in horror at the thought of professional sportsmen going for a drink the night before a game. But it was hardly a diabolical liberty. In fact we thought very little about it. We were in bed by one-thirty and got up about ten o'clock the next morning. That's a good night's sleep by anyone's standards.'

For Moore, Greaves and Dear, a few lagers and two glasses of wine during a long evening represented a very modest consumption of alcohol. Moore: 'Not one of us felt we had jeopardised the team's chances. No player would do that on purpose. If a player did I would consider him warped, I wouldn't want him in my team, he shouldn't be part of any team.'

'The problem was not the drinking. It was the result.'

The afternoon after the early morning before, West Ham walked into one of their familiar defeats by a lesser team. Moore and Greaves both played. Dear was substitute. Ironically the non-drinker, Best, was not picked. Blackpool won 4–0.

'There was only one winner from the start,' said Moore. 'We were totally outplayed. The pitch was bony with the ice. They were steamed up to have a go and West Ham were never in it. We were left once again with the feeling of utter disappointment at being beaten by a team from lower down the League.

'Our position in the First Division didn't mean much at the time and everything that season hinged on a good Cup run. But those results had become a regular occurrence. Ron Greenwood was upset with the performance because it was hardly a performance at all. It was a sick trip home but nothing much was said and that seemed to be the end of it.'

It was, in fact, the beginning. On the Monday Greenwood was confronted in his office by an irate supporter who had travelled to Blackpool, heard that players were in a night club and been sickened by the result.

'Normally,' said Moore, 'Ron would have dismissed that sort of thing. From that aspect Ron was too big a man to have truck with people phoning in or calling to tell tales on players just because the team had a bad result.'

This time, however, club chairman Reg Pratt walked into the manager's office in the middle of the heated discussion and the midst of his own disappointment with the Cup defeat. He demanded to know what the fuss was about.

The supporter also contacted several Fleet Street newspapers and on Monday afternoon Brian Dear received two phone calls from journalists seeking confirmation of the story. Dear denied everything and telephoned Moore to warn him that the newspapers were making enquiries.

An hour later Dear answered another phone call, this time from Greenwood, and admitted the indiscretion to his manager. Again he telephoned Moore with the news.

Moore drove early to Upton Park on Tuesday morning and at once sought out Greenwood in the manager's office.

'I understand there's something you want to see us about.'

'No, not really. I don't want to talk about anything.'

'Well, you've obviously heard. I know you have. It is true. I've come to apologise. We know we did wrong but it wasn't done with any ill intent. All we can do now is apologise.'

'You've hurt me. Let me down. I don't want to talk about it any more. It will be dealt with in due course.'

Greenwood, whose habit was to keep all West Ham affairs as private as possible, was confronted by a scandal already breaking in the press. He felt obliged to name the guilty players to journalists in order to protect the reputation of the innocent members of his team.

While Greenwood plunged into a round of meetings with the club's directors , B.B.C. television were making their usual secretive arrangements for that Wednesday night's *This is Your Life* programme, with Moore as the surprised subject. West Ham delayed announcing their verdict on Moore and company until

Thursday, thereby allowing the B.B.C. to go ahead with their programme unembarrassed. Moore: 'One night I'm a T.V. star. Next day, the big hammer.'

The punishment was a two week suspension for Moore, Greaves and Dear, plus a fine of a week's wages, in Moore's case £200. Best, rightly, was treated more leniently.

The repercussions were considerable. Greaves was hastened towards retirement. Dear ran out of clubs willing to take a chance that goals would keep coming despite a merry life style and expanding waist line.

Not only was Moore's golden image somewhat tarnished, but the suspension kept him from being match fit to lead his country against Malta in the European Championship. So Alan Mullery, with whom Moore was later to team up at Fulham, was given the honour of England captaincy for that one match.

All for what? At the risk of shattering whatever schoolboy illusions remain about this great game of ours, it is necessary to record that the fuss was over nothing at all unusual.

It would take a very naive or a somewhat dishonest manager to claim that none of his players has ever taken a drink the night before a big game. The crime in Blackpool was getting caught, compounded by losing the match. That is the British way, a heavy drinking society with a hypocritical response to any miscreant unlucky enough to be apprehended.

Greaves did not turn farther away from the game that made him famous out of a sense of shame. He was disgusted with the fuss made by holier-than-thou critics. Moore made no excuses – not even mentioning the rumours that the match would be off – because he did not believe any were necessary: 'Greavesy and I were nauseated by the way Blackpool was blown up out of all proportion. Whether people like it or not, whether they care to admit it, footballers are always doing what we did in Blackpool.

'It's been done many times before, both abroad and in England. I remember when I was first picked for the England team being a bit surprised to see that Greavesy always popped out for a couple of pints of beer the day before a big game. When you first get your chance you wouldn't dream of doing it but Greavesy didn't think anything of it and in fact it was what he needed.

'After I moved to Fulham and we had our long run of matches

to the 1975 F.A. Cup Final, we used to go to the local after training every Friday for a lager before travelling to the cup-ties. Nobody complained because we kept winning.

'It happens all the time. Our visit to Brian's club made not the slightest difference to the result in Blackpool. Perhaps it was exaggerated by my involvement. I know that when you are England captain people are always looking for little chinks in your armour, little slip-ups that they can cash in on, so I tried not to give them the chance.'

Like most of his contemporaries and successors, Moore resented the extreme reaction of the media and large sections of the public every time a player is known to have sampled the demon drink. Personally, he had a high tolerance to lager, his favourite poison, and wine, which he enjoyed with most meals. He was also a more relaxed individual after the first couple of drinks and even after a heavy night had a remarkable power of recovery which enabled him to cope comfortably with strenuous training early the next day.

Although some of his acquaintances damaged his reputation by telling exaggerated stories of his social life – even though he and I swam through a few liquid evenings together – Bobby usually kept his alcoholic indulgence within reasonable bounds.

Moore summed up his attitude to drink in a neat phrase of his own: 'A car needs petrol.' Elaborating: 'Of course some players have damaged themselves by too much social life. Two of the best players I knew, Jim Baxter and Budgie Byrne himself, did themselves no favours. But everyone is different. A drink helped me unwind the way it obviously helped Dave Mackay. You were always hearing stories of Dave being picked up off the pavement up and down Tottenham High Road every night of the week. It didn't stop him being a great player for Spurs every time he went out on to the pitch.

'As long as you don't regularly drink to excess, the problem is mental rather than physical. When I first started out as a young professional I wouldn't dream of taking a drink after Thursday.

'I wasn't really used to it because my dad never drank at all. Yet you saw the senior pros going for a couple of beers on a Friday and slowly it dawned on you that the whole business is just an attitude of mind. At first you think you mustn't do certain things in case it affects you. Then you realise everyone is different and it's an individual decision.

'I like a drink and as long as it's not to excess I feel better for it. But if you're seen holding a lager in this country people start shaking their heads and asking whatever happened to the clean-living sportsmen.

'That's not the case anywhere else. I've seen the Italian and the Brazilian national teams, for example, sit down to lunch before a big evening game with wine on the table. They say it helps the digestion. Here people make you think you shouldn't be doing it and create another problem in the player's mind.'

Discipline was left to the individual at West Ham. Greenwood wanted to treat his players like responsible men, wanted to trust them. Sometimes the response was good, often he was let down.

Yet, invariably, the football was entertaining.

During the 1965–6 European Cup Winners' Cup campaign they travelled to Greece for a return match against Olympiakos two weeks after establishing a 4–0 lead in the first leg of the tie in London.

Moore recalled: 'One or two of the lads were getting stuck into the bevy on the plane and we had to make a stopover in Switzerland. Before we took off again the pilot came through and asked Budgie how much more champagne he was likely to need. Budgie said: "Just one more crate."

'When we got to Greece they had to put Budgie to bed for two days. Two more of the lads went out on the booze the night we arrived in Greece and they were falling about with stomach cramp and all sorts.

'That was often the way in our European ties. For me, that was over-doing it. These were some of the most important games a lot of the West Ham lads played in their lives. When it was that big, I left it to the night after the match to go totting. And I love life as much as anyone.

'Yet Budgie was incredible the way he got away with it. It was a struggle to get him out of bed on the day of that match in Greece, yet he was brilliant. He murdered them again. We drew 2–2 and skated through on aggregate.'

The temptation to let pleasure interfere with the business of winning football matches had required Moore, Byrne and several more stars to salvage their distinguished names in more dramatic fashion on an even larger stage in the early summer of 1964.

Fresh from their triumph in the F.A. Cup, Moore and Byrne were key members of Alf Ramsey's England squad selected to travel to Lisbon for a prestige international match against Portugal on Sunday May 17, 1964.

As usual the players gathered under Ramsey at the rather anonymous Whites Hotel, near the Football Association offices in Lancaster Gate, four days before the match.

Again, as usual, Ramsey took them training on the smooth turf of the Bank of England sports ground at Roehampton. The manager then suggested they should spend half an hour in the bar with the club staff and members who always gave the England team whole-hearted co-operation.

Ramsey, as was his practice whenever he drank with his players, bought the round. He then ushered his squad on to the coach back to central London in time for dinner at the hotel.

It was a warm evening and after dinner Moore and those closest to him took a stroll along the Bayswater Road. They were a distinguished company; Moore, Byrne, Gordon Banks, Jimmy Greaves, George Eastham, Bobby Charlton, Ray Wilson.

It was still very warm. They jumped at the suggestion of a drink in the West End.

Again it was nothing too outrageous. The match was still four days away. Even the multiple distractions of the West End of London did not keep that elite company of footballers out later than a few minutes after midnight.

But Ramsey was not a trusting soul like Greenwood. At 11.30 he and his staff patrolled the hotel corridor to check the rooms. One of his assistants, Harold Shepherdson, discovered the empty beds.

Ramsey and Shepherdson simply placed each missing individual's passport on his pillow. To players accustomed to team officials keeping all travel documents, the inference was obvious. They were lucky still to be making the trip.

Alf then let them sweat. Moore: 'As soon as we saw the passports we knew we'd been rumbled. We flew out on the Thursday morning thinking we would be for it sometime that day. Alf said nothing. Friday, nothing. Then we had a meeting after training on the Saturday and right at the end he let us have it.'

As he dismissed the squad, England's manager said: 'There are seven players who I think would like to stay and see me.' One by one the rest of the squad walked out looking questioningly at the seven, who had kept the incident to themselves.

Ramsey said: 'If I had enough players in the squad none of you would be in the side. In fact, I don't think you would be here at all. But I haven't enough players. And I don't think you will do it again. Because I think you now realise it would not be worth the risk.'

Ramsey then named all seven in the side to play Portugal next day, as if daring them to fail. The public, unaware of the drama, thrilled to a dramatic match which England won 4–3. Johnny Byrne rose to the challenge with a brilliant hat-trick. Bobby Charlton scored the fourth goal.

Still Moore felt it was a storm in a beerglass. 'It would have been ridiculous if some of those great players had not gone on to the 1966 World Cup just because we had a few beers four days before a match.'

For Moore, in fact, it had been something of an achievement to get to sleep not long after midnight. His insomnia often led him to seek refuge in a long night's socialising and he played all the better for not spending several hours tossing and turning in bed.

Between Fulham's F.A. Cup semi-final and final he was seldom in bed after eleven o'clock but did not enjoy one good night's sleep. At home he often retreated alone to another room to avoid disturbing his wife.

'If you don't have trouble sleeping,' he said, 'you don't know what a hell it can be. Sometimes I'll go downstairs and fall asleep reading. So I'll stir and go back to bed. Then I can't get back to sleep again. There's no way having a drink is worse for me than all that nonsense.'

At such times, Moore was naturally keen to keep convivial company around him but he said: 'I hope I didn't influence other players, particularly younger players, to drink. I always invited a young player into my company if he was feeling left out of things. If he didn't want to drink that was fine by me. Every individual knows what he's capable of and what's good for him.

'It's like training. Slogging round the track all day, every day, might sound like good hard work but it can take the edge off you.

'It's a very delicate business, working out why you might be having a bad time on the pitch. At times like that I tried anything and everything. Extra training ... early nights ... late nights ... drinking ... not drinking ... eating well ... living like a hermit off the bare essentials. You name it, I tried it. And most times you just felt yourself going backwards. I went into extra training and strict diet but if I dropped below 12st 8lb I didn't feel fit and strong as I should. My best playing weight was 12st 10lb and just those couple of pounds made all the difference. In the end, however, you're living, all you need is to suddenly get one good game under your belt.

'If you're having a bad patch and people see you out in a pub or a club they start pointing the finger. But sometimes a fellow wants to forget all about it and he does himself good by going for a drink and going to the limits.'

What, one might ask, can the limits be to encompass such a philosophy?

'You can let yourself go so far and recover. Too far, and there is no going back, no sweating it out of your body and your system however hard you try.'

But how far is too far?

Moore groped for an illustration and found it in two well-worn words: 'George Best.'

He explained 'George should have been the best player in the world. For a time he probably *was* the best player in the world. All the skills, scored goals, courage. Complete. He was right at times when he said he *was* Manchester United. There were times I saw him dominate a whole game from start to finish. Other times he did enough in 20-minute bursts to win matches outright, even for Northern Ireland. He played teams on his own.

'What I couldn't understand was why he didn't enjoy doing that. He says he did, so why did he just throw it all away at the drop of a hat?

'He gave me the impression that he just didn't give a damn. That's wrong. He took liberties by just not bothering to turn up, say for training if he'd had a heavy night. He was not only abusing himself but abusing other people's respect for him.

'There's got to be something strange in a person who doesn't have feelings for his own team mates or care what they feel. These are the people you work with and spend a lot of your life with. Surely you must want them to like you and above all respect you.'

Moore's powerful sense of team identity was one of his abiding strengths. He did not like to let people down and did not appreciate such behaviour in others.

Of the paradoxical figure of Best, Moore added: 'Even after the crap hit the fan at United, George was still letting people down who were putting plenty of money his way. I was in South Africa in the summer of '74 and it was reported that a Johannesburg team were paying him £1,000 a game. Three thousand people turned up to watch George's first training session there. The only person missing was George.

'In the end, of course, he let himself down as badly as he let those people down. In one game he tried a few tricks but was badly out of condition. I asked him how someone with talent like his could let himself be exposed in that level of football. He couldn't see it. So sad.'

Moore accepted that Best's problems were exaggerated to self-destructive proportions by the hangers-on who were the bewildered little Irishman's substitute for a stable domestic life at that time.

'Those people who want to be seen out and about with the football stars are the biggest problem, bigger than smoking, drinking or anything else.

'Budgie had the same problem with them. Like George, he could never say no. He always had to go out, and go on.

'There were times when I'd start an evening with Budgie and I would love to have gone somewhere – but you've got to have the strength to say it's not possible.

'There are a million people who want to be with you because you're a name. The same people will disappear if you hit bad times. As far as I am concerned if they think the worst of you for going home, then you don't need them. If they take the point, and even encourage you to leave, they can be friends.

'It takes a bit of character to walk away from a good scene and I don't deny that being married young was a help to me. It's not a bad thing to have some responsibilities, to have somewhere to go home to, to have a family waiting. Overall I spend a lot more nights indoors. Going home to an empty house must have been hard for George. He couldn't do it. I don't know if I could have done it regularly.

'It might sound lovely being out chasing the girls every night and having a pad to take them back to. But it's not the answer. That's why I felt sorry for George.'

Girls are always mentioned in intimate connection with the social life of footballers, not least by Best himself. Moore said: 'Some players get involved, some players don't. But every time you're out late people think the worst. Take it from me, when they put two and two together they usually come up with five.'

That was how a lot of unofficial mathematics calculated the Blackpool business. Those malicious rumours annoyed Moore, most of all for the pressure they exerted on a marriage which had yet to reach its own crisis and eventual divorce.

6

A Boy to Take Home to Mother

If during Bobby Moore's first flush of manhood there was an approximation to the West End in East London, then it had to be Ilford. The town crowds around the High Road, a main artery darting away from the milling junction of trains, buses, cars, hamburger joints and people which is collectively identified as The Broadway. Half way down the High Road, spaced out between the old town hall and the public baths and competing for side-street parking with the cinema, throbbed the dance hall.

The chains of weekly newspapers recording the turbulent life of the East London sprawl, devote much of their space to pictures of hopeful newlyweds. In my time I wrote countless supporting captions hinged around the locally immortal phrase: 'The couple first met at a dance at Ilford Palais'. One such sentence of mine advised the worthy readers of the *Walthamstow Guardian* that Robert Frederick Moore and Christina Elizabeth Dean had been joined together in holy matrimony at the Church of St. Clemence, Ilford on June 30, 1962.

Since that fateful day, Ilford Palais has been renamed often and tarted up aplenty. Yet in essence it remains the same: a cross between the cavernous Palais-de-Danse, of which a vintage specimen survives at Hammersmith, and the intimate Club-de-Smooch suggested by the fashionable new names.

There was a big band and a brash group laced with an interval disc jockey. There were several gentlemen who never looked comfortable in dinner jackets designed for some previous occupant until they bounced a few locals trying to prove their manhood in a flurry of fists and bottles. There was a bar not far from the dance floor to ply the shy with Dutch courage. There were hot dogs on the balcony to supplement the first verbal sparring of the sexes and to save the cost of a meal later.

There were Teen Nights for the very young trying to look impossibly mature. There were Over-21 nights when stags ran into hen parties, mostly on Fridays, the traditional East End night for extra-marital flirtation.

Most of all there was Saturday Night. Girls dressed to kill but did most of the damage with withering glances at those boys who plucked up the courage to walk away from their mates and get turned down for a dance.

Saturday Night began full of hope, collected a bare handful of romance on the way and ended with wallflowers mincing down one side of the High Road and groups of rejected youths jeering from the other.

Tina Dean lived a brisk, well-lit walk from the meeting factory, Bobby Moore a threepenny bus ride away at Barking. Tina sat with the girls in the warmth and the dark, repelling unwanted dancers. Bobby stood with the boys, watching the fragments of light reflect from the spinning silver ball high in the ceiling and dart tantalisingly across the pretty young faces.

She was 15. He was 16. We have to report something less breathtaking than love at first sight.

To start with, Tina played hard to get. One night Bobby made a dance, a walk home, a peck on the cheek and a mad dash for the last bus to Barking.

Tina, however, was asked by a girl friend what on earth she saw in this rather square young footballer. Her stepfather consulted record books not yet alive to the arrival of Bobby Moore and insisted there was no such footballer at West Ham. Tina was not the slightest bit interested in football anyway.

So she did not go to the Palais next Saturday. Bobby waited all evening, stood up but undeterred.

He took to spending Saturday mornings in Ilford High Road loitering at the record shops where Tina loved to listen to music, browsing absently through the racks, being rewarded by no more than a brusque nod from the pretty blonde upon whom he had fixed his affection.

That was the limit of his success until the day Tina and her mother drove by in a taxi as Bobby strolled the street. Tina jabbed at the window: 'There. That's the boy who says he plays for West Ham.' Her mother looked out at a short-haired, clean-cut good-looking young man with an open face and clear blue eyes. She said: 'He looks a nice boy. Why don't you ask him home for tea?'

Like all mothers, Tina's wanted the best for her daughter. Her instincts about Bobby were proved right. She packed Tina off to the Palais that night, saw them married four years later on that day in 1962 when the reception celebrated not only the nuptials but also young Moore's return from the World Cup in Chile with his first England caps. She lived to see them flower into the first couple of English football and was remembered with affection by both her daughter and former son-in-law for her helpful influence on their early life.

First the death of Tina's mother, then the two strokes suffered by Bobby's father in the early Seventies, rendering him virtually housebound, strengthened the marital bond for some years. Those moments of private distress sharpened gratitude for their own good life.

The Moores first set up home in a classic example of the sub-urban semi in Gants Hill, Ilford's dormitory. They progressed to mock-Tudor splendour in stockbroker Chigwell's affluent Manor Road.

Then, in 1974, ambition to build their own prestigious residence and the urge to move their children away from the fast roads took them around the corner and further up status hill to the sanctuary of 'Morlands', a baronial family seat.

Their mutual progress always seemed well scripted. Tina faced the realities of earning a living in an employment agency, used her looks to advantage in sporadic modelling sessions and was ready to retire into maternity as Bobby began to reap the financial rewards of his own talent.

Roberta, Little Miss Bobby, was born on January 24, 1965. Dean arrived, to perpetuate Tina's family name, on March 24, 1968.

They were a seemingly ideal family, packaged into what Bobby described, accurately if not inventively, as 'the home of our dreams'.

Bobby and Tina looked at the cost together, took a deep breath and plunged into their £100,000 investment. By way of reward, they approached the new house through elegant white pillars, dined sumptuously behind rich velvet drapes, relaxed in deep sofas in a large cool lounge and dispensed hospitality in Bobby's favourite room, the bar.

Tina had domestic help, notably in the fully-gadgeted kitchen from which she always promised to produce a Cordon Bleu meal, dabbled in charity work, took care to look the part as Mrs. Bobby Moore, steered the children through everything from riding lessons to the best education money could buy, lunched with friends, holidayed in an assortment of sunspots and said: 'It's a hard life.'

Anticipating the public wince at the remark, she hurried on to the qualification: 'A good life, yes, but still a hard life. There were a lot of pressures. Not enough privacy. More time apart than I would have liked. Whatever Bobby got he earned the hard way. He was on show almost every minute of the day. It put us under pressure.'

The first Mrs Moore quickly perceived the growing gulf between so many of football's husbands and their wives and determined that she was not going to be one of the little women left behind by her husband's success.

She never much liked football, made no pretence about it and went to matches only out of a sense of duty to support her husband on the big occasions.

Bobby said: 'Tina would never want to come and see a match with me. Sometimes she would come along but only because we were having dinner later with some friends.'

Yet she stayed abreast of her husband socially, developed her own personality which Bobby recognised at that time as 'stronger than my own' and remained for some years his closest confidante, and most influential adviser.

By such means she sustained a turbulent marriage for 23 years, until it ended in the divorce which enabled him to settle into more tranquil happiness with Stephanie. He was not a man who could live alone, even though he was able to stand apart from his colleagues.

Bobby says: 'I was never a person to take football home to the house. I could lose a match or two and be a bit upset without regarding it as the end of the world. I could go home to Tina and escape from it all.

'But whenever there were real problems – on or off the pitch, then or later – I needed someone to turn to. There are some things you can't disclose to acquaintances, some things you could never tell a friend. Outsiders will be nosy enough to want to know what's going on but they can't come up with the answers.

'The only person who can do that is the one who cares for you and is deeply involved in the outcome. Stephanie became something deeper, more profound. Yet whatever the problems between Tina and I we were always able to talk things through. For a long time there was no one else I would have called a really close friend.'

Moore knew that the honesty of that remark revealed a great deal about himself and would rankle with those who claimed to be the closest of his social circle.

The man's latent suspicion of outsiders grew as each new success attracted a fresh crop of admirers. Tina admitted to having felt the cold draught as Bobby lowered the self-protective barriers: 'I knew he was hard to get close to, to get through to. Very, very few people succeeded.

'I got through to him but sometimes even with me I could feel him withdraw. Do his reserved bit. Go icy quiet.'

Tina recognised the mechanism as Bobby's way of living with external pressures. 'Everybody always said how easily he rode all the pressures. He did seem to cope very well. But down the years it took its toll deep down inside him. Most of the time he was worrying about not upsetting people, not letting them down. There always seemed to be people queuing up for Bobby to do. something for them.'

Moore said: 'If I agree to do something in good faith then I will do my damndest to be there.'

Tina became less tolerant and more demanding of some return for Bobby's time. There were people who felt more snubbed by Tina than Bobby. Her increasing irritation with Bobby's polite tolerance of hangers-on was tempered by her personal gratitude for his generosity. 'Bobby was a high-liver but never at the expense of myself or the children. He was a very generous man. He always put others before himself.

'I loved the way he always had a kind word for waiters or children, people who wouldn't dream of presuming. Did you ever see him refuse an autograph to someone who asked politely?'

In fact, Moore's civility withstood almost any effrontery. During the summer of 1975, he had just three hours to spare in transit from a Fulham match in Gibraltar to a six-week stint as a guest player in South Africa. Tina had been left to arrange a meeting for him at Heathrow with a group of Brazilians to discuss details of a contract for Bobby to play exhibition matches in Rio de Janeiro later that summer.

Tina also wanted to take the children to say hello and goodbye to their father. Still, it was as much as she could do to dissuade one of Moore's business partners, Freddie Harrison, from going to the airport 'just to buy Mooro a drink'. As yet undetected outside the tight family circle, cracks in the relationship were developing.

Tina said: 'There were all sorts of things to sort out in those three hours. Above all I wanted to see Bob because we'd had a row before he went to Gibraltar and I didn't want him to go off to South Africa for six weeks with us all upset.

'But people were pestering us all the time and when the Brazil people finally went we just had a few minutes left. We went to kiss goodbye ... and someone just barged up, pushed an autograph book in between us and said: "Sign that." I could have hit the man but Bobby signed because it was the quickest way of getting him out of the way.'

The Moores rarely moved about unrecognised. Not that they wanted to. A handsome couple, they looked good together which served only to sharpen the speculative daggers pointed at the hearts of all public couples. While football marriages creaked, groaned and collapsed all about them, Bobby and Tina succeeded for longer than they might have in deflecting the gossiping predictions of a crack-up.

Both travelled extensively. Both mixed freely. Both were aware of the dangers. She said, both revealingly and prophetically: 'I believe in fidelity in marriage ... and Bobby knows it.'

The Blackpool affair was a severe test of their trust. A rumour that girls were present to compound that indiscretion was shabbily hinted at in some sections of the media, suggested with a leer in some sniggering conversations.

Bobby said: 'There was nothing like that but I knew what some people would try to make of it. I rang Tina and told her: 'You're going to read some things in the papers which may not be true but which you're not going to like.'

'I told her what to expect but that didn't stop all the aggro. We had some bad moments. That sort of incident puts your marriage under stress, whatever the truth of the situation. If it had come early on in the relationship it might have presented even more problems.'

Nevertheless, it was a hint of things to come, although the difficulties were pushed to the backs of their minds as the social pace quickened most vividly after Moore led England to the World Cup in 1966.

Immediately they were invited on a goodwill visit to Malta. The itinerary was packed with ambassadorial duties. 'An engagement every hour, on the hour,' Bobby said. As the strain told he begged an afternoon off to relax on a boat but was due back in Valetta for an evening reception.

They changed aboard the motor cruiser. A launch brought them rippling back through the clear blue waters to where welcoming dignitaries clustered on the weathered jetty beneath the bleached buildings of the ancient city. It was an idyllic scene bathed in the amber sunlight of early evening.

Tina stepped up the gangplank to take the outstretched hand of a beaming bishop, tripped, and began toppling towards the water. The bishop held on to Tina, a priest clutched at the flying skirts of the bishop's frock coat. All in vain. Mrs. Moore and her attendant clerics plopped into the harbour in full regalia.

The bishop was blowing water and failing to prevent his steel-rimmed glasses sinking gently to the bottom, to join one lost shoe. Bobby was spluttering, not with water but with the effort of trying not to laugh: 'Everyone seemed so upset, I didn't like to hurt their feelings by bursting out laughing. Especially Tina's.'

Bobby was frequently, though secretly, amused by the depths of a public fascination with himself as the international symbol of a national triumph. He often recalled waking in a hotel room at six a.m., rising in preparation for a seven o'clock engagement and opening the curtains to a burst of applause from a Mediterranean crowd gathered beneath his window.

'They thought I'd done great to wake up in the morning,' he said.

'For a time I could do no wrong. In a restaurant everyone else would be sitting watching me. I'd cut a steak and a roar would go up like I'd scored the winning goal or something. Kind but crazy.

'People everywhere were so courteous and kind but sometimes kindness can be a cruelty. Once when I was invited to Israel they were desperate to show me everything, make sure I missed nothing. The trouble was they were trying to get twenty-five hours into a twenty-four-hour day. I was walking about like a zombie and by the time I got the plane home I was on my knees.'

Mostly, he accepted that pressure for the rewards. He never forgot the surroundings in which he soothed the wound of losing the World Cup in Mexico, 1970. He spent two healing weeks drinking in the view of Acapulco from a hotel suite which numbered among its luxuries an individual swimming pool sweeping from a private patio into the heart of a lavish lounge.

Such interludes became more frequent and more precious when he shared his life after football with Stephanie.

Even so, Bobby remained as meticulous in keeping appointments as in everything else he did. The measured perfection of his football was mirrored in his everyday life. The scrupulous appearance was matched by an almost obsessive tidiness at home. When Bobby opened a beer can, the metal top was *always* slipped back into the empty container, which in turn was *always* placed in the waste bin. Bobby's clothes were always hung up or folded away.

After a day by the pool or on the beach, Bobby would always fold towels and neatly stack away the reclining chairs, however many staff were hurrying to relieve him of the chore.

After training or a match, the kit boys with West Ham, England or Fulham always found Bobby Moore's kit put neatly away and his boots cleaned. His whole game was built on this methodical nature. Knowing his left foot to be comparatively weak, he spent countless hours perfecting a curved pass with the outside of the right foot to achieve the same effect as a pass with his left.

Knowing that he lacked a sharp change of pace, he painstakingly programmed into his make-up a positional sense which made it almost impossible for opponents to exploit that flaw. Never, for a moment, did he relax those standards. 'I never understood players messing about in training routines or five-a-sides. Bad habits are too easy to catch. If you waste a ball in training, the odds are you will waste it in a match. Even in the kick-in I passed every ball as if the World Cup depended on it.'

That intense concentration, that search for perfection, was just one of the investments which matured Master Moore into the best defender in world football.

Tina paid her price for the ensuing yield of creature comforts by accepting repeated separations from her husband, culminating in the decisive parting.

Within a year of becoming Mrs. Bobby Moore, she had begun learning from first-hand experience that wives and football do not mix.

7

The Days of Wine and Pansies

New York has been to the footballer what Las Vegas is to the businessmen: a place to make an exhibition of yourself, to pick up a fast buck, to mix business with pleasure. Only intermittently has Soccer in the States become a phenomenon to take seriously, and its future in the land of baseball and the gridiron will remain uncertain even after it has accepted FIFA's gift of the World Cup Finals there in 1994.

In the summer of 1963, West Ham were playing their part in educating our American cousins in the mysteries of the rolling ball game. They were competing in an international tournament against teams drawn from a representative cross-section of Europe and Latin America.

The football was more demonstrative than competitive, which was to West Ham's liking. After eight matches spread through the month of June they were top of the League. That minor achievement required them to return to New York in July to play Gornik, the winners of a second series of matches, then a grand final against Dukla Prague.

Perhaps moved by the relaxing spirit of the whole venture, West Ham's players opted to take their wives on the return trip, in lieu of a bonus.

The womenfolk had applied a certain amount of pressure to that end. Unhappily, some of the wives were scratching each other's eyes out within an hour of landing in New York. Bobby: 'There was more aggro in that hour than we'd had in the whole of the first month with just the lads out there. In the end, the players were getting at each other because of the girls.

'You couldn't even get organised to go out to dinner because one girl wouldn't go if her best friend wasn't coming. Two more wouldn't leave the hotel because a third wife was homesick. They were talking behind each other's backs, dragging the lads into arguments. It was a disaster. Would you believe we lost?'

Dukla won the first match 1– 0. The second leg was drawn 1– 1. The Czechs went home with the trophy. West Ham returned to England with a repair job to do on team spirit without which they could not have won the F.A. Cup ten months later, nor the European Cup Winners' Cup a year after that.

Moore and Johnny Byrne worked on that problem in their usual way, keeping the social wheels nicely lubricated.

For all that labour of love West Ham's form in the League was as unremarkable as ever. They eventually finished the 1963–4 season back in 14th place in the First Division. They were, however, blessed with good fortune in the draws for succeeding rounds of the F.A. Cup.

They beat Charlton, Orient after a reply with their poor East London relations, Swindon and Burnley on their way to Hills-borough and the top semi-final. That was a modest record fromwhich to challenge the brilliance of Manchester United. Most people forgot that, on their day, West Ham could beat anybody. Moore cherished that semi-final as West Ham's best day of all. United's all-stars were thumped 3–1. Ron Greenwood cried on the train home. West Ham laughed all the way to Wembley.

The 1964 Cup Final is remembered fondly in the environs of Upton Park as the highlight of West Ham's history, lent, by the distance of time, more enchantment than the 1975 Wembley victory which Moore tried so hard to deny them on Fulham's behalf.

Moore found no reasons down the years to change an opinion formed at the time, dispassionately, amid all the hullabaloo of Wembley.

'It was an anti-climax. A lot of finals are like that anyway because you pour so much into striving to be there that winning a semi-final and setting up a trip to Wembley seems like the major achievement in itself. But it was more than that.

'We were playing against Preston North End, a Second Division side.

'We'd been magic in the semi-final against Manchester United. Wembley should have belonged to West Ham. We won and it was good to win the first major honour. Apart from that it was a wash-out.

'We played badly. We spluttered. We didn't fulfil anything we had promised ourselves. Most of us felt let down. We were lucky to beat Preston, and bloody lucky Preston were no better than they were. Who could explain it? That was West Ham.'

Holden gave Preston an early lead as the veteran Lawton and the very young Kendall took advantage of the space offered as usual by West Ham. Sissons equalised but the burly Dawson sent Preston in at half time leading 2–1. Greenwood negotiated a tactical switch to subdue Lawton, West Ham strained for Hurst's equaliser and Boyce scored a rare goal from midfield in the dying moments to win the Cup.

Moore: 'The game looked certain to go into extra-time until Ronnie scored. I suppose it was exciting for the fans. I was pleased to see us get it over with. But I didn't feel any great thrill.'

He remembered collecting the trophy and going through the ritual of holding the glittering silver aloft before leading a lap of honour around the milling stadium. He remembered his abortive attempt to embrace Greenwood, the manager.

The perfectionist in him would not permit enjoyment of a substandard triumph. He remembered almost everything better than he remembered the football, even his irritation at the banquet that night: 'We went to the London Hilton and West Ham had kept down the guest list. There were about 300 of us huddled up in one corner of a vast room. It was like going to a funeral. Nobody enjoyed it as far as I could see.'

Hollow as it was, the victory over Preston opened up the playing fields of Europe to West Ham. It was in the following season, in competition with their fellow Cup-winners from all over the Continent, that the technical niceties of Greenwood's playing philosophy were to be displayed to best advantage.

Here, in Europe, they were not so likely to be bludgeoned out of their elegant stride. The European Cup Winners' Cup was more a contest of skill and science than our League football and

West Ham were perfectly equipped for the challenge.

Even so, they had to overcome the insular belief of the English that Continental clubs were second rate.

West Ham went to Ghent in the first round, beat the Belgian Cup holders 1–0 and played out a 1–1 draw in the second leg at Upton Park to go through on aggregate.

Moore recalled: 'So many people were disappointed. They had never heard of La Gantoise so they thought they must be a bunch of second-raters and figured we should have thrashed them.

'In fact they were the first pair of a lot of hard matches.'

West Ham slipped through by the odd goal against Spartak Prague of Czechoslovakia and were given all sorts of shocks by little Lausanne of Switzerland before winning 6–4 on aggregate to qualify for the semi-final.

Just as in the F.A. Cup the year before, the semi-final proved to be a classic tie. West Ham were pitted against Real Zaragoza of Spain and were a bare 2–1 ahead at the end of the first leg in London.

Moore: 'We put a brave face on it but none of us believed deep down that it would be enough. They called the Zaragoza forward line the Magnificent Five and we knew they would give us a real going over in Spain.

'Sure enough they wiped out the lead early on and we were left trying to contain them for most of the match. Suddenly John Sissons and Brian Dear broke away and knocked in a goal between them and we'd got a great result.'

His perpetual modesty disguised the truth. The Spaniards knew who to blame. They declared that the Magnificent Five had foundered on the Magnificent One.

Bobby Moore was as unbeatable for West Ham that day as he was to be for England so often in the future.

This time they went to Wembley and did themselves justice. By chance, the Cup Winners' Cup Final was scheduled for England in 1965 and West Ham were in irresistible form against the German Cup-holders, TSV Munich 1860.

Alan Sealey scored the two goals and Moore glowed with the memory of a gala night. 'We benefited from the experience of the previous year and took part in what many people believe was one of the best matches ever played at the old stadium. There was a lot of good football and we played really well against a good side with a lot of good players. We felt ourselves lucky to get the chance of satisfaction at Wembley so soon after the F.A. Cup Final.'

Greenwood acknowledged: 'This was Bobby Moore's greatest game for West Ham. Technical perfection.'

The club had also learned their lesson from 1964. This time there was no banquet. Everyone went off to celebrate in his own way. Greenwood went home to his devoted wife, Lucy. Bobby and the boys made tracks to their favourite watering holes and drank the night away, not knowing that they were celebrating the end of West Ham's brief flirtation with success.

The following season they scraped through to the semi-final of the European Cup Winners' Cup, where they were well beaten at home and in West Germany by Borussia Dortmund. West Ham were already sliding into long years of agonising self-appraisal. After 1965, they always seemed to be asking themselves: What's gone wrong?

Moore conceded that the answer was more involved than his basic belief that Greenwood bought erratically. The great enigma of English Soccer was enmeshed in the fine strands of a complex West Ham philosophy which was straining to produce football of stunning simplicity.

Like a delicate cobweb glistening in the sunlight, West Ham were beautiful to behold but inspired no feeling of permanence.

On so many days they spun a silken web of delightful football, only to be blown into tatters by a storm of old-fashioned British sporting aggression.

'It was well known,' said Moore, 'that everyone enjoyed playing against West Ham as much as they enjoyed watching them. We had endless discussions about what went wrong but nobody seemed able to put their finger on it.'

Moore suspected they should have sought the answer in the difference between the West Ham which won the F.A. Cup and that which won the Cup Winners' Cup a year later.

All the brilliance of West Ham was distilled into that performance against TSV Munich 1860. The difference between that and their earlier Wembley performance could be traced to the emergence of one more West Ham player of sheer class.

Moore: 'It still surprises a lot of people to be told that Martin Peters was not in our 1964 F.A. Cup Final team. Martin is remembered as being as much a part of West Ham as Geoff Hurst and myself. But Eddie Bovington was the wing half in '64 and Martin didn't get the position until we went into Europe.

'That worked out well in its way. In the Cup Winners' Cup you needed more skill and Martin added an extra quality to our game. Yet whenever West Ham have been successful at home they have had a strong man, a battler at wing half.

'In the mid-Sixties we had Eddie Bovington. In the mid-Seventies they came up with Billy Bonds. Its been loosely talked about as adding steel to the West Ham team but that's too simple.

'There was plenty of bite about West Ham if you knew where to look for it. Even Martin had a nasty streak in him if something made him angry.

'It was a question of emphasis in the minds of the management. Ron Greenwood and John Lyall shied away when you mentioned putting some stick about. The emphasis was on skill. That was also the thought in our minds.

'I look on tackling as a skill. Any time I see a defender just whacking through the back of a forward's legs to get at a ball, that to me is ignorance. You can't win the ball if you've got a body in front of you. You don't have to go around kicking people up in the air to be a good tackler. The art is to deny a forward space and force him to knock the ball away.

'One of the problems was that sometimes West Ham didn't do this as a whole. They were so obsessed with creating space for themselves that they could not or did not recover when moves broke down.'

That failing conspired with a lot of Northern antagonism to undermine West Ham. The delicate football they played and the glamour surrounding some of their players made them bear the brunt of the anti-London feeling which exists in most football centres outside the capital.

Moore noticed it even before he got into the first team. 'I was a reserve standing in the tunnel at Upton Park one day when Bolton Wanderers came down with a team of hard nuts. They were all saying: "We're going to wipe the field with you pansies."

'Every team seemed to feel the same. Wherever we went they

seemed to want to get stuck into us; got all steamed up about giving West Ham a kicking. We were everybody's London hate team.

'Maybe we brought it on ourselves. In midwinter, we'd get to some of those tough, cold grounds in the North and we'd upset the locals by going out to play wearing gloves. They just thought we were a bunch of fairies. It was like a red rag to a bull with their players. They couldn't see the sense of it. Ron used to say "Put the gloves on; you can't concentrate on playing football when you've got cold extremities."

'The teams lower down the League were as bad. All wanted to stuff West Ham. That Johnny Quigley seemed to have all his best games against me. Turned us over again when he was with Mansfield and we went up there for a cup-tie in the mud.

'In the end our own fans turned against us. In 1967 we got a home draw with Swindon in the third round of the F.A. Cup and Geoff Hurst got a hat-trick but we still only drew. Went up to Swindon for the replay and lost. Awful. When we got back they had smashed in the windows of my sports shop opposite the ground. I couldn't be angry. It was as hard for us to understand how a team with three World Cup-winning players kept getting it wrong.'

What bothered Bobby most was that when he looked through the West Ham team he, like the fans, could find no really glaring weakness, no excuse for repeated failure. 'You looked at a few of the individuals and felt there might have been room for improvement. But the eleven pieces of the jigsaw fitted when we won the cups. They'd put the ingredients in the cocktail shaker and the team had come out right.

'It's like a drink. Sometimes a cocktail is fabulous, sometimes it's diabolical. But when you get it right it's a crime to let it go.

'Our successful team had the right mix even if some of the lads didn't seem too brilliant. If you wanted to be really critical you could find better goalkeepers than Jim Standen ... but at £6,000 from Luton he was perfect for West Ham.

'Ken Brown was far from being everyone's ideal at centre half but he was right for us. He was powerful in the air and his priority was always to get the ball the hell out of the danger area.

'Sometimes he would whack it away when I thought we should

capitalise on a situation and I'd say: "Brownie, what are you doing?" He'd say: "Don't worry, it's no trouble up there." But he was always positive and it took a long while to replace him.

'He had a good understanding with Jim Standen and with John Bond. It's no surprise they went on to work together as coach and manager at Norwich. Understanding is vital at the back. Ken and Jim Standen were good together and Jackie Burkett at left back was a very limited player and shy sort of person who was happy just to do what was asked of him and balance out the rest.

'Ronnie Boyce kept things ticking in midfield. Peter Brabrook or Alan Sealey took 'em on and knocked in some goals. Johnny Sissons kept threatening to be the best left winger on earth.

'Why didn't West Ham make something more of that boy? When he came into the League side as a teenager Johnny was pure gold. Specially that fabulous left foot. Early on he played against Liverpool and went to go down the line. As he went past Chris Lawler, the full back, Tommy Smith came hammering across and knocked him clean over the low wall at Upton Park into the crowd. I thought: "Jesus, Poor little feller. That's the last we'll see of him." But he picked himself up and came back to run Lawler and Smithy ragged. It was one of the sweetest sights I've ever seen.

'He scored a goal in the F.A. Cup Final and was still only nineteen when he played in our European Final. At that time he would have been in my squad for the 1966 World Cup. But he never got any better. Ron Greenwood was still calling him young John when he was twenty-five. Perhaps it was because he was still young. But we should have been demanding things of Johnny Sissons as one of our experienced players.

'I'm sure there were many times in those five or six years when Ron made up his mind to leave John out of the side. Then you would see him Monday to Friday in training, up front in the road runs, fastest in the sprints, drilling them into the net with that left toot in five-a-sides, showing you ball skills which demanded a place in the team. Come the Saturday afternoon, nothing. John Sissons was non-existent. He was a thoroughbred who never matured.

'Against that, Ron had his successes. He had a lot to do with me and he turned Geoff Hurst from a bit of a cart-horse at wing-half into a truly great forward. None of us thought Geoff was going to make the switch. It took him years of hard work and patience to become the man who scored three goals in a World Cup Final.

'For a time he got away with it because he was just a foil for Budgie Byrne. He was so willing he ran himself into the ground and we used to give him terrible stick for all the things he was doing wrong. He was so willing it was untrue. He ran and ran and ran and was always just short of everything. I don't know how he put up with the abuse but it was worth it because in the mid-Sixties he became for a few seasons a genuine world class player.

'Playing behind Budgie and then playing up alongside him must have helped. That man was magic. Real touch, real class. If it hadn't been for the drink aggravating his weight problem Budgie would have been with us in the 1966 World Cup Final as well. Always chatting us through it, joking about. He virtually finished his top-class career with horseplay. We were over in Canada in 1965, had a few drinks and Budgie jumped off a stagecoach. Did his cartilage.

'So we had all that going for us and then up popped Martin Peters. Such talent. Played in every position for West Ham and was obviously best known as a midfield player who scored goals. Yet he could be a tremendous centre-half because of great ability in the air and long legs for tackling. Not the quickest man on earth but would never leave himself in a position where he could be vulnerable. Martin was a natural sportsman from the start, good at any game he tried. We might be travelling somewhere and see people playing an unusual game and Martin would ask to try it and be good at it straight away.

'It's laughable that people don't remember who scored the other goal in the World Cup Final. Martin's subtlety was probably the very reason he was never a big hit with the fans. Yet he was virtually a complete player. In addition to all his talent he had vision and awareness and a perfect sense of timing.

'In fact he was so subtle that when he moved on to Tottenham I felt the players there did not appreciate all his gifts and did not cash in on Martin the way we used to at West Ham.'

Sometimes, when West Ham were cashing in on all their varied attributes, they were irresistible. One Bank Holiday when Budgie was really on song, they put seven goals past the invincible Leeds United. Don Revie, the Leeds manager who later took charge of England's national team only to defect to the Arabian desert, went to the West Ham dressing room to offer congratulations and was disappointed to find Greenwood leaning against a water pipe, apparently unmoved by the brilliance of his own team. Revie went back to the Leeds dressing room and told his players: 'You will never lose to that man's team again.'

A few days later, in the return holiday fixture, Leeds thrashed West Ham by a similar margin. Yet the day came when West Ham hit form at Leeds to win a League Cup replay and Moore said: 'That was a real pleasure because they were the best side in the country and they had been hammering us stupid ever since we put those seven past them.'

There were other days like that, when the touch of genius was upon West Ham. But they dwindled in frequency. Other teams cloaked the increasing violence of their play with the euphemisms of the times: full blooded, competitive, professional. Other teams turned more to defence, ironically enough in the wake of what Moore, Hurst and Peters helped Alf Ramsey to achieve for a methodical England team in 1966.

Greenwood stuck to his principles. West Ham, somehow, clung to the lower reaches of the First Division. Moore: 'Often we had to play championship-class football just to get out of trouble at the end of the season. Then we would go away congratulating ourselves we had put everything right and sometimes we even started the next season the way we left off. No problems, until half a dozen games had gone by and slowly we lost the momentum.'

So what did go wrong?

Moore was unhappy with many of the signings Greenwood made to try to put matters right. 'After Jim Standen and Ken Brown went we always had trouble with goalkeepers and centre-halves.

'They never replaced Budgie up front. Even when they did find a striker who might have done the job they didn't know how to handle him.

'When Ted MacDougall came down from Manchester United it was obvious he was' the sort of player who needed to be geed-

up, encouraged. But when Ted had a bad time Ron just dropped
him and said: "The best gee-up any player can have is to be left
out of the side. It will make you more determined to get back."
That worked with some players but it killed off Ted MacDougall
as a West Ham player. All Bryan Robson needed was to be told
how good he was. But he was sold.'

Alternatively, there were plenty of fingers pointed at Moore
himself. The man who captained England so majestically was
accused of being less than interested in the fortunes of his club,
of pacing his game to come to a peak for international matches.

Greenwood confessed he thought of Moore as a big-occasion
player. Moore said: 'Some of my best games were played on cold
days in the North of England when we were well beaten because
we went out with hardly any sort of team at all. No one said a
word about those games. They just listened to the other rubbish.
I wanted a League Championship medal so badly I would have
lifted West Ham to the top single-handed if it was possible.'

If not culpable as a player, Moore may, however, have been
partly to blame off the pitch. West Ham certainly lost something
by the mutual failure of Greenwood and Moore to build a secure
relationship between manager and captain.

Bobby's mixed feelings kept him firmly in the players' camp.
When he did feel obliged to bridge the gap – as on the day he
agitated for Greenwood to sign Maurice Setters – he was more
often than not met by resistance. So West Ham had a captain
unable to act either as an intermediary between the management
and players or as a powerful influence on policy.

Those qualities hallmarked the captaincies of Danny Blanchflower in the Spurs League and Cup Double-winning team of the
early Sixties, Frank McLintock in the Arsenal Double team of the
early Seventies, Billy Bremner in the Leeds United team which
spanned more than a decade of greatness.

Moore had the insight to put his finger on the flaw in his own
make-up: 'I would have liked more powerful, more dominating
people around me at West Ham. People like that inspired me to
involve myself and to enjoy life. I needed to react to big personalities because I knew that deep down I was not like that
myself then. Not when I was alone.'

That goes a long way towards explaining the change which

came over him when he played for his country. It was with England that Bobby Moore found himself surrounded by characters substantial enough to help him develop into one of the most important personalities in world football.

8

Guess Who's Coming to Chile

The moment Ron Greenwood held open the door to the England team, Bobby Moore could cheerfully have relieved his mentor of a few front teeth.

The problem was that West Ham's manager amused himself by giving the bad news first. Greenwood called Moore to his office, looked stern and said: 'You won't be coming with us on the trip.'

Bobby had worked hard for the club in that 1961–2 season and, like any inquisitive young man, was looking forward to the reward of a summer tour of Rhodesia and Nigeria. It was more a challenge than a question when he said 'Why? What the hell have I done wrong?'

He should have asked what he had done right. At 21, he was the apple of his manager's eye. For some months Greenwood had been alerting England team manager Walter Winterbottom to the rapid progress of his protege.

Greenwood was doubling as manager of the England under-23 team, so the then-traditional eve of Cup Final match between England and Young England gave Moore the chance to justify Greenwood's propaganda. Moore did them both proud even without realising how much was at stake: 'As far as we all knew the World Cup party had been picked. The under-23s were always ready to have a go at the seniors and that year the lads in the full squad were still out to impress because places in the actual World Cup team were up for grabs.

'It was a good game. I felt I'd performed well and went home happy. For me, that was that.'

Not for Winterbottom. He and Greenwood discussed Bobby at length that Friday night. As the pre-selected squad for the 1962 World Cup in Chile gathered in London, he bounced Moore's name around with his assistants Jimmy Anderson and Harold Shepherdson.

By Tuesday morning, Winterbottom had played out the necessary charade with the members of the international selection committee, the archaic cross England managers before Alf Ramsey had to bear, and Moore was summoned to Greenwood's office at Upton Park.

Greenwood smiled at Bobby's flash of anger and came on with the good news: 'Walter wants you to go with him to Chile.'

Moore always acknowledged his debt to Greenwood: 'I don't doubt that Ron worked on that chance for me with everyone at the F.A. He and Walter were particularly close.'

Winterbottom relieved the publicity pressure on his recruit by doing nothing to dispel the public impression that young Moore was merely gathering experience by training with his elders and betters in the England party.

It was not in Bobby's nature to trumpet his own arrival. He joined in the training, studied everything and everyone, said little or nothing. The deception grew as the rest of the party kept returning to their hotel while Bobby stayed at home to deal with injections, suit fittings, and the collection of playing gear and to finalise personal arrangements for an unexpectedly long absence from England.

The rest of the players were too preoccupied with their own prospects, some dreaming of victory, others just hoping for a game, to realise that the greatest career in the history of English football was beginning in their midst.

Not until Moore's third day with the squad did captain Johnny Haynes realise Winterbottom was talking to Bobby as well as the rest of them about the travelling arrangements. Haynes at once went to Moore and said: 'Look, I'm so sorry. I didn't know you were coming with us. I thought you were here just to make up the numbers in training. But welcome.' That was the fumbling start of a long-running mutual admiration society.

Even after that, many of the players remained unaware that Bobby had been added to the playing party because the members of the squad were allowed to go home for the last weekend before their flights to South America.

At that time the Munich air crash which wiped out the bulk of Manchester United's great team was a vivid scar on every footballer's mind. It became the practice of most teams, England included, to divide their party between two flights in the belief that half a disaster was better than losing every player in a single crash.

Winterbottom had told Moore to be ready for the first plane out, then realised how that move might give away his private intentions. Moore reflected: 'When that late call-up came I thought it would be an experience to train with these players and see them play against some of the best teams in the world, a privilege just to be with them preparing for a tournament like that.

'Then Walter sorted out who was going on which flight and it seemed logical to me that the team for the warm up match in Peru would be chosen from those on the first plane. It arrived 24 hours earlier and gave people a day longer to acclimatise.

'When he put me on the first plane it just stirred in the back of my mind that I might have an outside chance of being a surprise selection. But when we got together again on the Monday I was switched to the second flight a day later. I accepted he'd made a mistake and I was going along for the ride, I was a player for the future.'

Winterbottom had everyone fooled. Moore stepped off the late flight to Lima and into the right half position in the England team. Jimmy Greaves provided what Moore described as 'his usual three goals'. Ron Flowers scored a penalty. And Bobby Moore was a fixture in the England team by the end of his full international debut.

He was blessed with a disarming knack of using understatement to emphasise the measure of his achievements without appearing a braggart. He said of his first effort in the white shirt of England: 'Walter was also pleased with the defensive performance and kept virtually the same team for all four matches in that World Cup.'

That team comprised Ron Springett, Jimmy Armfield, Moore, Maurice Norman (who also made his debut in Peru), Flowers, Bryan Douglas, Greaves, either Gerry Hitchens or Alan Peacock at centre forward, Haynes and Bobby Charlton.

Together they travelled high into the Chilean mountains for ten days' acclimatisation to South American altitude and were promptly beaten by another European nation, Hungary.

Winterbottom, however, saw nothing in that 2–1 defeat to shake his faith in Moore. He simply replaced Hitchens with Peacock and let the rest of them get on with it against Argentina.

Flowers converted his customary penalty, Greaves and Charlton both scored and England were 3–1 winners of a match Moore expected to be the hardest in their group.

Moore was adjusting more readily than he had dared hope to the rarefied atmosphere of the World Cup, helped by an instant rapport with Haynes who 'always wanted the ball, just like me' and Greaves 'who showed where he wanted it and usually stuck it away'.

His instant education programme continued from a successful debut in Peru, defeat by the technicians of Hungary and satisfying triumph over the brooding Argentines into a purely political match against Bulgaria.

The experience saddened him far more than losing an attractive match to Hungary. 'Right to the end of my England career that game stuck in my mind as the worst international I ever played in. Bulgaria had lost both their other group matches and we only had to draw to qualify for the quarter finals. They wanted to salvage something to go home with, a point at least. So they played with nine men in their own half.

'We started off trying to play the game but as soon as we realised what they were up to we knew we would go through if we didn't take any chances. So we kept nine men in our half. It made me feel terrible. We would have a dozen passes at our end and then try to hit the ball up to our one forward. He was bound to lose it. So they had fourteen passes at their end and tried to hit their one forward in our half. It was one of the poorest international matches of all time.'

Nevertheless Moore, an optimist by nature, felt England were ready for Brazil. He could be forgiven his mistaken judgement.

Until that quarter-final day in Vina del Mar, he had never seen
the Brazilians play.

Moore had slipped so comfortably into the England routine,
had seemed so exactly talented for international football that he
was already regarded as a well-integrated cog of the machine.
Brzail provided a timely reminder that he would never stop
learning about the game: 'Thank goodness there was no Pele.
But they had the Santos boys, Garrincha, Didi, Vava, Amarildo,
Zagalo ... most of the team that had won the World Cup in
Sweden four years before.

'I really felt we were doing quite well against them. Garrincha
got a goal in the first half but Gerry Hitchins got us back on level
terms and I felt we could hold them. But when we came back out
Garrincha suddenly produced one of his famous free kicks. It
bent all over the place. I'd never seen anything like it. The ball
hit Ron Springett in the chest and Vava was in like a flash to make
it 2–1. We felt we had to push forward for the equaliser and
Garrincha used the space to take another goal off us. Like candy.
Goodnight.

'We came home. Didn't stop to see them win it. I knew they'd
win it. Easy. Stuck four past Chile in the semi and three more past
Czechoslovakia in the Final, always having plenty in hand to
turn on the magic when they went for the kill in the second half.'

Moore came home enriched by an experience which ironically
put the skids under Winterbottom.

Bobby was putting his life in order that summer. The rookie
who boarded the plane to Peru returned a World Cup veteran, a
five-cap international, to marry his girl and set up house. By the
time England played France that October, Moore's existence was
neatly packaged to the liking of his tidy mind, a mind already
coming to the conclusion that England were a bad side.

In every player who settles down to a long international career,
the initial exhilaration at being picked for his country sooner or
later gives way to a realistic appraisal of the quality of the team.
With Moore, it was sooner.

Bobby's natural acceptance of his own success and his calculating nature set his mind to assessing England's shortcomings
even as he lazed on his honeymoon beach. In theory he was the
new boy. In practice his thoughts were coincidentally grooved

into the same channels as those of the England manager.

Winterbottom had been pondering his own and England's future for many weeks when France came to Sheffield Wednesday's Hillsborough ground on October 3, 1962. The occasion was the first match in the Nations Cup, the Championship of Europe which would also become a blight on Alf Ramsey's record and those of Revie, Robson and Taylor when they succeeded to this precarious throne.

The first great team in the history of French football – hinged around Kopa and Fontaine and good enough to reach a World Cup semi-final against Brazil in 1958 – was past its physical prime but still rich in class. England were spared home defeat only by a Flowers penalty and Moore said: 'Even though we drew 1–1 we were played off the park. An awful performance. No organisation. No nothing. It was clear to me I'd come in on the end of an era.

'A little earlier England had a tremendous run after adopting a 4–2–4 formation using Haynes and Robson in midfield. I'd seen them beat Spain 4–2 at Wembley a couple of years earlier and thought they were a helluva side. I'd understood why when I first spoke to Walter. He was a warm, outgoing man who loved talking about techniques, tactics, skills, attitudes. You could bet your life he knew every good player in every country by his Christian name, knew every individual's strengths and weaknesses.

'The man was a walking education on football. But he was at the end of his reign. Walter had impressed me because he knew so much about the game, every aspect of it. I had been with him on youth and coaching courses and he was responsible for getting coaching organised in this country. He made people think about football. He did such a great deal for English football that I couldn't understand how he allowed himself to be messed about by the amateurs of the F.A. selection committee.

'I felt he'd lost the will to fight the system. Some of the lads were already asking how much he had to nod to the F.A. It was obvious to me he had to answer to the selection committee, which made it hard for him to retain his respect. His time was up.'

Winterbottom knew himself it was time to move over. The fire was going out in his team. Loyally, he stirred the embers

sufficiently to achieve formal, predictable wins over Northern
Ireland and Wales in the next two months while his employers
opened negotiations which brought Ramsey from astonishing
success at Ipswich Town to the far more profound challenge at
Lancaster Gate.

Ramsey had seen how Winterbottom had been undermined by
the interference of the selection committee and took the England
managership on condition that he had the sole right to pick the
team.

By February 27, 1965 the word 'selection' had been dropped
from the title of the F.A.'s senior international selection committee
and Ramsey was exercising his prerogative in Paris, against
France, in the return match in the European Championship.

Bobby Smith and Ron Henry were brought into the side from
Ramsey's old club, Tottenham Hotspur, and all England waited
for the kind of tactical miracle which had spirited Ipswich Town
from nowhere to the First Division Championship.

Moore recalled all the players being wary of Ramsey, a much
quieter, more introvert character than Winterbottom. Within a
few minutes of the kick-off Moore had his suspicions confirmed
that he was still part of a bad team. By half time England were 3–
1 down and Ramsey faced his first real test. Moore: 'France were
still going strong and we were diabolical. Everyone waited to see
how Alf would react. He stayed very calm, told us we could still
win the game if we went out and started to play a bit and believed
we could do it.

'There was none of the ranting and raving you might have got
from some managers in the middle of a bad defeat.'

For a few minutes, at least, it worked. Bobby Tambling, Chelsea's all-time record scorer, added an England goal to the one
scored by Smith in the first half. But the organisation was weaker
than the belief in recovery and France swept gracefully to a 5–2
triumph.

Superficially, it was anything but an auspicious start to Ramsey's stewardship. But while the world mocked the result, Alf
began seeking the answers. He was already in no doubt of whom
to ask the questions.

Moore had no sooner settled into his seat in the coach taking
them sadly from the stadium in Paris than he looked up to see

England's new manager sitting alongside. Bobby recalled: 'Alf started asking a million things about the way things had been done under' Walter. I was playing a sort of old-fashioned right half at the time, neither functioning properly in midfield nor in defence. I was falling between two stools and he was obviously going to sort that out. Ron Springett had a bad night in Paris and he played in goal for England only occasionally after that. Gordon Banks was one of the new faces introduced to the side.'

Ramsey had already settled on Moore as his lieutenant, partly because he knew he had not been involved with England long enough to store up tight-lipped loyalties to Winterbottom. The foundations were laid of a long relationship which never once became blurred by emotion.

The icily resolved ambition of both men to conquer the football world had to survive one blistering test, six weeks later. Scotland came to Wembley full of literal and metaphorical spirit – the fans with fumes on their breath, the players breathing fire – to give Ramsey his first bitter reason for hating the Auld Enemy. A goal from Douglas was not enough to stop Scotland winning 2–1 and inevitably making a great deal of noise about it.

A month later the tide of results turned. Douglas scored again at Wembley and this time his effort sufficed to hold Brazil to a draw. There was method and morale, organisation and optimism about the new England as they embarked for Ramsey's first summer tour.

The cornerstone was laid on May 20, 1963, without ceremony, in grey and distant Bratislava. Jimmy Armfield was injured. Ramsey leapt at the chance to give the England captaincy to his young lieutenant, Bobby Moore.

Those closest to Moore advised the world and his wife to put their mortgage on England beating Czechoslovakia. Those who thought they knew better compared records, studied the teams and deferred judgement.

Moore recalled: 'I loved that first experience of leading England out. The atmosphere was magic. The crowd are fanatical in Bratislava. I decided we'd only get beat over my dead body. The Czechs were still a great side. It had taken Brazil to beat them in the World Cup Final the previous summer and the stars were all there, Popluhar, Novak, that magical man Masopust.'

Jimmy Greaves, two, Bobby Smith and Bobby Charlton shared the goals in a 4–2 win. The way Moore presided over the match had the accompanying jostle of journalists writing about Englishmen holding their heads high on foreign fields once again.

Chauvinism was reinforced as England went on to Leipzig and 2–1 victory over the East Germans. The testing Iron Curtain stretch of the tour was over and Ramsey was able to omit Moore, among others, to give loyal reserves a game in Switzerland, which was duly won 8–1.

Moore returned for a string of autumn wins over Wales, the Rest of the World and Northern Ireland. The latter 8–3 romp, on November 20, 1963, celebrated Wembley's first floodlit football match.

Already the milestones were piling up. So was Moore's confidence in Ramsey's administration. 'For the first time since I'd come on the scene, England were really getting organised. I don't mean that to be disrespectful to Walter but I'd come in at the end of his reign, when he'd done it all. Alf was fresh and full of ambition.'

Scotland popped up in the spring of '64 to dent a few mushrooming egos, beating England 1–0 at Hampden Park. Yet even defeat seemed to serve Moore's purpose.

That was Jimmy Armfield's last international and there was no longer a valid rival for the captaincy.

Other faces in other places changed as the games ticked through Ramsey's meticulous preparations for the World Cup itself. Pickering, Wignall, Bailey, Hinton, Baker ... all came and went as the caps mounted up for Bobby Moore.

Only once did Ramsey detect in Moore's attitude to England the subtle drift from convincing arrogance to worrying complacency which sometimes afflicted his football for West Ham. Corrective treatment was at once forthcoming.

By June 1966 Ramsey had crystallised his eddying pool of talent into a final squad of 22 players who left for a warm-up tour of Europe. Moore recalled: 'Alf numbered everyone from 1–22 and the feeling was that those who were numbered from 1–11 were going to be the World Cup team. I was number six and full of myself. And Alf left me out of the first game of the tour.

'From being Jack the Lad I was now on the run. A lot of people had been punting to get Norman Hunter into the team in my place. A lot of the press were saying I wasn't good enough and Norman should be in. When they won 3 – 0 in Finland everyone thought the writing was on the wall for R. Moore.

'It made me sit up. From that day on I never *expected* to be in an England squad until the letter from the F.A. dropped through the letter-box, never took it for granted I would be in the team until I saw my name on the sheet or heard Alf call it out.

'Alf was driving it home to me that there are always enough players for any team to get by without any one player. I was disappointed. So sick. I'd gone through all those games. The preparation had become really intense during ten days in the training camp at Lilleshall.

'No one was more relieved when he brought me back in Oslo. No one was more on his toes.'

Moore led England to wins over Norway and Denmark, then on to Katowice. Gornik were doing well in European club competition and most of the critics thought Poland were too tough a choice for the last test of Ramsey's World Cup team.

Roger Hunt's goal gave 1–0 victory to Banks, Cohen, Wilson, Stiles, Charlton, Moore, Ball, Greaves, Charlton, Hunt and Peters. Yet it was Moore who made it possible. A performance of chilling, almost brutal authority declared the studs as well as the skills of England's captain well and truly sharpened for the conflict ahead.

There was just one problem. Secretly, not even Alf Ramsey was sure if Bobby Moore was eligible to play for England in the 1966 World Cup Finals.

9

Arsenal and Old Lace

The Hendon Hall Hotel is secreted in the outer fringe of north west London, a short, nervous and invariably silent drive in England's team coach along the North Circular Road to the turreted portals of Wembley.

It would have provided apt headquarters for the English footballers in 1966, had the footballers been typical Englishmen.

Normally, there is a sort of hushed reverence about the dark brown rooms, the modicum of noise generated by the regular inmates being absorbed as much by the cloistered atmosphere as by the Regency carpets. It is the kind of hotel you imagine creaking, even if the doors are well-oiled and the floorboards firm.

Periodically, Hendon Hall used to be shaken out of its metaphorical mothballs by the glamorous and muscular presence of the cream of England's footballers. This was Alf Ramsey's hideaway for his beloved team, vine-clad security from public eyes prying into private little dramas, like that which clouded the dawn of England's World Cup. On the morning of July 7, 1966, with the nation waiting for England to set the jamboree in motion, Bobby Moore was football's equivalent of a stateless person.

West Ham and their most famous son had been playing brinkmanship with each other for months, right through Moore's preparations for captaining England in their finest hour.

Other, bigger, wealthier clubs had sensed Moore's dismay as defeat in the semi-final of the European Cup Winners' Cup had turfed West Ham out of the honours for the first time in three years.

The season at Upton Park had ended on a flat, sour note. The pressure on Moore to seek a move to a grander club had been intensified by his deep involvement with the England squad, whose meetings are a notorious tapping ground for unsettled players.

Moore was not only ripe for tapping – a clandestine approach from another club, in this case via one of its own players – but also concerned that Norman Hunter's success with Leeds United might edge him out of the England team.

He went to see Ron Greenwood but recalled: 'There was no way we could negotiate. West Ham said they would not let me go in any circumstances. Ron and I had it out for hours. Finally we agreed to let it ride until after the World Cup.

'Our differences were supposed to be our secret. But then a big story broke in the newspapers. I stormed in to see Ron and he admitted he'd let it out because he was so sick of the whole business and all the talk and rumours that he wanted to get it off his chest. So I dug my heels in and refused to sign a new contract.'

With a dramatic sense of timing, Moore's contract with West Ham expired on June 30. For the first seven days of July he was working with Alf Ramsey towards the pinnacle of their mutual ambitions, yet he was not officially contracted to any club in the Football League. So, legally, he did not exist as a player in the eyes of the Football Association, whose team he was about to lead into the World Cup Finals.

Ramsey's whispered and frantic consultations with F.A. officials ended with him urging Moore to regularise his position by signing a contract for one month; long enough to get their hands on the Jules Rimet Trophy.

All of a lather, Greenwood was summoned to hurry the appropriate forms to Hendon Hall. He found England's manager and captain waiting in the foyer. Ramsey pointed to a dark, panelled door and told Greenwood: 'You can have him in that room for just one minute.'

Moore signed the form in seconds, barely exchanging a word with Greenwood before returning to the business of the moment, the struggle with Uruguay.

West Ham's manager escaped, the reason for his visit undetected, silently cursing the clandestine attempt to recruit his
captain which had inveigled him into that embarrassment.

Moore admitted: 'I knew perfectly well which club I was
going to join if I could twist Ron's arm to let me go ...
Tottenham Hotspur. I'd had a good run in the cups with West
Ham, got the England captaincy. And everyone knew Spurs
were interested.

'The Hammers looked like they might be going on the blink.
A lot of people were suggesting that Norman's form made me a
bit iffy in the England team. Tottenham caught me on the rebound
from our Cup Winners' Cup defeat. I'd heard a lot of rumours
that they would like me. It was easy for Spurs because I used
to see a lot of Terry Venables. After talking to Terry and to
other Tottenham players it was obvious there was a genuine
interest.'

Venables' stay at Spurs was not wildly popular with the White
Hart Lane crowd. He was *en route* from Chelsea to bigger things
at Crystal Palace and Queen's Park Rangers and enormous affairs
as manager of Barcelona. Eventually, he was destined to return
to Tottenham as the highly-celebrated football manager who
summoned up the cheek and the capital actually to win control
of the club after a contentious takeover battle.

Back in the Sixties, he was already a deep thinker about the
game and became a confidant of manager Bill Nicholson.

Venables lived near Moore's Chigwell home and the pair were
warm acquaintances, moving in similar social circles. Moore said:
'Spurs were supposed to be above these things, but the fact
remained that they wanted me and I was itching to go there.
Tottenham would have suited me down to the ground. They were
the team of the Sixties. No trouble.'

Tapping, of course, infringes the laws of the football authorities,
who try to insist that players are the last to know about transfer
negotiations supposedly conducted in seemly fashion between
the gentlemen in charge of their clubs.

Moore's sympathy for West Ham's chagrin at the trouble
caused by Tottenham's interest would have been more acute had
he not had solid grounds for suspecting that Greenwood was
himself a skilled player of the transfer game.

The first evidence for that had come in 1960 when Greenwood was assistant manager at Arsenal and vitally interested in relieving West Ham of their future England captain.

Moore was then making headway in an England under-23 team managed by Greenwood. He said: 'Ron used to talk to me a lot at that time. He never actually said anything I could put my finger on but I kept going home from those under-23 sessions with the distinct impression that he wanted me to go to Arsenal. Then one of the Highbury lads in the squad gave me a pull one day and said: "You know they'd like you at our place." Finally one of Ron's pet journalists came on my ear about getting away from West Ham to Arsenal.

'If the chance had come I would have loved to have gone to Arsenal for the same reason that Spurs appealed ... a big club. But I suppose when they made the official approaches West Ham knocked them back.

'The funny thing was that Ron came to West Ham instead. He told me that the chance to work with me in club football was a big reason for him moving from Highbury to Upton Park. That was a twist.'

That was in the spring of 1961. Within a year Greenwood was using Moore to help him sign another player who was to have a profound influence on West Ham's cup fortunes in the mid-Sixties: Johnny Byrne.

Moore and Byrne were combining well in England's under-23 team and Moore recalled: 'We were even rooming together on the trips so it was easy for me to establish that Budgie was as interested as West Ham in a move of this kind.'

Even so, West Ham still had to pay a then-record fee between British clubs of £65,000 – that's right, all the zeros are there – to secure Byrne from Third Division Crystal Palace.

Moore, like most people in football was involved in covert negotiations and felt no remorse whatsoever for his part in breaches of football's vaguely ludicrous laws.

He said: 'Is it wrong? Maybe it would be if clubs had the decency to keep you informed of everything that might affect your career. It is a player's life yet often he is not even told when another club has made an offer which could change his whole life.

'They probably feel they are playing it straight because they are the guvnors. Yet managers move, like Ron did from Arsenal to West Ham. How infuriated a manager would be if a big club went after him and he did not find out until six months after the approach was made to his board of directors.

'The facts of the matter are that for a century football was just about the only business which denied a craftsman the freedom and liberty to work for whoever he wanted. Whatever opportunities came my way, if West Ham said No, that was the end of that.'

Much as Moore wanted to join Arsenal and Spurs early in his career, he felt the keenest frustration when, much later, West Ham denied him a transfer to Derby County.

On that occasion Brian Clough, a gentleman with about as much reverence for officialdom as Al Capone, did not so much tap Bobby Moore as beat him about the head with a sledgehammer.

Clough's latent interest in adding the England captain to his championship team at Derby was fanned to life by Moore's performance in West Ham's 1–1 draw at County's Baseball Ground towards the end of the 1972–3 season. Moore said of his efforts that day: 'I played more than well. Derby paralysed us but they only got a draw with a penalty in the 84th minute. Even Ron Greenwood came up to me and said well done. Praise indeed.'

The image of that majestic Moore performance was still alive in Clough's mind that summer as he strolled the tea lawns at Wimbledon as a paying spectator at the 1973 Lawn Tennis Championships.

By chance he fell into conversation with Nigel Clarke, a soccer reporter and occasional tennis writer for the *Daily Mirror*, and one of the few members of the media in whom Moore invested any trust.

Clough expressed his interest, Clarke telephoned Moore with that juicy piece of intelligence, then relayed his friend's eager response to the Derby manager, complete with Bobby's ex-directory telephone number.

One morning that July, Moore picked up his home 'phone to hear: 'Hello Bobby. This is Brian Clough. If you want to play for Derby will you pop up to London and meet me.'

Moore: 'I'd love to. Where?'

'Churchills.'

Churchills is about as quiet as any American-orientated hotel can be. It is plush and velvet and a trifle garish, yet kissed with a touch of aristocratic class and comfortably expensive. Clough could have made no better choice of venue to sell his deal to a working-class boy who had grown accustomed to doing things in style.

Clough has a habit of coming to the point. The men shook hands in the bar and this was Moore's recollection of their conversation. Clough said at once: 'I hear you're interested in winning a League Championship medal.'

Moore, touched on the sensitive spot of his one unfulfilled ambition: 'Who wouldn't be?'

Clough: 'Would you play for Derby County?'

'Why not?'

'That'll do me.'

The pair headed for lunch in the restaurant and were at first turned back by the *maître d'hôtel* because Moore was dressed in a casual shirt and sweater.

Clough brushed the protest aside: 'My team will never stay here again if *my* player can't sit in this restaurant.'

Moore protested: 'I don't play for you yet.'

Clough: 'Shut up. You're my player. That's no trouble. I'll ring Ron up now.'

Moore was astounded: 'I'd only been with the man five minutes and I shouldn't have been with him at all. Yet he phoned the West Ham ground and asked for Mr. Greenwood. He was on holiday. Cloughie asked where but they didn't know. He left a message for Ron to ring him the minute he returned.'

Clough's larger than life behaviour and burning passion for the game were already exciting Moore. He was deeply flattered when he asked why Derby wanted another central defender when they already had the future England pair, Roy McFarland and Colin Todd.

Clough said: 'I'll play Toddy alongside you at full back and tell him to watch, listen and learn from the Master.'

Bobby was hooked. 'All I could see was a white shirt with a ram on the chest. I felt at the time that I needed lifting, a gee-up, needed a boost. I felt all through my career that my own pride had carried me on. It had been self-motivation. Now I needed help to maintain my position in the game. Cloughie was generating that enthusiasm within a few minutes. I was impressed by the man. I loved him for wanting me. The pen was as good as in my hand.'

West Ham did not quite see it that way. The next Moore heard was that the directors had agreed in principle to a Derby bid in excess of £400,000 for himself and Trevor Brooking.

Then he heard that Greenwood had blocked the deal and once again he was knocking on his manager's door. 'They were huffing and puffing through another season and Ron said he felt they couldn't let me go.'

Greenwood, echoing the public suspicion of the time that Moore would not relish a move away from his favourite watering holes in London, asked: 'Why do you want to go to Derby?'

Moore: 'Because it would be good for me.'

'Is it money? Has someone spoken to you?'

'No,' Moore lied. 'But if it's true I'd like to know and I'd like to go. It's more than money. I want to speak to Brian Clough. Can I go if the deal's right?'

Again the answer came in the negative. Moore: 'I had to accept a sort of compromise. If I stayed to help them through that season they would let me go on a free transfer at the end. So I would be able to negotiate a good deal for myself.

'Transfers are often about luck and timing. It wasn't long before Cloughie left Derby and Ron was telling me what a favour he'd done me by stopping me from going up there. Who knows?'

The mutual respect between two men who hardly knew each other was brought back into focus when Fulham were drawn against Nottingham Forest in the 1974–5 F.A. Cup. Clough, in his capacity as Forest manager, went to study Fulham's replay against Hull City, Moore was warmed to see an evening newspaper interview in which Clough was asked what he thought of Fulham and replied: 'Bobby Moore plays for them, doesn't he?'

Fulham came through that round of the Cup into a four-match saga with Forest. After one drawn match, on February 3, 1975 in Nottingham, Clough walked into the Fulham dressing room and quickly pressed a packet into Moore's hands, saying: 'Just a little present for Tina.'

Moore unwrapped a tablecloth of finest Nottingham lace and wondered if it was some sort of a joke, until he read the attached note.

Dear Bobby,

Just a little bit of Nottingham lace for your wife. I didn't have time to have a word with you the last two times we were at Fulham but judging by your performance you are in excellent condition. It was a tragedy we could never get together as a team but that's just one of the barmy parts of football.

Brian

It was a barmier part of football that Moore had gone into the 1966 World Cup Finals knowing that the better he played for England, the less his chances of the transfer to Spurs on which he had set his heart.

'At the moment I was signing that one-month contract in that room at Hendon Hall, I felt convinced that Ron was so sick of the whole business that he would let me go. If England had done badly I would have been on my way to Tottenham the minute the World Cup was over.'

No one watching Bobby Moore at Wembley could have guessed at his dilemma.

10

Home Sweet Home

Bobby Moore's capacity for playing great matches to the background of personal drama was matched only by his unfailing sense of occasion.

The vulturous critics of this most successful young man were about to be confounded at the one place which Moore knew mattered most in English football: Wembley.

The lushest turf. The twin towers. The 100,000 worshippers filling cathedral terraces. Never mind the cracks of obsolescence, feel the atmosphere. Here was the grassy Shangri-La of all our boyhood dreams.

Moore had grown up with those fantasies, and with them the ability to have realised already the ambition of playing to full houses at the famous stadium.

By the summer of '66 he was ready to unfurl the full standard of his greatness and make the place his own. Many splendid talents were to grace the World Cup stage that July but by the time the drama was done Wembley belonged to Bobby Moore just as surely as the Old Vic to Sir Laurence Olivier.

Don Revie was among those campaigning at the time for Moore's replacement in the England team by his own awesome Leeds United defender, Norman Hunter.

Later, much later, after Moore had finished amassing international caps and Revie had succeeded Sir Alf Ramsey as England manager, owning-up time came over drinks in a London penthouse.

Revie admitted the impact of Moore's World Cup: 'Had I been

England manager earlier, I would have picked you in front of Norman. Because you could produce it for the big one. Week in, week out for Leeds I would have gone for Norman. But it would have been you at Wembley.'

Moore: 'If I'd been at Leeds instead of West Ham there would have been no ordinary matches. Every game would have been a big game. Every game might have meant a championship medal. I'd have given you a Wembley, every game.'

Either by accident of the draw, or devious design of the Football Association, every England game of the 1966 World Cup was at Wembley.

The world put tongue in cheek and said: 'Lucky England'. Moore relished the experience, yet recognised the demands Wembley made on the limbs of England players straining to satisfy the expectations of the home nation.

'There had been talk of the semi-final going to Everton's ground if the groups worked out that way. As it happened we did eventually play all our games at Wembley. I'm not saying that didn't help in some ways. But at the same time it was an exhausting achievement to play six games in eighteen days on such a tiring pitch with all the tension and atmosphere surrounding the World Cup.

'It was nice not to have to uproot ourselves from the hotel and travel to another centre. Yet at a club ground we would have felt closer to the crowd and sensed their support far more. Wembley is wearying and the tension was heightened because London was the focal point of all the interest and pressure.'

Pressure? Moore's computerised resilience under fire supplied priceless support for the man under the most savage strain of all ... Alf Ramsey.

Ramsey had turned the screw on himself two years earlier with the uncharacteristically rash prediction that England would win the World Cup. 'That was one of the few times he let his pride show through,' said Moore. 'He had also spent two years getting together the players he wanted and felt in his heart that we would not be beaten too often in the next few years.

'We didn't lose many and Alf knew the way it went in players' minds. If you don't lose you start believing you are unbeatable, especially if you are playing a big tournament in front of your home supporters. Then the other teams start worrying about you, think you're the big obstacle, the team to beat.

'Alf had it all mapped out. The players and the matches he needed to win the Cup. So he went and blurted out that we would win. That was bad enough. Then he took stick from the critics all through the build-up because it didn't look as if he was getting the right team together.'

Oddly, the hounding Ramsey was receiving from the press – whom most star footballers the world over tend to generalise as the enemy – helped cement the corporate will to win and community spirit of mutual aid which became the trade marks of Ramsey's team. Moore recalled: 'The spirit in the camp had been good from way back, but with every new blast at Alf the sprit grew. We believed we had a great chance. Alf believed in us. We would show 'em.'

Not at first, they didn't. England got the show on the road to a great roar of anticipation which fizzled into a 0–0 draw with Uruguay – 'We just didn't function at all.' Then came a 2–0 win over Mexico – 'We were struggling until Bobby Charlton got a goal out of the blue.' Then they beat France 2–0 to qualify for the quarter finals in a blaze of anxiety – 'France hadn't won a game and were not a good side at all by 1966, yet we weren't very convincing against them.'

Ramsey was convinced of only one thing: his wingers were not good enough. Moore: 'Everyone refers back to the 1966 team as the wingless wonders, yet Alf played wingers in all those first three games.'

Ramsey had first picked a team without a semblance of a good old-fashioned winger for the last preparatory match in Poland. Prophetically Alan Ball had worn No. 7 and Martin Peters had won his first cap at No. 11, both functioning as wide midfield players coming late to support attacks. It had worked well, creating unusual spaces in a packed Continental defence which could be exploited by intelligent players. Yet it deprived the press and the public of the drama of ball-playing wingers plying the penalty area with crosses and incidents.

So against Uruguay, Ramsey, who paid more heed to the critics than he ever cared to admit, replaced Peters with John Connelly. Peters came back against Mexico but Ball was dropped to make way for Southampton winger Terry Paine, Ramsey confiding in Moore: 'I'm going to have to leave out Ballie. I know he'll be sick but I need a winger.'

Against France, Paine was replaced by Liverpool's Ian Callaghan. Still everyone knew the blend was far from perfect. Moore: 'The sad part for Alf, looking back, is that he wanted to play wingers but he was crucified for doing away with them.

'Paine, Connelly, Callaghan. Peter Thompson was also in the party. They all had their opportunities but Alf got no success with any of them. He wanted wingers because they give you a way to get round behind defences, create chances and win games. But the ones who were available didn't have the right attitude, the right temperament . . . the right something.

'What do you do if the people you play aren't good enough and aren't doing the job for you and you've got other people you can utilise better in a different way? I tell you. You use Ballie and Martin Peters.'

That was Ramsey's solution for the quarter-final match which had the entire country in an advanced state of jitters. One other decisive alteration was made for Ramsey by injury. Jimmy Greaves, whose genius never quite compensated in Ramsey's mind for his unwillingness to run as far or tackle as hard as the others, was injured against France.

Greaves was Moore's room-mate at Hendon Hall and Bobby had to console him as well as congratulate his West Ham team-mate, Geoff Hurst, on being selected for his first appearance in the World Cup.

'Greavesy was sick at being out,' said Moore. 'He was to be a lot sicker by the end of the tournament.'

Yet before the match against Argentina the betting shops were conspicuously empty of people rushing to put their mortgage on Hurst ending England's goal famine.

Argentina were the menace crouched in the undergrowth. A dark, brooding, panther of a team, spitting, snarling and waiting to devour the unwary with an explosion of lithe and powerful movement.

England had watched with grim fascination as Argentina and West Germany kicked a goalless draw out of each other in their group.

Ramsey's team talk amounted to one sentence which was something of a parody of the British war-time spirit against the odds. Like a Blimpish colonel at a briefing, he said only: 'Well, gentlemen, you know the sort of game you have on your hands this afternoon.'

'That was enough,' said Moore, whose recollection of his own doubts summed up all England's anxiety. 'The players didn't say anything or admit anything publicly or even among ourselves but deep down we all had secret fears about Argentina.

'We accepted in our guts it was going to be hard. Maybe brutal. We hadn't conceded a goal in the tournament so we didn't feel that they ought to beat us on overall quality. The problem was that this was a sudden death, knock-out quarter final and that while we were going for the win they might upset us, frustrate us, and catch us unawares. We even knew the public doubted we could do it. Because we hadn't looked like scoring goals.'

The Argentinians were nursing similar neuroses about England and set about their problem in a way which was to draw an uncharacteristic outburst from Ramsey. After the match, England's manager lost his head and called the Argentinians: 'Animals'.

Even during the heat of the battle Moore retained his composure and held the rhythm and the temper of his team together. Moore's splendid form had done much to get England that far without conceding a goal, and the captain was not about to let his men throw it all away because of Argentinian intimidation: 'Animals? I don't know. The South Americans play the game by a different code. They were sure as hell not very pleasant to play against. They did do nasty things. They did tug your hair, spit at you, poke you in the eyes and kick you when the ball was miles away and no one was looking.

'It wasn't nice, but it wasn't worth losing the game over. I managed not to get involved. Around and about me I could see lads like Ballie and Nobby Stiles and big Jack Charlton getting steamed up and finding it difficult to get on with the game.

'I just said that the only way to deal with them was to beat the bastards. That was what would hurt them. Because their attitude was simply not to lose. Not at any cost. Off the pitch they were supposed to be charmers. I just said that off the pitch we didn't even have to look at them. Just beat them out here.'

Even under such steadying leadership, even with the latent understanding Hurst had built up at club level with Moore and Peters, England might still have been playing Argentina today but for the intervention of a short and balding referee.

In the midst of all the mayhem, Rudolf Kreitlin of West Germany sent off Antonio Rattin, millionaire aristocrat, midfield thoroughbred, captain of Argentina almost by birthright.

For what?

'Who knows?' said Moore. 'Swearing? Taking the mickey? Anyway the little bald fellow gave him his marching orders. They argued, they strutted about. It seemed to take for ever. It was probably four or five minutes. I looked around and saw Ray Wilson sitting calmly on the ball. Liked that. Someone else was asking if I thought we'd start again. They had FIFA officials down out of the stand. Ken Aston, chairman of the referees' committee, was on the touchline putting in his two pennyworth.

'I watched Rattin go. Alf had great admiration for Rattin as a player. During the game he'd lived up to it all. An upstanding, strong man. Powerful, fine skill, good appreciation of what was happening around him. Knew the game inside out.

'As he went down the tunnel he left the door open for us. Just a crack. Even with ten men they still put up a hell of a struggle. But then the understanding between Geoff and Martin got us through.

'They knew each other's play by instinct and they found a chink of space they'd used a million times for West Ham. Martin laid in a near post cross and Geoff got that priceless goal. The game was as good as over, the hard part done. It taught a lot of people the value of having the understanding of good club units in the England team.'

Moore, Peters and Hurst represented West Ham's strong thread of understanding through the team. Bobby Charlton and Nobby Stiles elevated their midfield partnership with Manchester United into a vibrant international force.

That was why Ramsey fought so hard to resist the political chicanery designed to force Stiles out of the team. That, and the small matter of Stiles' murderous tackling scaring the living daylights out of Eusebio, the one man Portugal prayed could fire them to the Championship.

'Nobby had this thing with a lot of Continental forwards,' said Moore. 'He was a tough little nut and they didn't have the heart to try to go past him because they knew it would hurt.

'They felt it was easier to get him banned than to take him on out there in a match. So there was a lot of pressure from the world press and a lot of talking in the corridors of power.'

The waves of trouble barely washed against the shores of the England camp. To the players it had become unthinkable that they should go into a major match without their Nobby and footballers by and large pay little attention to football politics until it affects them directly.

Stiles had become a sort of playing mascot. A comical little ferret of a man with no front teeth on the pitch and owlish spectacles off it, he was also the first out-and-out ball winner, a destructive, abrasive species which blossomed under Ramsey in the face of withering criticism from the rest of the world.

Ramsey was left to conduct Stiles' defence.

He did so by having no truck with the charges that the little man was too robust. He said simply: 'If Nobby Stiles doesn't play, then England don't play.'

The team loved their manager for that and Moore said: 'Everyone felt that was great. All right, we were biased. All right Nobby was there first and foremost to spoil, to mark people, to niggle and upset people. But he could still play the game. Nobby did a great job for Alf. Nobby was there to get the ball and give it to Bobby Charlton to go and do something constructive for us. And on top of all that he had the Indian sign on Eusebio.'

Portugal themselves had hacked Brazil, and more particularly the great Pele, out of the tournament. Eusebio was challenging to become the new Black Prince. In the early games he looked full of muscular grace, lithe athleticism, fluent skills and explosive finishing.

England were so sure that the unlikely-looking Stiles would cut him down to size that Moore was convinced they would survive their semi-final: 'For the first time that Wednesday we felt the country was getting behind us. The morning papers at last looked as if they thought we could win the thing.

'I had no doubts by then. I never felt that Portugal could beat any England team. They were the sort of side I would think about playing against with England the way many League clubs thought about playing West Ham … that it would be a good game but not a hard fight and we would probably win in the end.

'They had a lot of good players: Torres, Coluna, Auguso, that terrific winger Simoes. Their top club side, Benfica, were having a great run and this was probably their best side ever. Yet they had needed Eusebio to pull them out of trouble against North Korea, of all people. And Eusebio didn't have the stomach for Nobby Stiles.

'For the first time we felt the crowd rising, sensing we were all on the verge of a World Cup Final. Thank God we finally thrilled them, gave them something to cheer. Portugal were a good team who wanted to come forward, not physical at all. It was a good, open game and we were the only winners.'

Bobby Charlton converted England's expectations into giddy reality with two goals. Eusebio was left with the dubious consolation of scoring the first goal of the tournament against Moore's immaculate defence. That penalty, ten minutes from time, helped establish Eusebio as the leading scorer of the championship but was too late and too little to keep England from the Final.

That night, as secretively as they had done after most of the earlier matches, several of the players' wives joined the restrained celebrations at the Hendon Hall Hotel.

As usual, Ramsey bought the drinks. Just sufficient to reward and relax his gladiators, never enough to erode their fitness. The manager's gesture ended by midnight with the wives slipping quietly away in the darkness.

They were not allowed near the bedrooms. 'There was,' said Moore, 'no fun and games. We'd been with the squad for the best part of eight weeks and not a soul had stepped out of line. Now there were only three days to wait … and that one game to play.'

11

1966 and All That

The happenings at Wembley on July 30, 1966, have long been copiously treated with purple prose, dissected by expert analysis and replayed into the memory banks of the English people on any and every screen big enough to take pictures of the World Cup Final.

You had to be devoid of all the senses and incarcerated on a forgotten island to be alive in England and yet avoid contact with the finest hour of our national game. It was not enough to be dismissive of the working man's obsession. For in its way, that afternoon's sport changed the society in which we live.

The emotional magnitude of the occasion broke through the barriers of class and culture to harvest thousands of wealthy and influential converts to the muddied arts of the round ball game; people who would help Soccer survive a later depression.

Just one of the many economic spin-offs was the beginning of the boom in colour television. England awoke that day to the rattle of the tumbrils, the flutter of Union Jacks in tens of millions of patriotic stomachs ... and countless early morning deliveries from rent-a-set.

It was less public knowledge that the man who was about to be acclaimed as the world's paramount footballer started his day of coronation trying to console a friend.

Bobby Moore woke that Saturday morning to find his roommate, Jimmy Greaves, packing his bags. Greaves was fretting for the place he had lost to injury and Geoff Hurst. Moore, the ice man, suffered with his friend: 'Jimmy was hurt. I don't care what people say about Jimmy, about how he didn't work and didn't care, how his attitude was all wrong. I knew the man and I knew what he was going through. All he wanted was to play in the World Cup Final. He believed he could get the goals to win it for England. He believed he was something special and it broke his heart not to have the chance to prove it.

'That moment began Jimmy's disenchantment with football. I knew that if he'd stayed fit or got his place back the Germans would have been frightened of him. I believed Jimmy Greaves could have won us the Cup. But I also knew Alf Ramsey couldn't change the team.

'Geoff had come in and done too well. It was helpful to have someone else in the team who knew me and Martin Peters as players. From the start he had a good understanding with Roger Hunt and their running had opened the way for Bobby Charlton to start scoring vital goals.

'Alf had been given that bonus out of nothing. He couldn't turn it down now. Not for this match.'

Just as Nobby Stiles had a psychological advantage over Eusebio in the semi-final, so Bobby Charlton held the key against West Germany.

Moore knew it. 'The preparations virtually took care of themselves. There wasn't much for Alf to say by then. He just reminded us that Franz Beckenbauer was more worried about Bobby Charlton than we were about Franz Beckenbauer. That was their mistake. Franz was the man who made it all happen for the Germans but he was weighed down by the responsibility of playing against Bobby, with all his fantastic reputation abroad.

'We all felt keyed up and confident going to the stadium. Alf seemed all right. Everyone seemed more or less in control of themselves. And when the coach got through the people and up to the dressing rooms you had no chance to notice how any of the lads were being affected, because it was complete and utter chaos.

'The old favourite dressing room was jam packed with photographers, arc lights, T.V. cameras. Okay, you accepted it at first. But come 2.15 I couldn't believe Alf hadn't thrown them all out. I think I'd have stood for it until then. Co-operated. Perhaps even hoped it would give us something to occupy our minds. But most

players like half an hour of more peace and quiet to get changed
and prepare themselves to go out.

'At half past two there were still a hundred people in the
dressing room. Terrible panic. At twenty-five to three I said to
Jack Charlton: "This is the most important game of my life and
look at this lot. I can't even start getting changed yet."

'Big Jack grinned and said: "That's why it is the most important
game of your life, isn't it?" It was half an answer but not good
enough. Everything was a rush. It was bothering me so much
that even now I don't remember going up the tunnel. The hand-
shaking. Tossing up. Nothing. A blank until I woke up to the fact
that we were kicking off, somehow still confident of winning.'

Moore was relieved to find his brain functioning again, ticking
over the endless permutations of covering positions, attacking
ploys, clinically vital tackles, switches of play.

The game hurried by as quickly as the words came spilling out
to paint the images of the drama from the inside.

'We believe this is our destiny and all that. Yet we get off to a
bad start. Helmut Haller gets a goal for the Germans from a bad
headed clearance by Ray Wilson. Pride stung because its the first
time we've conceded a goal in open play. Not the best day to go
behind for the first time in the tournament. Yet all I thought was
that Haller shouldn't be the sort of player to score against us and
certainly isn't the class of player to win a World Cup Final.

'It wasn't right. So I still feel confident and Hursty proves me
right by getting on the end of my free kick and heading us back
on terms. That's better. Going nicely. No fuss at half time. Keep
working to break the stalemate and get in front midway through
the second half.

'Again it's not a good goal. Not nicely worked. But it will do.
Geoff tries a shot from the edge of the box which is blocked and
spins into the air. It falls perfect for us in oceans of space in the
goalmouth. Martin Peters and Jack Charlton are tanking on to it
and Martin wins the race to blast it past two full backs and a
goalkeeper, all marooned on the line.

'At that moment I felt we'd won the World Cup and felt proud.
Time was running out nicely. For the first time I noticed the
crowd. A hundred thousand singers. Happy voices. Makes you
realise there's only minutes to go.

'Out of the blue they get a free kick. Out of nothing, danger. You know the decision should have gone in favour of Big Jack because the other fellow's backed into him. But there's no percentage in arguing. Only a minute left. Get lined up right. Only a minute left. Deal with this and we're home. Crowded back here. Keep our heads. Here comes the free kick. Make it ours. Someone's trying to clear. Too frantic. The ball hits a body. Schnellinger handles. Come on, ref, bloody handball. No whistle. It spins across the goal. Like running too slow in a nightmare. Everyone heaving and scrambling to get there. Weber scores.

'I'm looking round and I'm asking them all: "How the hell did you let that happen?" Then comes the whistle and time to think.'

Ramsey's most serious words of warning about West Germany were haunting the players as their manager came stonefaced and steady of pace on to the pitch. Moore: 'He'd reminded us how many times we'd been outplaying the Germans but they had come back at us simply by believing in the things they were doing and by staying patient.

'By the end of ninety minutes I was sure we were the better side. Yet they were so methodical and composed that even at 2–1 down with a minute to go they took their time over a free kick. Most teams in the world would have been panicking and rushing all over the place. They had done exactly what Alf admired them for. He always used to say: "You're better than them. You can beat them. But never forget they're not beaten until the final whistle goes and you're one goal in front."

'If he'd gone on about that right then, he could have killed half our team stone dead. They were gutted enough as it was. I didn't know what he would do. You never know absolutely and for certain how people are going to react until the really big moment comes. Alf was unbelievably good. He could have come on screaming and shouting, hollering and hooting, saying "I thought you'd know better. I thought you'd have learned after all these years as professionals." Instead he said: "All right. You've won the World Cup once. Now go and win it again. Look at the Germans. They're flat out. Down on the grass. Having massages. Flat on their backs. Just have a look at them. They can't live with you. Not for another half an hour. Not through extra time." '

So Ramsey pushed England on from what should have been

a simply satisfying triumph towards great drama and heavy controversy.

Wembley had gone limp in those interval moments. The players could afford no such luxury. 'I believe it was worse for the spectators,' said Moore. 'Watching would have been worse for me. We were all pig sick but the people in the stands had time to think ... and get sicker and sicker. Even when extra time got under way and the ball went out of play they had a few seconds to sit and wonder how the Germans got the ball into our net.

'Being involved was just a matter of getting on with it. Alf was right. We did overpower them. Still there was that debate over Geoff's goal, the third goal, the one that mattered.'

Moore's typical understatement refers to disagreement which at the time seemed violent enough to cause yet another breakdown in international relations between the United Kingdom and the Federal Republic.

Hurst shot against West Germany's crossbar. The ball bounced down and out of the goal. Roger Hunt turned away to celebrate his belief that the ball had crossed the line. And one Tofik Bahkramov, a grey-haired, long-shorted Russian who many Germans suspected of harbouring grudges from the Eastern Front, raised his linesman's flag to declare England the World Cup winners. (By another extraordinary numerical coincidence, Bahkramov was to die a month after Bobby, at the age of 66.)

West Germany protested. Referee and linesmen conferred. The goal stood and Bobby Moore later risked re-igniting the entire controversy by admitting: 'We won the World Cup on the best appeal of all time.

'I believe Roger Hunt got us the verdict. I was fifty yards away on the halfway line and in no position to offer an honest opinion at the time. From my viewpoint it had to be a goal because of Roger's reaction. He was right there, a yard from the line, and the ball came out his way. Yet he made no attempt to knock it back in. Just turned round with his arms in the air.

'If the goal hadn't been given that would have been the biggest ricket of Roger's life. As it happened, I believe old Bahkramov was convinced by that reaction.

'I've watched the film a million times. At normal speed it looks as if it might be a goal. In slow motion it's much more debatable.

I don't know how the linesman could decide. At the time I was in no doubt but on reflection I've got to say I wouldn't have liked a goal like that to be given against England.

'We went to West Germany the following year and all the time their people were coming up and clapping me on the shoulder and saying: "Look at this picture. It didn't cross the line. You never won the World Cup." What could I say a year later? Only that we deserved to win. I believe that. And remind them that we got a fourth goal.

'I'm glad we got that goal. It took the pressure off that linesman's decision. It came with the last kick. A lot of people have said it didn't matter and that it was a bad goal anyway. But to me it was a great goal.

'It was another West Ham job. I couldn't count how many times I knocked that same pass into that same space for Geoff to make that same run. They were shattered and it split them wide open. Geoff was exhausted but he was stronger than them. He set off for goal but said he knew it was near the end. He intended to put everything in the shot and not care if it missed as long as it went a long way back up the terraces, out of harm's way.

'It ended up a diamond of a goal.'

The positively final whistle sent Hurst towards immortality as the first and still, more than a quarter of a century later, the only man ever to score a hat trick in a World Cup Final. It sent Moore towards the Royal Box steps through a chaos of extravagant emotion: 'The scenes right at the end were very vague. I dunno. Sort of misty and unreal. I saw Jack Charlton dropping to his knees and putting his head in his hands. I saw Bobby crying. I remember seeing Ray Wilson's face but not what he was doing. I could see myself running round to all the lads and saying: "All right. It's okay. We've done it."

By the time he was climbing the steps to lay claim to England's golden, glittering prize, Bobby Moore was being elected supreme player of the tournament, by a landslide. And Bobby Moore was worrying that his hands were dirty.

'It had been a wet afternoon and when I got about two yards from the Queen I saw her lilywhite gloves. I thought: "My God, My hands are filthy." All the front of the Royal Box was decked out in velvet and there am I more worried about scraping the mud off my hands on the velvet than getting hold of the World Cup.

'Once I did, nothing else mattered. We were down the steps giving Alf a look at the trophy and hugging and bursting inside and trembling. Everyone elated but most of us trying to be correct. Not get carried away by it all. Typically English. Perhaps that was me and Alf. Don't show people too much. But even seeing the film years later still gave me the shivers. It is the be-all and end-all of football.'

That night the Royal Garden Hotel seemed like an enchanted palace, seen through starry eyes. Limousines nosed through crowds choking the streets of Kensington and spilled their celebrities into a laughing throng of guests illuminated by sparkling chandeliers, flashing cameras and the sheer dazzle of success.

The official banquet was stag. The wives dined sumptuously but separately in an ante-room while the players basked in the back-slapping acclaim and strove to keep their beaming smiles within modest proportions.

'It was,' said Moore, 'just fabulous. We all felt, well, expansive. The memories of the Royal Garden are sharper. That was when you realised what you'd done. When it first started to sink in. Only one thing was wrong. No Greavesy.'

Jimmy Greaves had finished packing on that morning, disappeared from Wembley as soon as the Final was over, fleeing to lick his wounds of personal disappointment on some distant holiday with his wife, his brother and his sister-in-law, shying away from questions, from inquisitive eyes, from sympathy even.

Ramsey took Moore's elbow and quietly expressed concern for Greaves and about the little man's motives.

Moore said: 'Don't take it wrong, Alf. He's not doing anything malicious. It's not a protest. He's not walking out on you. He's not even angry. Just disappointed. Jimmy's hurt and doesn't think he can take all this. Accept it, Alf. He's better off away from all the fuss.'

Moore felt better about Greaves for having the chance to put his friend's case. He led the rest of the players on to the balcony to wave to the cheering crowds packed solidly round the hotel.

As in most good fairy stories, the best moment came at midnight. Bobby came out of the hotel entrance to find thousands of people still waiting for a glimpse of their heroes. 'I couldn't believe they were still there, still standing in the street after all those hours. It made me realise how much it meant to them. It really touched me. Moved me. I'd never felt, what can I say, such a bond with the fans. It was a real lump in the throat moment. Never forget it.'

The players went several different ways through the early hours. Moore, like most of them, drinking in smaller groups at quieter West End places.

'Next day,' he said, 'We all went to the T.V. studios. Then, suddenly it was over. All breaking up. We tried to drag it out. A few strained jokes and silly laughs and handshakes. But that was that. One went to this plane, one to that train. This one gave a lift to that one in his car. All gone.

'Apart from the odd weekend at home we'd been together for the best part of eight weeks. The spirit had been fantastic, I can't remember one moment of bad feeling. We'd all become part of each other. It left a funny, empty feeling.'

Where do you go from the top of the mountain? Bobby drove home to Chigwell that Sunday evening. He wrestled with the growing depression and sense of anti-climax; poured a lager; fidgeted with the television switch; sat thinking about the men whose personalities had become extensions of his, names which the events of the day had linked with his own forever.

'I remembered Alf saying some time during the interviews that he was lucky to have three world class players in key positions in the team. He meant Gordon Banks in goal. He meant Bobby Charlton in midfield. And I figured he meant me. There were others on the verge of world class yet you could look at the team man by man and say oh yeah, there were better players than this one or that one. But we fitted together like the best jigsaw you ever saw.

'I remembered Walter Winterbottom saying that if you got eight world class players and stuck them in a team then they would take care of themselves. But was that the case? Some world class players need a bit of guidance. They can be irresponsible. Put eight irresponsible people together and then what have you got? Even if they've got the right attitude it might not work. Denis Law and Jimmy Greaves were both great players, great goalscorers, world class. Would they have worked together? Alf got eleven to work together.

'Gordon Banks? The complete goalkeeper. Best ever. Easy going but brave. A quiet character but a dry sense of humour.

'George Cohen? Old Oddjob. Could find plenty better right backs for going forward on the overlap. More often than not George hit his cross on to the terraces behind the goal. It was a bad ball for George if he got it into the penalty area. But how many wingers went past him? He was there to stop them. And he stopped them.

'Ray Wilson? For my money, Ray was also a world class player. It was a comfort to have him at left back. A quick little tackler and tremendously fiery little fellow who was so much better going forward than he was ever given credit for. You knew his character would stand up to all the pressure. Always looked good. Meticulous. I saw him years later, after he became an undertaker. He gave me his card and said: "You don't look so good. Better put that in your top pocket." Nothing could shake him.

'Nobby Stiles? Not a bad passer of the ball in his own right but prepared to do the marking and the ball-winning job we needed ... and take all the stick without complaining. We needed him to feed Bobby like he needed contact lenses on the pitch. It was argued that his bad eyesight made him look a dirtier player than he was; made him mistime tackles. But he would keep going in, full of heart, honest, competent. Definitely a better man to have with you than against you.

'Jack Charlton? A big man and a big character. Some days we'd be going out and I'd look at him and wonder how the hell this giraffe played football. But he was tremendously effective. We used to argue black and blue because I wanted to get the ball down and play the game and he wanted to hoof it away to safety. But we made a pair. They talked at Leeds about Don Revie being a great manager but if my grandmother had Giles, Bremner and Jack Charlton in her team she'd be half way to being a great manager.

'We all knew Jack had the personality to end up as a manager himself but in 1966 some of his ideas about facing up to free kicks were hilarious. Alf was petrified about the way Continentals and the Latin Americans could bend free kicks round or over our defensive wall to the half of the goal Banksie wasn't covering. So Big Jack suggested he should stand on the line behind the wall and head the ball away. Then he wanted two walls of three players each to block both ends of the goal, leaving a gap a yard wide in the middle for Gordon to peer through. We were falling about laughing, even more so because Jack was perfectly serious. But what a pillar in your team. And what a manager he became.

'Alan Ball? Ballie had been showing us tremendous promise and potential. Even as a lad he was full of bounce. A firework character under that red hair. Just the busy little man you needed to ginger up the squad when we were together so long. The Final was the making of him. Ballie was marked by Karl Schnellinger and that was no picnic. But he ran that good man Karl ragged. Turned him inside out. Really captured the crowd. Never stopped running but still chased a long ball from Nobby down to the corner flag in extra time to lay on that third goal.

'Bobby Charlton? What a footballer, what a tremendous tournament, including the goal which broke the ice for us against Mexico and both goals against Portugal to put us in the final, where West Germany were terrified of him. A lot of pros had their arguments against Bobby, but he was world class all right, in every way. Sometimes he would lose possession by attempting the impossible or doing naive things instead of playing the simple ball. But he had all the lovely skill and talent and that lovely habit of suddenly getting a ball in a nothing position on the half way line, dropping one shoulder, then the other, drifting past two people and plonking it in the back of the net from thirty-five yards. You'd find yourself still screaming at him to give the simple pass. So you'd break off in mid-sentence and go pat him on the cheek. Bobby had two tremendous feet, could run all day, was better in the air than people thought and scored magical goals.

'I'd seen him play his first game for Manchester United. He scored three goals against Charlton from outside left. At times he looked like the best winger in the world. But his irresponsibility was worse out there. Playing midfield for Alf, he used to run the game. I don't know how he achieved all he did in the game after being carried out of the horror of United's air crash in Munich. No wonder he was the quieter brother.

'Martin Peters? The emergence of Martin was the factor which settled us into a very efficient formation. When Alf said he was ten years ahead of his time he was on about his perception. Martin was never afraid to play the killer ball. He would look for the decisive pass and even if it was dodgy he would still try a curly little ball or a dinky little chip to try to create a vital goalscoring chance. They used to call him the ghost even though he was always involved in the game. People didn't notice him because he played so many perfect first time balls. We'd lose count of the time he made great runs into ideal positions and just kissed the ball off to present another forward with a great chance. A player with the same skill but who didn't see things so quickly would pull the ball down, roll it under the sole of his boot and then have the crowd in raptures before playing it into the same spot, a few second too late. Martin was a really clever finisher. He would never be panicked into hammering a shot. He always hit the ball sweetly and invariably at the right spot. It seemed crazy that people forgot he scored the goal which put us in front in the World Cup Final.

'Roger Hunt? The goals fell to Geoff but it could just as easily have been Roger scoring off Geoff's running. They came together through the circumstances of Greavesy's injury, not through planning. Yet it was the final touch to the team. Roger worked himself into the ground for the players around him. He didn't score a goal in the tournament but all the lads knew the value of his contribution. You couldn't keep us away from his testimonial match up at Liverpool a few years later. It was teeming with rain at 5.30, sleeting when the game kicked off at 7.30 but we were all out there. Anfield was packed and there were 10,000 people locked outside. Everyone loved Roger Hunt.

'Geoff Hurst? The Final changed Geoff's life. On that day a wonderfully honest trier became a truly great striker. From that day on Geoff drew confidence from his achievements and went out to live up to his reputation as the man who got a hat trick in the World Cup Final.'

All of which leaves one man, the leader who even made a virtue of his economy of words on the pitch. Against teams whipped on by voluble captains, England rallied to the blond, imperious defender whose very presence injected essential arrogance into the team, whose superior attitude pervaded Wembley with an aura of invincibility and whose football breeding blessed the team with a special intellect.

To lead successfully from such an aloof position he just had to be the most accomplished footballer in the tournament. Bobby Moore was the only rational choice as the outstanding player in the World Cup. Deep down he knew it.

'I felt the award must go to an Englishman. Perhaps to Gordon or Bobby. I can't honestly say I was surprised it went to me. I'd enjoyed the World Cup so much and you only enjoy things if you know you're doing well. Sometimes your team can win a trophy but you feel you could have done better personally. Perhaps some people who were watching in 1966 could point out some slight errors on my part. Yet a player knows best of all when he's on top of his job. At the time, I didn't regret a single thing I did. Looking back, I can't recall putting a foot wrong. What more can I say?'

The world was getting ready to say it for him. The East End kid was about to rub shoulders with princes, politicians and the tin-gods of his jet-set age.

12

Room at the Top

Overnight, footballers were in fashion.

There always had been an upper crust patronage of Soccer, visible at big matches in the patriarchal shape of a smattering of aristocrats looking down benignly on these gladiators of our time.

Below them cavorted the fringe element of *nouveau riche*, social climbers and showbiz risers fussing round the edge of the game for their own various purposes, like carrion after the feast.

Footballers could always rely on being entertained by those who believed their own appearance to be enhanced by reflected glory.

Now, however, the *right* doors were opening. With the help of television's intensifying focus on their deeds the cream of England's footballers were becoming international celebrities.

Just as pop groups had surged above film stars on the social ladder, so footballers were on their way to ousting vocal guitarists as the cult figures of their generation. Their glamour was enhanced, most of all for the faintly bored majority of society ladies, by their robust athleticism. It was quite the thing to have a pet footballer.

Rough diamonds were in demand for adding sparkle to a host of swank functions and putting a kick in many of the the best parties.

Most mornings, the Bobby Moores found their doormats ankle deep in gold-encrusted invitations. They were *persona* most *grata* at the best clubs. Annabels at first, Tramp later.

The late Sixties were English football's golden age. The abhorrence of the maximum wage was long gone, the austere struggle for economic survival was in the unforeseeable future, the descent of the national game into hurtling, snarling, guileless aggression still unimaginable.

The world had been conquered at Wembley. Commerce queued up to put the smiling faces of our heroes on the breakfast table, the beer mats, the billboards and the bottles of after-shave. The money poured in, the drink flowed and no one stopped to wonder where the next extravagance was coming from.

There were invitations to the Palace and Number Ten.

Moore remembered: 'Some of the parties at Downing Street were riotous affairs. There was one at Number Ten to honour the American astronauts who were the first men on the moon. To start with the political people were thinking about their image. Harold Wilson had asked Kenny Lynch, Harry Fowler, Sean Connery. All the chaps.

'The bigwigs stood together while the chaps started telling jokes and doing impressions. Once the Prime Minister started laughing they were all falling about, the drink was flowing and everyone ended up nicely oiled.'

Some footballers plunged so deeply into the social whirl that they never regained their feet, not noticing the erosion of will and muscle, not realising how quickly the society which plied them with drinks would turn its back when they slipped from the pinnacle of their form. Bobby Moore had seen the opportunities ahead and worked too hard getting there to be that foolish. Early on, Greenwood had described his protege as 'a very ambitious young man'. Moore's career had flourished from the roots of several calculated decisions in his youth.

Not the least important came in November 1960, when Bobby was nineteen, a few days after he was sent off for the first of only two times in his senior career.

'We played at Manchester City that November 4. Never forgot that day. David Wagstaffe was playing on the wing for City. He was at it from the first minute, shirt pulling, niggling. I kept my head until the last minute. Then Joe Kirkup took the ball off him and pushed me a pass down the touchline. I played the ball forward and some second later, as he was running back past me, Waggy kicked me across the back of the legs.

'That was me gone mad. I turned and gave him exactly the same treatment. Of course Waggy went down in a heap, putting on the agony. I got my marching orders. He didn't. I got suspended for a week. He didn't.

'I detested that in a player. The niggling, the aggravating, the feigning injury. So-called professionalism. I was due to join an England under-23 party the next day and it was a great consolation to me when one or two of the lads who were a bit older than me said they had the same trouble with Wagstaffe. But it was a lesson in itself.'

Still it was a lesson which needed translating into Moore's benefit. When he returned to West Ham a few days later he was buttonholed by Jack Turner, then a sort of *ad hoc* counsellor and advisor at the club who wanted to attach himself to Moore as a business partner and financial aide.

Moore said: 'Jack had been biding his time and waiting his chance. At the time I was in what I now call my blue period. I'd been dropped from the side once by Ted Fenton, the old manager, and when I came back I was so keen I was getting stuck in, kicking everything.

'West Ham didn't have any players who did that and the other, older lads in the team were delighted to have someone doing it for them. I was quite an aggressive player at the time and the rest of the team kept congratulating me. The wilder I got the more they encouraged me and I got carried away with it all.

'Jack had the press cuttings ready when I got back from the under-23s. They were asking if I was the right sort of man to be playing for England. Jack asked me if the kicking was really necessary. He pointed out how it could damage my career. I sat down, thought about it and made a conscious effort to steady down my game.'

Turner had made Moore realise just how far his career could go. It was the start of a deliberate climb towards the England captaincy – and all the social advantages that go with the title.

Moore drank his public rewards to the full. Unlike many others he slaved away in private to stay at the top. All the beautiful people were still sleeping in some of the smartest holiday resorts in the world as his lone figure pounded across the sands and pumped along the water's edge.

This was his philosophy: 'England would come back from an overseas tour towards the end of June and people would be expecting us to join them on holiday somewhere exotic and West Ham would let me start late on summer training because I was still match fit. But I'd know when the rest of the lads were starting. Say July 12. And that date would be burning a hole in my head. We'd have some spectacularly late nights but from July 12 I'd be up at six every morning, running round the bay, stomach exercises in the surf, sprints on the sand.

'When I finished they'd all still be asleep and I'd shuffle into the room like a sand dancer. Was it worth it, that hour's training that day? Maybe, maybe not. But it seemed important not to miss it.'

There are no stories told at West Ham or Fulham of Bobby Moore missing a single morning's training, however profound the ravages of the night before.

So, ten years on, when others had fallen by the wayside, Moore was still walking in high places. He did not delude himself that he was sought after socially for his stunning wit or towering intellect, admitting: 'In truth, it was years before I developed real interests outside football. I'd like to play golf well but that's a game at which most men have a fancy for looking the part. I can't read a book which isn't light and easy and gets hold of your interest quickly. I read Robbins, Fleming, Wheatley. Books you can pick up and put down with no problems. But eventually I realised that if I made an effort to read more widely it would broaden me as a person.' So it was that Moore's single-mindedness preserved him for another Cup Final, in 1975, and more celebrated encounters. The social preamble to his Wembley appearance for Fulham against West Ham again threw him into conversation with the Prime Minister: 'All Harold Wilson wanted to talk about was football. He made a joke about knowing he was a bad politician but how he was a good forecaster. So I asked him who was going to win the Final and he said he'd have to see the state of the pitch first. I said I could tell him that already.'

That touch of irreverence – 'I'm not politically minded, in case you hadn't guessed' – was withheld only from the handful of men Moore idolised. They are a small but revealing collection.

South African golfer Gary Player epitomises all that Moore appreciated in a sporting professional. 'I admire success and I've found the common theme to success is putting in some private sweat, and actually enjoying what you are doing. Look at Gary Player. Practice, practice, practice. Working hard at what he loves. He wanted to go on forever.

'It must have meant the world to Gary to give up so many pleasures in life to keep himself so fit. Fantastic dedication. How could you have anything but admiration for a man who kept himself at a peak for so long?'

Muhammad Ali, the greatest sporting showman of all time, excited Moore's esteem. 'It was impossible to agree with everything he said and did, but he was all talent. Great for boxing and great for his people. The man was electrifying. I went to a dinner in his honour in London and was talking to one of his henchmen about his training. The fellow said that Muhammad had four trainers but no one trained him. If he felt like training one day he would drive himself for hours. If not, all the shouting and pleading in the world wouldn't get him off his backside. He'd pretend he was listening but he knew what was right for himself.

'Whenever he needed to be driven through something special he went to his old masseur who no one ever heard about and sweated it out behind locked doors. Before he fought George Foreman the masseur gave him hours of abdominal exercises every day. Come the fight all he was worried about was stopping George hitting him in the head. He let the big man punch himself out on his stomach and then put him away. Muhammad was in a class of his own.'

It was not a sportsman, however, whose presence turned Moore's legs to jelly. 'I'd idolised Frank Sinatra all my life and then got a chance to meet him in Los Angeles when I was over in the States with West Ham. It was nothing really. I was doing a regular column at the time for the *Daily Mirror*. Their photographer Kent Gavin managed to fix up with one of Sinatra's entourage for us to have our picture taken together.

'We didn't say much more than hello but it was the most nerve-wracking moment of my life. Worse than any big match. Worse than going into the World Cup Final. Sinatra oozes professionalism and he loves his business so much that he can't bring himself to give it up.

'We were lucky that while we were in L.A. he was doing one of his countless farewell concerts. Geoff Hurst and I bought 100-dollar tickets as soon as we got the chance. Later in the day the West Ham team were offered tickets at half price and I couldn't believe that some of them wouldn't pay fifty dollars for a unique experience. I couldn't understand them having no sense of occasion. How often do you live?

'It delighted me when he decided to make a comeback. I saw the T.V. show of *Old Blue Eyes is Back* from Madison Square Garden. He got a terrible press. They were on about him slipping from his pedestal. What rubbish. The man was knocking on but he was still all class. Still that aura about him. All right, so he's past his best. All right, so he's been a bastard in his time. So who else is there?'

Apart from the almost childlike trauma of meeting Sinatra, Moore was as much at home in opulent surroundings and celebrated company as on a footballer's binge. He became the prime example of a social phenomenon spawned by the frivolous ideals of the inflationary Sixties.

Soccer was no longer just the opiate of the masses. It was the creator of gods. Moore wore the mantle with the greatest conviction. He dressed with more panache than most footballers, a little less flash than others. The manners were more studied, the carriage erect, the demeanour quiet. He looked and lived out the part of England's captain. 'In public I never forgot who I was.'

Bobby Moore was pleasant to have around, even if it was impossible to put your finger on the real man behind the watchful blue eyes.

To the world, he appeared self-possessed and unapproachable. Yet it bothered him that he was not loved openly: 'Henry Cooper was a pal of mine and look at him, lovely feller and everyone loves him. Yet people seem so nervous of me, so on the defensive when they approach me that they have to hide behind snide remarks. Later, when they got to know me, they admit I'm different from what they expected.

'It's like my old relationship with football crowds. I enjoyed the adoration, same as every player, but I knew I mustn't let it affect me. Adoration can make players want to do too much with the ball. At times I had to shut them out just to get on with the job the way it should be done.

'I used to love playing at Manchester United and Liverpool, 52,000 people and not one of them on my side, every one a challenge to overcome. Success is about overcoming challenges. That's why I was delighted Norman Hunter and Colin Todd were elected as the first two Professional Footballers' Association Players of the Year. That was one of the biggest compliments I could be paid. I kept those two fine players out of the England side. The only positions for which there were several real challenges were goalkeeper and my No. 6.

'That was the satisfaction of the England job. It would have meant nothing to me to be picked only because there was no one else. I wanted to be picked because I was the best.'

Moore's unconscious air of superiority and his unshakeable belief in his own ability were a powerful combination. Yet he needed only the occasional jolt to keep his ego in check.

The Scots, who resented Bobby Moore's golden boy image as passionately as they hated the England team, were falling over themselves to oblige.

13

Bloody Foreigners

It is a much-loved part of football's folklore that Denis Law, Manchester United's undiluted Scot, was at pains to spend the afternoon of the 1966 World Cup Final playing golf in his homeland.

Sanity insisted West Germany were unlikely to prevail at Wembley. Chauvinism therefore decreed that Law put himself beyond reach of any television, radio, newspaper, or even passing stranger likely to broadcast the details of England's triumph.

The stark result in itself was enough to stick in Scotland's gullet through the ten months they had to wait before flinging themselves upon the new world champions.

To their perverse satisfaction, England remained undefeated through that time, beating the Irish and the Welsh but being held to a home draw by Czechoslovakia.

By April 15, 1967, the Wembley stage was perfectly set for the Scots to play like dervishes, Law himself to score their first goal and Scotland to win 3–2. Bobby Moore's memories were acute: 'They went absolutely mad over it. The eyes of some of the players were wild. Their supporters came pouring off the terraces to cut up the pitch, waving lumps of earth at us and saying this was the turf on which they destroyed the world champions. Some of them were seriously suggesting we ought to hand over the World Cup.

'Playing the Scots was a thing apart. For so long their football was retarded by the belief that beating England was all that mattered. They used to drop numerous daft results against foreign teams because they never charged themselves up to play with the same heart as they did against England. In a way it was tremendous. The atmosphere was unique. It built up a magnificent tension and it took each new lot of England players a while to come to terms with the experience.'

For a long time the Scots had relished puncturing what they regarded as the arrogance of Moore and the supersilliousness of Alf Ramsey. Moore's first game against Scotland, at Wembley in the spring of '63 was England's first Home International under Ramsey's managership.

'We lost 2–1,' recalled Moore, 'to what I believe was the best side Scotland ever had. Jim Baxter was in his keep-the-ball-up heyday and scored both goals. They also had Dave Mackay, John White, Denis Law, Ian St. John. What better players to build your side round? Alf was sick about losing to the Scots from that day on but most of the players appreciated the way Scotland played and my worst memory of that match was the collision which broke Eric Caldow's leg and quite seriously injured Bobby Smith.

'It was the next game against Scotland, a year later, which got under the skin of the players. We went up to Glasgow the following April and the irritation started as soon as we were walking to the coach at the airport. There was a lot of abuse. Chants about Bobby Moore's handbag. Bloody foreigners. All that rubbish. You couldn't be sure it was all meant in fun.

'You had to admire their supporters for their fanatacism, up to a point. But they carried things too far. Everyone admires Liverpool's support because it's fanatical for Liverpool, not abusive to others. If another team goes up to Anfield and plays well the crowd show their appreciation. Not the Scots of my era. Their support spilled over into hatred for the opposition.

'It was the first time several of the side had been up to Scotland for a full international and it was quite something. For the next couple of days their papers were full of a dozen pages of gibberish about how great the Scots were and what a joke we were. Then we lost the game 1–0 and of course they made the most of it. In the end it rebounded on them.

'There was a start, there and then, of a changing attitude in the England team towards playing the Scots. Me and one or two others slowly became more and more determined to ram it back

The promising youngster. Above (front row, centre with shield): Bobby aged 11 with The Crisp Shield, won by Barking Primary School in 1951–2 (*A.P. Batten*). Right: In his second year with West Ham, 1959 (*Press Association*).

Ron Greenwood leads West Ham on to the pitch for the F.A. Cup Final against Preston North End, Wembley, 1964.

Holding aloft the F.A. Cup – his first major trophy – after West Ham's victory (*Daily Mail*).

The European Cup Winners' Cup held high for West Ham's civic welcome, May 1965 (*Hulton Deutsch*).

The classic Moore tackle, dispossessing Charlie Cooke (*Daily Mail*).

The 1966 World Cup line-up, with trophy. Back row, left to right: Harold Shepherdson (trainer), Nobby Stiles, Roger Hunt, Gordon Banks, Jack Charlton, George Cohen, Ray Wilson and Alf Ramsey (manager); front row: Martin Peters, Geoff Hurst, Bobby Moore, Alan Ball and Bobby Charlton (*Hulton Deutsch*).

Captain Moore leads his team out onto the pitch, July 30, 1966 (*Daily Mail*).

The Queen presents the Jules Rimet Trophy to Bobby, seconds after he had wiped his hands on the balustrade before touching her lily-white glove (*Gerry Cranham*).

A moment of pure ecstasy for a great captain and his great team (*Press Association*).

A classic shot from English soccer's most glorious day: Alf Ramsey is offered the cup while a toothless Stiles smiles on (*Hulton Deutsch*).

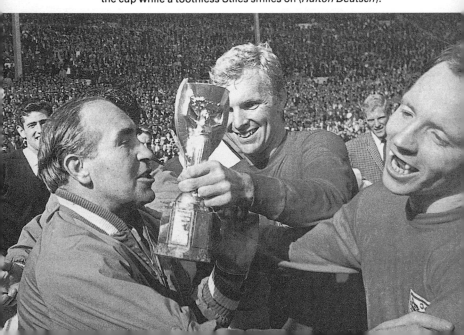

The fans came in droves to meet their hero at the Royal Garden Hotel (*Daily Mail*).

The manager and his captain proudly hold the Jules Rimet World Cup during a reception at Elstree Studios (*Hulton Deutsch*).

February 1967: a proud moment for both Bobby and Tina as he received his O.B.E. at Buckingham Palace (*Hulton Deutsch*).

With children Dean and Roberta (*Daily Mail*).

down their throats, shoot them down, silence them.'

Ramsey, determined to pull the Scottish thorn from his side, promoted that attitude. One of his diplomatic gems came at the time of another landing at Glasgow airport when a Scottish journalist began the interview procedure with the pleasantry: 'Welcome to Scotland, Sir Alf!' Ramsey replied: 'You must be joking.'

'It took a time for us to get the upper hand,' said Moore. 'But by the time I finished with England we were not only in the habit of beating the Scots, but of thrashing them by big scores. It was all the more satisfying because while it was very important for England to beat Scotland, it was just one of many important matches. For Scotland in those days it was the end of the world to lose to England.

'In a way we did them a favour. When they realised they couldn't beat us every year they started to appreciate the importance of little things like World Cups, building experience against countries who play the game differently, learning what it takes to beat Latin teams as opposed to Iron Curtain countries, pitting your wits against obstruction and finding the concentration to break down a deep defence, understanding what it takes to become a world class team.

'Tommy Docherty really made the breakthrough for them when he was Scotland's manager, making them concentrate just as hard on games against Continental opposition as against England.'

The first really instructive lesson in the niceties of international football had been applied by England in Glasgow in February 1968. Then a 1–1 draw – 'We were never in danger of losing but at first they couldn't work out why we were happy not to win' – put England into the quarter finals of the European Championship of Nations.

Scotland's emotional win at Wembley in '67 already counted for nothing beyond its own sake. Yet, ironically, England were to find the European Championships as bitterly frustrating as so many of their previous encounters with the Scots. Each succeeding failure ended with Moore in an unfamiliar and uncomfortable role ... in the dock at the inquest.

In '68 England safely negotiated a two-match quarter-final with narrow wins over Spain at Wembley and in Madrid. The closing stages were compressed into a summer week in Italy and England were camped at Florence for their semi-final against Yugoslavia. Ramsey warned his team that the Slavs were a dangerous mixture of fine skills and uncompromising strength but England's reputation as World Cup holders had gone farther ahead of them. Moore: 'They were so wary of us that they chose to play the game much the same way Argentina played against so many teams, clinging to the ball at the back, frustrating us and putting the emphasis very much on the physical.

'For all our territorial advantage we had too few chances and late in the game they got a breakaway goal which was down to me. They floated a long ball out of the ruck in midfield. It came in above me, the last man at the back. I knew someone was making a run behind me. I could have reached up and pulled the ball down with my arm. But I wasn't sure if I might be just inside the penalty area. And anyway that's not my way. I still felt I could get up to the ball with my head. Strained. Didn't make it.'

Moore turned to see Dragan Djazic, Yugoslavia's world class left winger, finish the job. 'Djazic was a very talented player. No way he would miss a chance like that. Cracked it perfectly past Banksie.'

England had grown unaccustomed to losing games that mattered. The goal inflamed their already aggravated feelings. Alan Mullery lost his head with one of the Yugoslav hard men in midfield and the shame of having a player sent off further soured the taste of defeat.

The failure was compounded when Yugoslavia went on to lose a replayed final to Italy, the host nation. Moore was one of many trying to pin down an explanation: 'We had been beaten so few times since two years prior to the World Cup that we felt we must have a great chance of winning the European Championship. Alf had every confidence in the team and we had every confidence in each other. We all believed in the way we were playing, the things we were doing.

'The problem was that the system of football in England didn't give us time to put the same care and thought into this competition as into the World Cup. The old club *v.* country problem. Nothing changes. The Continentals cancelled their League programmes, moved heaven and earth to give their national teams time to prepare. We got caught a bit cold. It kept happening but all the managers who succeeded Alf ran into the same problem in the same competition. But with Alf it became an obsession.'

The spring of 1972 deepened Ramsey's neurosis about the European championship into something approaching a per-secution complex. A quirk of the draw paired England and West Germany, the old rivals, in the quarter final. Roy McFarland, his exciting new centre-half from Derby County, was declared unfit at the last moment and he took the calamitous gamble of pairing the similar talents of Moore and Norman Hunter at the heart of his defence. Worse still, Ramsey was under mounting pressure to adopt a more adventurous style of play and he made the concession of dispensing with a midfield ball winner on a day when the team needed a Nobby Stiles lookalike to put the clamps on one Gunther Netzer.

'On reflection, both decisions were mistakes,' said Moore. 'Instead of calling up any tall, dominating, orthodox centre-half you care to name, Alf went for experience with me and Norman. I think he always felt he owed Norman a game whenever he could give him one, for being so loyal and patient even though I had his position in the team. There was a lot of rubbish talked about a tactical mix-up between me and Norman but the simple truth was that we couldn't play together because we were too alike.

'Then it was one of those rare occasions when he picked three attacking players in midfield. We had Alan Ball, Martin Peters and Colin Bell. And we hadn't been told a thing about Netzer.'

Ramsey's suspicion of strolling ball players had apparently led him into the trap of overlooking the potential impact at Wembley of the blond, languid problem boy of West German football. Unexpected and unmarked. Netzer ran riot. Moore: 'The way we were playing gave Gunther the freedom of the park. He hated being marked tight, but in the circumstances he found at Wembley his skills and brain could take any team in the world to the cleaners. He was just allowed to carry the ball from his own half, at our defence.

'I'll put my hands up and admit it was one of the worst games I ever played for England. But we were set up all wrong and any defender struggles if midfield players are allowed to come through at him and strand him between two opponents.

'It was a whole day of mistakes. Franny Lee got a goal but we were stuffed 3–1. Even their goals came from mistakes. I was responsible for the first. There was a bad penalty. And Emlyn Hughes made a ricket on the third.'

Ramsey plotted a warped revenge. He decided recovery was beyond England in the return match and went to Berlin with a negative, bruising team which made it impossible for the Germans to please their own supporters and goaded Netzer into saying: 'Every Englishman except the goalkeeper has autographed my legs with his studs.'

To the men who had cost him goals and prestige at Wembley, Ramsey said very little. 'You don't expect to win matches if you make mistakes which give away bad goals,' said Moore. 'But Alf would never criticise you for making errors. He knew the players didn't need to be told they had made mistakes.

'The only ones worth pointing out are when a man doesn't know he's doing wrong. Like getting caught in false positions.'

That is an ironic phrase. No one doubted that Bobby Moore would personally survive England's crisis. In many ways he had built his football game and his life style around a capacity to extricate himself from just such difficulties.

The experience had already proved invaluable when a careless visit to a Latin American jewellery shop had trapped him in the tightest corner of his life.

14

Whodunit?

Bobby Moore lost his temper as often as Brazil lose World Cups. Maybe once every eight years.

For those accustomed to marvelling at his Aryan self-discipline, that stiff-jawed control of his emotions, one spring night in 1975 was memorable for an eruption of anger.

Moore was in Bournemouth with Fulham, sheltering on the golf course from the pressures of their F.A. Cup run to Wembley. Footballers, however, are lost without football and they spent one night off watching Bournemouth and Boscombe Athletic play a Third Division fixture. Then Moore went on to a bar with Harry Redknapp, once a team mate at West Ham, among a handful of Fulham and Bournemouth players.

Inevitably, the more pushing members of the local drinking fraternity attached themselves to Moore's company of sportsmen. Predictably, one man was emboldened by the night's consumption.

A somewhat reddened face pushed itself at Moore from the fringe of the group and said: 'I know it was a long time ago, but I believe you've still got that bracelet.'

Moore's struggle with his more primitive reflexes was revealed by a clenching of fists and a strained, stilted, almost formal reply. 'If you're going to speak like that then please leave the company because I'm not interested in talking with you.'

The man recognised the danger signs but his continued presence and bumbling apologies compounded the insult. Moore reacted by using the appropriate and explicit two syllable sentence. The gentleman duly obliged.

It had taken almost five years to fracture Moore's restraint; five years of forcing a smile at bad jokes, walking past jibes in the street, closing ears to the taunts of the crowd, living with the knowledge that tens of millions of people believe he stole a trinket he could have bought with the end figures of his bank balance.

The England plane spiralled into the mountain city of Bogota. Bobby Moore sat half listening to advice on avoiding the plague of street corner salesmen, those black marketeers whose stolen goods might deposit an unsuspecting buyer in a Latin American jail.

The players were warned to fight shy of the fly boys and look for presents only in reputable shops, establishments with polished showcases behind plate glass facades like the one which caught the eye of Bobby Moore and Bobby Charlton as they checked into the hotel Tequendama, the best the capital of Colombia had to offer in 1970.

English football's two most famous players settled into their rooms, changed, and were back down in the lobby with an hour to spare before dinner. They drifted casually to the window of the shop, the very name of which hinted at intrigue as much as at specialised dealing in emeralds: Green Fire.

It was 6.25 p.m. Monday, 18 May 1970. Moore preserved a precise image of the scene in a compartment of his tidy mind. 'Bobby was quite interested in getting a present for Norma, his wife. So we went into the shop, looked in a glass showcase or two, made a few inquiries about prices from the girl behind the counter. She was like any assistant in any good class shop. Dark-haired, quite nice-looking, smartly turned out. Miss Average for a decent jewellers.

'Some of the other lads looked in. Only for a second or two. There wasn't even much of the larking about you sometimes get in shops when footballers are out together.

'I admit players sometimes do get boisterous and joke about. It was late afternoon and we had had a tiring journey. But we were just browsing the way you do to kill time in any hotel with its own shops, the way I did dozens of times in the jewellery shop in the foyer of the London Hilton. We didn't even ask the girl to get a single piece out of a cabinet. There was nothing that excited Bobby. We ambled out and sat down in armchairs, no more than twenty feet across the foyer from the shop window.

'We were just chatting idly. I watched an elderly woman go into the shop, come out again and walk towards us. She asked Bobby and me to step into the shop. We said yes, thinking they had found something to interest Bobby for his wife. As we stood up the woman fumbled with the cushions where we'd been sitting. Still nothing registered. But as we got back inside the shop she said: "There's some jewellery missing." '

Moore was the advocate from the start, instinctively turning defence into attack. 'Well, what do you want to do? Search us? Call the police? We'll co-operate: whatever you do makes no difference to us because we don't know what you're talking about.'

The shop proprietor had materialised. 'There is a bracelet missing.'

Moore: 'We haven't touched anything.'

Sir Alf Ramsey came on the scene rather like Neville Chamberlain down the aeroplane steps, outwardly reassuring but inwardly in a turmoil of anxiety for his England.

Those who find the analogy a little extreme might reflect for a moment on a saying of the late Bill Shankly, Liverpool's remarkable and obsessive manager: 'It's ridiculous to say that football is a matter of life and death. It's much more important than that.'

There was a grain of truth as well as a great deal of wit in that observation. It is safe to assume that had a third great war been declared in Europe in that summer of 1970, it would have troubled Ramsey less, personally, than the fear that England's defence of the World Cup was being undermined by some Central American chicanery.

Moore stood back and watched Ramsey go to work on the owner of the shop, the hotel manager and the police in his stern, acquired, English-gentlemanly way. Yet Moore knew his manager and was not completely deceived by Ramsey's unruffled exterior: 'Alf handled it like an expert and everyone thought it was done and forgotten the minute Bobby and I finished making our formal statements to the police. But there was something about Alf that

made me feel he was upset. He already sensed that something
was up, that it was a take-on. Felt it there and then.

'No doubt Alf was the first to react. At first Bobby and I were
just dumbfounded. Then it started to get to me that perhaps
somebody had done something we could be blamed for. We were
spending another three days there and we had a match to play
and it was on my mind that one of us might get back to our room
and find a bracelet had been planted. Bobby was openly worried.
Very edgy. I told him to try to put it out of his mind because it
was finished. But I wasn't sure I believed that.'

The few among the England party in the know maintained
tight-lipped security to keep word of the incident from the ears
of the accompanying party of sports journalists who, two days
later, blithely reported that England's footballers began tuning
up for the Mexico World Cup with a 4–0 win over Colombia,
Martin Peters scoring twice, Bobby Charlton and Alan Ball once
each.

Had they had any reason to listen more closely, they might
have heard sighs of relief escaping Messrs. Moore, Charlton and
Ramsey next morning as their plane climbed away from Bogota's
8,560 feet and lifted them still higher into the mountains, to Quito.

The capital of Ecuador is the eagle's nest of Central America,
perched at 9,350 feet but worth the climb for those wishing to
plunder its eggs. In England's case the rewards could be counted
in the number of red corpuscles pumped into the bloodstream of
every player.

The World Cup was to be played at around 6,000 feet and
100 degrees heat in Mexico. England were mountain-hopping in
Colombia and Ecuador to combat the physical disadvantages
which would otherwise cripple sea-level Europeans used to tem-
perate climes.

Under the direction of Dr. Neil Phillips, who practised medicine in Redcar and fussed over the fine tuning of footballers for
Middlesbrough and England, Ramsey's men were busy accli-
matising to rarefied atmosphere. In much simplified terms,
England were playing games and spending days at extreme altitude so that nature could increase the percentage of red corpuscles in the blood. That adjustment would help their bodies
make the most of every last drop of oxygen available in Mexico. It

would reduce the likelihood of the England footballers collapsing with knotted leg muscles and burning lungs.

Once that change in metabolism had been established, Dr. Phillips planned to bring them down from Quito to Mexico in time to adjust to the higher temperatures. There, with the help of salt preparations and special fluids, they would combat a sweat loss of up to half a stone a player during a 90-minute football match.

That layman's diversion into sports medicine explains how England were so preoccupied in Quito that the Bogota bracelet was pushed to the back of a few notable minds.

On May 24, four days after their win in Colombia, England found themselves sufficiently at home in the mountains to beat Ecuador 2–0. Amid all the delight over two impressive results it hardly seemed important that in order to fly from Quito to Mexico next day Bobby Moore and company would have to change planes at Bogota.

By the time England had snatched every last hour of altitude acclimatisation in Quito, Ramsey was so untroubled by the affair of the bracelet that he arranged to fill a five hour gap between connecting flights at Bogota with a showing of one of his inevitable Westerns, back at the very Hotel Tequendama. Like many an accused man, Bobby Moore was returning to the scene of the crime.

The thin air was soured by the whiff of conspiracy as soon as the England party strolled into the airport building. The arrivals area was alive with plain clothes police armed with a warrant and Keith Morris, the British Charge d'Affaires and head of the welcoming delegation, had only narrowly averted an arrest in full view of waiting newsmen and photographers.

Morris spoke quickly and quietly to Ramsey as the team's baggage was checked through transit. England's manager took Moore to one side and said: 'Mr Morris will be coming along to the hotel just before three o'clock to take you to the police station. It is only to confirm your statement and you will meet up with us again at the airport at four.'

No one was surprised as Bobby loitered in the hotel lobby instead of taking a seat for the screening of *Shenandoah*. He had long since tired of Ramsey's penchant for horse operas. No one noticed as Moore slipped into the embassy car. The plot was thickening inside as well as outside the curtained room.

Still Bobby was fairly unconcerned. Alf had seemed calm enough. Mr Morris talked mostly about football. The alarm bells did not start ringing until it dawned on Moore that he was walking into a court-house instead of a police station.

The traditional nervous wait ended in a small bare room. White walls, dark wooden desk, Spanish-speaking judge, French-speaking lawyer commissioned for Moore by the embassy, a student translating into pidgin English. The cross-talk darted bewilderingly about Moore's ears. The watch raced on his wrist.

4 p.m.: 'I should be at the airport now.'

4.30: 'Please, I'm late.'

5.00: 'My plane is due to leave.'

5.30: 'What on earth's happening?'

Always just a few more minutes. Unintelligible arguments. No sensible answers.

England's plane was in the air before the whisper began that one of our players was missing. Most of the journalists would have given their writing arm for the pilot to turn back. Others, mostly those closest to Ramsey, began claiming they had known all along. If they did, it is hard to understand what they were doing on the aeroplane at all. Collectively, they would hit the panic button when the plane stopped to refuel at Panama City, racing through a downpour to commandeer telephones, telex machines, telegraph operators.

The departure time long gone, Moore felt isolated and abandoned. He had no way of knowing that Dr. Andrew Stephen and Denis Follows, respectively chairman and secretary of the Football Association, had stayed in Bogota. The room, no more than 15ft. by 12ft. began to take on the aspect of a prison. As yet he did not know that a cell was his intended destination.

At last, late in the evening, it was spelled out that he had been arrested because the shop girl, the dark-haired and highly-strung Clara Padilla, claimed to have seen Bobby Moore, not Bobby Charlton, toying with a glass wall cabinet, the supposed resting place of a gold bracelet studded with emeralds and worth £625.

'I knew right then it was a frame-up,' said Moore. 'I knew the cabinet they were talking about. A main display case. It was one of those to show off just a few nice pieces of jewellery. Not a clutter. I had looked at it and I could easily remember the four pieces inside. Just four. They would stick in your mind. I knew the truth then but I thought, how the hell am I going to prove it?'

Bobby's unswerving loyalty, it transpired, made that all the more difficult. Years later, at the mellow end of an especially long evening, he confided to me: 'Perhaps one of the younger lads with the squad did something foolish, a prank with unfortunate consequences.' He would not have made such a remark lightly.

The name of the suspect was never disclosed, not even in privacy. In public Moore maintained an implaccable insistence that 'there never was a bracelet', drawing support for that proposition from a body of evidence about similar attempts at frame-ups in Bogota. Also, he recognised that if anyone could cope with such a trauma it was Bobby Moore, the captain. If there was a culprit, he knew the young dolt could be relied upon to keep quiet. So he took on the accusations single-handed.

Without Moore's stature and reputation to stand against the charges, the consequences were likely to be all the more unfortunate.

A little over six thousand miles away across six hours of time zones it was two o'clock on the morning of May 26 as the insistent ring of the telephone disturbed the peace of a mock-Tudor household in Chigwell, Essex. The call had been placed by a late duty reporter from the news desk of the *Daily Mail*. Tina Moore fumbled in the dark to answer the bedside phone.

'Mrs. Moore?'

'Yes.'

'It's the *Daily Mail* here. Sorry to wake you, but something dreadful has happened to Bobby.'

'Oh God. He's been in a car accident?'

'No, no. He's been accused of stealing a bracelet.'

'Don't be stupid. I don't need bad jokes at this time of night.'

The central characters in the headline dramas of our times are very often cut off from normal contact with the outside world. They become so enmeshed in their own extraordinary predicament that even if they are used to bathing in publicity they cannot imagine the torrent of interest they are generating.

By 10 p.m. in Bogota, after seven hours of judicial waffling unrelieved by so much as a glass of water, Bobby Moore felt very alone and very forgotten. That sense of depression was deepened as his ear deciphered the single word which Judge Pedro Dorado was repeating with an exasperated wave of his hand: 'Detention, detention, detention.'

In a sudden flurry of activity Bobby was hustled through a side door, into a police car, through the darkness and up the dimly-lit steps of another, altogether more sinister building. His recollections ran in this stream of conciousness. 'I know there's problems but the subtleties have been lost by the student interpreter and I don't know how bad it is. I'm in a reception area, which is like a madhouse. I'm having to fill in a form with personal details and all around me they are jabbering away in foreign languages. The embassy man's sticking close to me but there's not much he can say because it suddenly dawns on me where we are. Like coming out of a daze. Sort of into focus. There are cells in this place. They're chucking me in jail.

'For how long? For how long?'

Unbeknown to Moore, Morris's aides at the embassy as well as Stephen and Follows had spent the night urgently negotiating a compromise which was clinched as the cell door was swinging open. Under discreet pressure from the Colombian government Judge Dorado permitted Moore the unusual privilege of house arrest.

Senor Alfonso Senior, Director of the Colombian Football Federation, arrived breathless to sign for his country's most celebrated prisoner, an imperative step if Moore was to retain any semblance of fitness for the World Cup matches ahead. In addition to Senor Senior's personal guarantee Moore was to be under surveillance at all times by two armed guards. Again he was driven through the darkness, this time to coffee, a snack and the hope of some sleep.

As he was shown to his room in Senior's cool and welcoming hacienda he had company: 'The guards were watching me like I was going to pull a pistol out of thin air. One of them just came on into the room with me and when I got into bed he got under the cover of the single bed next to me. Fully dressed. Boots on. Hat over the bedpost. One hand on his holster. Watching me. I heard the other guard jam a chair under the knob outside the door and flop into it. I felt like the captured hero out of one of Alf's Westerns. It didn't make sleep any easier but it did make me laugh for the first time that night.'

As Bobby Moore lay wrestling with his insomnia, it was 5.00 a.m. in Chigwell and Tina was woken again, this time by a hubbub from beneath her bedroom window which was out of character with the expensive calm of their tree-lined avenue.

She peeped through the curtains and was astonished to see television cameramen and their equipment, reporters and photographers crowding the driveway.

Tina checked the time in mild disbelief, went downstairs, opened the front door and inquired in general: 'Is it right, then? Bobby's been charged with stealing a bracelet?' She heard the answer and closed the door before they could come hammering across the porch with their questions.

Fleet Street is not so easily deterred. As if on cue, the telephone resumed its ringing.

At 6.00 a.m. Bogota time Bobby gave up the struggle to sleep, pulled on his dark blue leisure suit – a somewhat flattering description of the misshapen cross between a lounge suit and a track suit which the F.A. required England players to wear in transit – walked past one snoring guard and tapped firmly on his bedroom door to send another jumping out of his chair.

In English words and universal sign language he told his startled captors: 'I'd like to go for a walk. Walk. I need fresh air.'

They went out together through the walled garden of Senior's delightful home into a beautiful blue morning smiling on the richest residential district of Colombia's capital; the captain of England's football team and, half a pace behind each shoulder, a policeman with dark, wary eyes and a hand on his gun.

With each step the vision of the prison cell was receding and Moore's self-assurance returning. They passed a milkman on his rounds. Bobby sought out some coins in his pocket, bought a litre of milk and the incongruous threesome went on their way, taking turns to drink from the cooling bottle. The state penitentiary was never like this.

Upon their return to the house Moore's Colombian host loaned a clean shirt, socks and underwear to supplement the clothes he stood up in. The rest of Moore's belongings had been loaded aboard the England flight with the rest of the team's baggage.

He set about placing a call to his wife in England. It came after the usual delay.

'Hello? Tina? Can you hear me?'

'Yes, yes. Are you all right?'

'All is well. How are you and the kids?'

'We're okay, but how are you? What are they doing to you? What's happening?'

'Look, its all right. There's no need to worry. Don't worry because ...'

At that critical moment the line was interrupted by the voice of the international operator: 'Mr Moore? One moment please. Long distance for you.'

'What the hell ...?'

'Hello? Bobby? Its the London *Evening Standard* here. We just wanted ...'

This time Moore terminated the call by slamming down the receiver. 'I had to do that. I wasn't sure what the score was with the Bogota legal system but I knew I couldn't afford to upset anybody by being quoted in the newspapers.'

Whitehall would have been proud of Moore's diplomacy. The Foreign Office was already applying pressure for the release of England's captain. Tom Rogers, who had taken over as Britain's ambassador in Bogota on May 22, in between the alleged theft and Moore's arrest, was at once facing a major test. The Prime Minister, Harold Wilson, intervened personally and was accused by Conservative MPs of trying to attract votes by taking up diplomatic cudgels on behalf of such a *cause celebre*.

Moore was isolated from the negotiations and kicked his heels through the first day of his confinement. By now, however, it was apparent that he was under the loosest form of arrest and Stephen and Follows took what steps they could to break the monotony and thereby nourish Bobby's morale. Arrangements were made for their party to dine with the family of a friend of Follows, a former airline pilot domiciled in Bogota. Moore's guards were now thoroughly enjoying their work. 'They changed a couple of times a day but I called each pair Pedro and Jose and they came to dinner and got stoned and loved every minute of it. They were like friends.'

When the household retired that night, Senior offered the guards a bottle of scotch. When Moore rose at 6.00 a.m. walked downstairs and shook them by the shoulder, the guards groaningly declined an invitation to join him on his morning constitutional. They went back to sleep soundly convinced that their prisoner would report back from his walk.

So on other mornings, rising even earlier in his insomnia, he just left them slumped in their propped-back chairs, hats over their eyes, while he went running to keep up his morale and his World Cup fitness. He also wanted to be mentally fit for May 27 – the Day of Confrontation.

When the line went dead, Tina Moore pumped frantically at the receiver for long minutes before accepting that Bobby's call was lost for good. She telephoned the Football Association who advised her to call the Home Office who re-routed her to the Foreign Office. She was then told that Bobby could be released at any hour, a message which was to be repeated to herself Ramsey, Stephen and Follows many times in their various parts of the globe in the ensuing days.

Morris Keston, a wealthy supporter of Tottenham Hotspur and social acquaintance and admirer of Moore, called with an offer to pay for Tina to fly to Bogota. She recalled: 'I felt helpless sitting at home. I wanted to be as near to Bobby as I could but they kept saying he might be released and if I went to Colombia I could miss him altogether.'

For the sake of the children, or more specifically the older and more aware Roberta, Tina attempted to keep the day on a normal course: 'Dean was only a baby but Roberta had just started school and I was worried about the effect on her and what the other children might say to her. Kids can be cruel without thinking.'

The headmistress of the private Braeside School gave reassurance that Roberta would be treated as if the newspapers were not beside themselves trying to find type big enough to express her father's plight. In the event, the only mild tremor was when Roberta came home from school one afternoon and mentioned: 'One little girl says Daddy has found a necklace.'

Nevertheless, the close attention of the media was making it impossible for life to continue unaffected. 'Everywhere I went,' said Tina, 'crowds of reporters followed. I felt I had to get away. And I felt I ought to visit Bobby's mother because she was very distressed.'

That family visit proved anything but a simple procedure. It needed the help of the police to arrange and required Mrs. Moore to become a mistress of disguise. A plain-clothes policeman arrived at the house with a dark wig and left minutes later in Tina's car accompanied by the au pair girl wearing Tina's hat and large sunglasses.

As the majority of the reporters and cameramen set off in pursuit of the decoy, Tina, in the wig, slipped out of the side door, crawled across the grass on her hands and knees, clambered over the fence and made a run for the neighbour's garage.

Another plain-clothes man was waiting with a plain saloon car. Tina was hidden beneath a blanket in the back and driven to Moore's family home in Barking.

Finally, the activity in Manor Road became oppressive and Tina effected another clandestine getaway, this time decamping with the children to the home of Judith Hurst, her closest friend and wife of Geoff Hurst: 'Until then I'd more or less had to have control of myself. But round at Judith's I watched the news on television and it was all about Bobby and for the first time I started crying and I couldn't stop.'

The Confrontation is one of the more entertaining twists in the long course of justice in Bogota. It brings together accuser and accused at the scene of the incident in question and attempts to reconstruct the happening.

In theory it should take place *in camera*. In practice, in a major case, the time and the date leak out and The Confrontation takes place for the cameras. So it was that everyone from the head of Colombian television news to the head porter of the Tequendama Hotel knew that the re-match of Bobby Moore versus Clara

Padilla was scheduled for the Green Fire shop at 10.00 a.m. on the morning of May 27.

The only person they forgot to tell was Bobby Moore.

'I was pacing up and down the house,' he recalled, 'wondering when on earth somebody was going to do something to get me back to the England team, when the phone rang. It was Denis Follows asking where I was. They were down at the hotel after being told there would be a meeting with the prosecution and I would probably be released to fly to Mexico. I couldn't get down there fast enough.'

It took Bobby several minutes to fight his way through the crowd in the hotel foyer and into the jewellery shop. There he was well and truly confronted by the Padilla girl, shop owner Danilo Rojas and a supplementary witness, one Alvaro Suarez who had been rounded up during England's sojourn in Quito. Once again, Judge Dorado was the referee. Painstakingly he traced the events of May 18.

Padilla claimed she saw Moore open the glass wall cabinet, remove the bracelet from a display stand of white coral and slip it quickly into his pocket. Suarez, who was dubiously described as a dealer in native Indian craftwork but was subsequently discovered to be known to the police as a trafficker in black market emeralds, swore he saw the whole thing through the shop window. Danilo Rojas insisted that one of his bracelets was missing.

Moore was invited to cross question his accusers. A career in top football had taught him to pressurise the weak link in the opposition. He concentrated on the fidgeting, chain-smoking Senorita Padilla. 'It was like a hot-house in the little shop and scores of people were pressed up against the door and window. I knew she was jumpy and she had told so many conflicting stories that I couldn't understand anybody taking her seriously. I gave her the old Muhammad Ali stare for a few seconds and broke her story down.'

After hours of waiting, Moore relished a chance to indulge his competitive instinct. The nature of her job in an international hotel demanded that Padilla spoke fluent, if somewhat accented, English. Bobby's rush of questions paved the way to the key point in his interrogation, a glaring flaw in her initial statement.

'Can you show us which way I was facing when I was standing by the showcase?'

'This way.'

'And what do you say I did with the bracelet?'

'You put it in your pocket.'

'With which hand?'

'This hand. Your left hand.'

'In which pocket?'

'The one away from me. The left pocket.'

Moore was again wearing the England leisure suit. He raised his arms from his sides to show the judge a suit with only one pocket. On the right hand side. And he burst out laughing, confident that that would be the end of it. Whatever Judge Dorado thought of the evidence, he was not amused by Bobby's sense of humour. He described the England captain's attitude as 'unhelpful' and adjourned the charade from the limelight of the shop to the relative calm of his chambers in the court house.

The Confrontation had lasted ninety minutes. The legal arguments raged on for another seven hours. Again Moore was driven through the night to Senior's house. Still the judge could not decide if there was sufficient evidence to warrant a trial.

Bobby's next, unguarded early-morning jog was coloured by the knowledge that he was still under formal arrest and that England's first match of the 1970 World Cup was only five days away. Concern about his fitness became a determination to begin repairing his physical condition: 'I'd hardly had any sleep at all thinking about this thing until my head hurt. In fact the hardest part was being alone in my room, but for the first couple of days I'd simply been delighted that I wasn't locked in a cell. That would have been a hell of a physical and psychological problem. I never felt at any point that they would keep me beyond the start of the World Cup but I began to worry that if they let me go at the last minute I would be out of shape. I knew I had to have some better sort of work-out.'

Senior secured permission and equipment for Bobby to train on a local open football pitch that morning. As usual, the Bogota bush telegraph was in good working order. By the time he turned away from a punishing and self-inflicted session of sprints and exercises, he found his smiling guards and a gaggle of wide-eyed boys waiting with a football. The police left their hats behind a goal but kept on the guns. The boys padded hopefully across on bare feet. So began a kickabout friendly match which had very little in common with World Cups but which was a magnificent if unintended exercise in public relations by England's captain.

Cameramen and reporters arrived in time to record a smiling moment. It hardened the suspicions of the majority of Colombian people that Moore was the latest victim of several notorious attempts to frame visiting celebrities into paying the costs of alleged thefts.

Public opinion added its weight to diplomatic pressure. Colombian newspapers denounced the charge against Moore as a national scandal. Later that day Judge Dorado offered conditional release, subject to Moore signing a declaration that he would make himself available for future questioning at Colombia's consulates in Mexico or London and return to Bogota if requested.

Moore signed – 'I have nothing to hide and no reason to fear returning to Colombia' – and was booked on a flight to Mexico next day.

May 29 was the only day in Moore's memory when Bogota's international airport lived up to its name: Eldorado. The airport precincts were packed with thousands of Colombian well-wishers. Women struggled to get their children within touching distance of the departing footballer. 'Overnight,' he said, 'I was transformed from a jailbird into a national hero.' He passed through them like a cross between a messiah and a prospective Member of Parliament, kissing babies on the forehead, shaking warm, brown hands and waving to the throng.

Word of Moore's release was brought to Sir Alf Ramsey as England emerged dripping from one of several training sessions conducted in the heat of the day in Guadalajara, Mexico's second city. Since the arrest of his captain, England's manager had kept his team moving steadfastly through their scientific preparations for the World Cup.

The initial, shocked disbelief of the players had quickly been replaced by a sense of anger. At first, some of those in the know had been reluctant to board the plane from Bogota without Moore, a protest which might have precipitated Bobby's release

but which Ramsey feared was more likely to disrupt their schedule.

Once in Mexico, the anger of the players became an ally,
Ramsey did nothing to discourage the feeling in his camp that
Moore was the victim of a Latin plot to unsettle England and
thereby make it easier to relieve them of the world championship.
The players were damned if they would let them get away with
it, whoever they were supposed to be.

There was some mild speculation that Norman Hunter might
have to deputise for Moore in the defence and some debate about
whether or not Alan Mullery could assume the captaincy after
being sent off in England's colours. But by and large the other
England players shared Moore's belief that he would be returned
to them in time for the first match of their qualifying group,
against Romania, on June 2.

Nevertheless, the Colombians had cut it fine enough to inten-
sify Ramsey's anxiety and when they told him Moore was on his
way Sir Alf replied: 'I will not smile until I see Bobby walking
towards me.' He had another twenty-four hours to wait for that
pleasure.

Bobby would cheerfully have travelled in the hold of any flight
to Mexico but as it happened there were only first class seats
available that morning. So he left Bogota in style and, by chance,
in the company of an ideal fellow traveller.

Omar Sivori, a splendid veteran of Argentina's midfield, was
also bound for the World Cup. He was the first reassuring voice
from Moore's own fraternity of footballers.

'Hello, Bobby. We all knew you would be out today or tomorrow.'

'I wish I'd known, Omar.'

'Ah, it is normal out here. They always try these tricks for the
money. Some people are so worried for their reputation they pay
a few thousand dollars for the jewellery they are supposed to
have stolen. It is good you fought them. Now, do you think you
can stop Brazil in our part of the world . . .?'

The illusion of a return to normality at 30,000 feet was shattered
on touch down at Mexico City. Moore was required to make a
night stop. Again the airport was seething with journalists and

sightseers and the authorities had contingency plans to spirit him away to a British embassy safe house with the minimum of fuss and exposure. Of the waiting journalists only the delightfully eccentric Geoffrey Green of *The Times* got close enough to exchange a few words. Forever nourished by his favourite beverage, Green would not have been panicked out of his benign stride by the end of the world. He called out:

'Roberto. Nice to see you back, baby.'

'Thank you, Geoffrey. Where have you been while I've been away?'

'Over the rainbow, baby.'

'That's lovely, Geoffrey. See you in Guadalajara.'

With that Bobby hurdled two barriers, sprinted across the tarmac to his designated car and sped away, leaving Green to weave a long, lyrical and absolutely captivating piece of prose from that shred of an interview.

Moore was driven briskly to the home of Eric Vines, Information Officer at the British Embassy. As safe houses went it was about as secure as a piggy bank in prohibition Chicago. It's whereabouts were such a secret that anybody who wanted to find Bobby Moore in Mexico City had only to read the newspapers. And Lou Wade certainly wanted to find Bobby Moore.

Bobby was standing in the lounge of the Vines home with Stephen and Follows, discussing arrangements for flying to Guadalajara next morning, when he was confronted by a bespectacled gentleman of some six feet, seven inches wearing patent shoes, rust trousers, green check jacket, pleated yellow shirt and wide, multi-coloured tie. The guards had been so dazzled by Lou Wade's appearance that they had forgotten to arrest his progress through a back door of the house.

Wade's mode of attire belied his enriching involvement in the rag trade. He, too, lived in Chigwell and spent a small fortune literally following the career of his friend and neighbour round the world. Moore was still dressed in England's leisure suit, nylon shirt and slim tie. Wade straightened Bobby's collar and proclaimed: 'My boy, you're all over the front pages and look at the way you're dressed.'

The tension broken, Moore subsided into laughter. Stephen and Follows, amazed by the apparition before them, were con-

founded to hear Wade advise them: 'Don't worry, gentlemen, I'm
Mooro's insurance broker.'

Wade, who like that Russian linesman would himself die
within weeks of Bobby's passing, had tracked down the embassy
house in company with Jimmy Greaves, who had arrived in
Mexico City twenty-four hours earlier as a driver in the World
Cup saloon car rally. Greaves strolled through the same rear
entrance and said: 'Come on, Mooro, you've got your release.
Let's go out for a drink for an hour.'

Wade plus Greaves was more than the embassy staff could
bear. The housekeeper said: 'What are you doing in here? It's
supposed to be a complete secret where Mr Moore is staying. I've
been told not to let anyone in. Who are you?'

Moore interceded: 'Please. Mr Greaves is a great friend of mine
and we've played together for many years and there's no one I'd
like to see more than him.'

'No. No one's allowed in. Worst of all he just walked in the
back door. Where does he think he is?'

'I don't know about it being a secret,' said Greaves, 'but I
couldn't get in the front door because of all the TV cameras.'

'Out. Out.'

Greaves on the front doorstep, under the arc lights. Rings the
doorbell.

Housekeeper: 'Yes? What is it?'

'My name's Jimmy Greaves and I'm a friend of Bobby Moore's
and is it possible to see him?'

'Please come in, he'll be delighted to see you.'

More laughter helped Moore's repatriation, the last phase of
which was completed the next day. The morning flight from
Mexico City to Guadalajara was greeted by Ramsey and his
assistant, Harold Shepherdson. It was a brisk reunion. England's
manager said to his captain: 'Nice to have you back. Delighted
to see you, Bobby. How's it been? The lads can't wait to see you
again. Let's get off and see them.'

The scene was witnessed by a mere handful of the journalists
attached to the England team. Moore: 'I can only remember the
two *Daily Express* men, Desmond Hackett and Alan Thompson,
being at the airport.' The rest were waiting at the team hotel for
a high-powered press conference which was to provide another

test of Moore's diplomacy. He had been advised that the case was legally *sub judice* so the details could not be discussed. However, he and Ramsey were aware they would have to give the media something to get their teeth into if they were to be left in comparative peace to prepare for the tournament. Bobby trod the tightrope of questions carefully enough to win a whole new crowd of admirers. One senior reporter, Laurie Pignon, then of the *Daily Sketch* and later of the *Daily Mail*, declared: 'I used to have my doubts about Bobby as England captain but the way he handled that conference was marvellous. He was the best football ambassador we've ever had.'

Ramsey himself was moved to pronounce his first glimpse of Moore as the most welcome sight in all his years in football. Coming from the man who sat impassively on the touchline bench at the very moment England had won the 1966 World Cup, that was quite an admission.

The vagaries of the time zones and the complexities of airline timetables conspired to usher Tina Moore through Mexico City a few hours behind the final lap of Bobby's ballyhooed flight from captivity.

It had long been planned for her to travel in a foursome of players' wives – herself, Judith Hurst, Kathy Peters and Frances Bonetti. The news of her husband's release had sent Tina tripping gaily up the aeroplane steps in London onto a flight also conveying Ramsey's wife, Lady Vicky, to the World Cup.

It was an unwritten law of major England tours abroad that even if players' wives travelled to see the matches they would rarely, if ever, see their husbands. Ramsey was far from happy at having the womenfolk at all – 'We are here to do a job.' – and they were billeted in another hotel across the city. That evening he made an exception, calling Moore to one side and saying: 'Go over and see your wife and reassure her, Bobby. The rest of the lads understand.'

That was the end of their separate traumas and they were not to know then how much more of the Bogota Affair they would have to face together in the coming years. They were no sooner home from Mexico than the telephone was being rung by newsmen seeking reaction to all kinds of improbable developments. Clara Padilla was sacked from her post at the shop and fled for a time to her father's home in the United States. The Green Fire shop itself closed after a total of only six months' trading, much to the shame and chagrin of its owner, Danilo Rojas, for whom very few people felt very much sympathy at all. All of that happened during thirty days of deliberations by a tribunal of three judges as to whether Moore should be brought back for trial under an extradition agreement between Britain and Colombia.

That worrying possibility did not recede until the August of 1970 when Captain Jaime Ramirez, Chief of F.2, the special branch of the Colombian police, published evidence of a plot to frame Moore. The intervention of the secret police gave vent to a whole spate of wild stories in the world's press. There was talk of an unidentified double of Bobby Moore snatching the gems, of the bracelet itself being seen on the Bogota black market, of intervention by Interpol, the FBI and even the CIA.

Moore carefully refrained from commenting on successive rumours as the Colombians tried to find some way of extricating themselves from the case with a minimum of national embarrassment. Instead of extraditing Moore the judicial triumvirate under Judge Jorge Cardenas Ramirez insisted on Moore and Bobby Charlton reiterating their statements under oath at a British Court. That was duly done at Bow Street Magistrates' Court, London, on December 18th, 1970.

Still the case remained under review for two more years. Then, on November 17th, 1972, Judge Ramirez declared that the charges had been shelved. Moore said: 'The same old voices came on the phone and the same old faces were back on the doorstep in the early hours of the morning wanting to know what I thought.'

'Well, what I thought was that it wasn't good enough because it left a question mark against me that I knew didn't deserve to be there. It wasn't conclusive and I guessed we hadn't heard the last of it. So I more or less kept quiet.'

Sure enough, Judge Ramirez re-opened the case in October 1973 and it was another two years before Moore was let off the hook. On December 2nd, 1975, the Foreign Office sent a letter to Bobby expressing their delight at notification from Colombia that, at last, 'the case could be considered closed for all practical purposes.'

By then Moore had incurred legal expenses approaching £1,000 for a specialist solicitor in international law to handle the London end of the argument. The Foreign Office insistence that the case had come to an end persuaded him the time had come to pass on a bill for the final reckoning to the Football Association.

Yet the conclusion left a sour taste in Moore's mouth. 'It was all very well getting a letter saying the case had been dropped for lack of evidence but that wasn't good enough. It wasn't what I was looking for. I wanted my name cleared. People kept advising me I should let it drop but I didn't like the feeling that whenever I walked into a jeweller's to buy a present I had to keep my hands behind my back and point to the goods with my nose. I didn't like being told it would be dodgy for me to go to a certain part of the world in case they arrested me all over again.

'I was innocent and I wanted the world to know I was innocent. It made me sick to my stomach that some people thought I still had that damn bracelet.'

Oddly, that belief was more powerful in Moore's own country than in Latin America, where they know about such matters. When Bobby resumed training with England he was approached by Joao Saldanha, immediate past manager of Brazil, who said: 'We all know exactly what happened. It happened to me recently in a different shop in the same hotel. So I locked the door, threw away the key, called in the police and made them try to find what they said was missing. They wanted money but they were not getting any from me. That is what you must do in future.'

'Thanks,' said Moore, 'but I hope it never happens again.' And he went back into full training in a manner which amazed and delighted Ramsey.

England's opening game was only two days away. Moore had lost 7lbs, the only visible sign of his acute anxiety under arrest, and would sweat away as much again in the heat of the first match. Ramsey had said little but was privately and deeply concerned about Moore's reduced weight, loss of sleep and loss of five days' acclimatisation to heat and preparation with the team.

The automated perfection of Moore's football was under its heaviest stress. His singlemindedness prevailed: 'Even the training was a relief, an escape from all the pressures and emotion. When you're indoors at home or in a hotel people can reach you with phone calls. When you're in the street people can shout at you about the bracelet. It was marvellous to get back to work. I knew it would be even more of a release to get into an important match.'

By the afternoon of June 1, by the end of what was only Moore's second spell of activity in soaring temperatures, Ramsey was no longer in the slightest doubt about who should captain England against Romania the following afternoon.

15

Montezuma's Revenge

Modesty, never the most conspicuous quality in England's footballers, was virtually a forgotten word among the strutting peacocks who were defending the World Cup in 1970. The close-cropped champions of '66 had become the nouveau aristocracy, preening themselves in their wide ties, flared trousers and belief in their own invincibility. As if that conviction needed reinforcing, Bobby Moore, the prime example of their species, had come unscathed through the green fires of Bogota.

Bring on the world.

'We all knew,' said Bobby, 'that we were at least as well prepared, no, probably better prepared for the tournament than any other nation. The acclimatisation had been perfect. It was hot, it was high and it was supposed to be the easiest place in the world to pick up stomach bugs, yet everyone felt in great shape. Even though I'd missed five days with the squad I had no physical problems coping with the heat so I knew the other lads must be okay.

'I looked around the squad and felt convinced we were stronger than in '66. We had most of the best players from Wembley, with all that experience. We had learned from our mistakes in the European Championship. Now players like Terry Cooper, Alan Mullery, Colin Bell, Allan Clarke and Franny Lee had emerged.

'We all believed we had the best squad in England's history. We all believed we were going to win it again.'

The way they started the tournament convinced a growing number of outsiders. The first test was provided by the hatchet men from Romania. Moore, as usual, led by example, aloof and disdainful of some wicked tackling. Geoff Hurst, reliably, came up with the only goal. It was a performance of chilling English efficiency which gnawed at the confidence of even the Brazilians.

The Mexicans, who knew in their hearts that even as the host nation their own team's involvement was unlikely to last beyond the quarter finals, shared the universal affection for Brazil's lyrical football. They took steps to support the cause of their favourite visitors. Or, rather, they took a drive in their motor cars. The Brazilians had come among the Mexicans dispensing smiles, compliments and souvenirs. Sir Alf Ramsey, who as a public relations man would have made a splendid concentration camp commandant, presented the face of England resenting the intrusion of the Mexican press and scowling with suspicion at their food, their weather, even their modes of transport.

Brazil *v.* England on June 7 was to be the showpiece of the Guadalajara group. So, on the night of June 6, hundreds of offended Mexicans took their cars into the streets, encircled the England team's hotel and kept their hands firmly on their hooters. It was, in its way, a modern parallel of one of Ramsey's beloved wagon train scenes. Stoically, the players huddled into back rooms on the top floor, snatched what sleep they could and came out to face the favourites as if nothing had happened.

In most considered opinions, England have never played better than they did that day. By common consent, Bobby Moore produced the paramount performance of his own career, his tackles being captured on film and relayed down the generations as classic examples of the defensive art. To world-wide acclaim, Gordon Banks defied a header from the incomparable Pele with a reflex save which has its own place in history. Yet England lost; lost by the only goal on a day when the tall, gangling Jeff Astle might have secured for himself a niche in the folklore of the game by despatching the simplest of scoring chances in his first moments on the pitch as a second half substitute.

Nevertheless, there seemed no need for despair. Both teams could still qualify for the quarter finals and the scenes at the end expressed with warmth and dignity the respect between the greatest footballer of all time and the best defender in the world. Pele and Moore stood bare-chested, exchanging shirts, streaming with the sweat and strain of their classic duel, unable to speak each other's language yet declaring mutual admiration with a hand on each other's cheek and a slow, shared smile. Such moments restore the faith of the people in a game forever threatened by cynicism and brutality.

Later, Pele said simply: 'Bobby Moore is the best defender I have ever played against, and a gentleman of honour.'

To Moore, Pele was the ultimate challenge. 'I used to love playing against him because there is no greater satisfaction than impressing against the best in the world. His mere presence on the pitch had to bring out the best in you because only your best could ever be good enough. Pele was the most complete player I've ever seen. Had everything. Two good feet. Magic in the air. Quick. Powerful. Could beat people with skill. Could outrun people. Only 5ft. 8in. tall yet he seemed a giant of an athlete on the pitch. Perfect balance and impossible vision.

'When you play against people of that ability, at the highest level, for those stakes, you don't have to speak the language to come to know each other. At that time Pele hardly spoke a word of English yet, without thinking, I knew him as a nice, quiet, sincere man, a gentleman and a sportsman. Later I had the privilege of going across to Brazil to see his two retirement games. For me it was a compliment to be asked to be there, to see what he meant in his own environment, to sit in his home town of Sao Paulo among tens of thousands of people all with tears in their eyes.

'He was the greatest because he could do anything and everything on a football pitch. I remember Saldanha being asked by a Brazilian journalist who was the best goalkeeper in his squad. He said Pele. The man could play in any position. And when he had to, he could take care of himself. England played a mini-World Cup in Brazil in 1964 and we went to watch them play Argentina. They tried to do terrible things to Pele. Had some of the tackles caught him properly they might have crippled him for life. After twenty minutes he waited for one Argentinian to go for him, miles off the ball, and he just laid him out on his back, nose splattered, on the edge of his own penalty area. I didn't like the incident but he had to protect himself. He hated having to do it because his concentration was gone from that moment and he did very little more in the game. He looked sad. Yet he remained the greatest of all players, even though he was the most marked man.

'Portugal were not really a violent side but they were so scared of Pele that they kicked him out of the World Cup in England in 1966. He said that if that was what World Soccer was coming to he did not want to know. He would retire. He was a millionaire but thank goodness he loved the game so much he had to come back. Brazil were always trying to find a replacement, Edu the little bird. Paulo Cesar. There were great players like Gerson, Rivellino and Jairzinho. But there was only ever one Pele.

'I like to think our admiration was mutual because I never resorted to foul tactics against him. It would have been an insult to myself. The way I was brought up to play the game was as a contest of skill and ability and thought ... unless someone took too many liberties. Then you've got to do something like Pele did that day against Argentina. But at the highest level it should be a test of ability, not who is the biggest and strongest and kicks the hardest. It was the right way with me and Pele. The best man wins.'

When they left the pitch that day in Guadalajara both men believed that one of football's most noble contests would be rejoined in the Final. That was the way of the draw if they came first and second in their qualifying group.

England duly finished runners up to Brazil. In the last match of the group they had only to draw with Czechoslovakia, who had been beaten by both Brazil and Romania. In the event they eked out a cautious victory by virtue of Allan Clarke's clinical penalty. In the sudden-death quarter finals, fate pitched them once more against West Germany.

Any worthwhile attempt to chart the decline of England's football under Ramsey must begin that day, 14 June, 1970. It was a day which began in a mood of arrogant optimism. The memory of the '66 victory sustained England on the long and dusty road from Guadalajara to Leon, where the Germans had won their group. Helmut Schoen, West Germany's gentle St. Bernard of a manager, appeared to have only his team's limited familiarity with the Leon surroundings in his favour.

Schoen had no way of knowing that morning that Montezuma's revenge for England's disdainful attitude towards Mexican cooking was entirely concentrated on the stomach of Gordon Banks, the most daunting of goalkeepers. Even the England players ignored the first warning sign when Banks first complained of gastroenteritis the night before.

Moore recalled: 'In all that time away there had been only one other hint of sickness. Peter Osgood missed a morning's training with a mild tummy upset. Like the rest of the lads I was sure Banksie would be all right on the day. Sure enough, he said he felt better next morning. I forgot all about it until we were getting on the coach to drive to the stadium, no more than an hour and a half before the kick off. Suddenly Gordon had been taken bad again over lunch. Suddenly we were on the coach and no Banksie.

'Even then it didn't seem that important. We all felt sorriest for Gordon at missing a World Cup quarter final but we knew we were in good shape and everyone was still bubbling with confidence. We'd put on the best performance of our lives against Brazil and the Germans weren't quite in their class.'

Peter Bonetti, Chelsea's cat of a goalkeeper, deputised for Banks, as he had done several times in the previous four years. After the first hour of the scheduled ninety minutes there was still no reason to doubt that England could live up to their own expectations. Mullery and Peters scored the goals which had been missing against Brazil and Moore was as certain as any man has ever been that he was in a World Cup semi-final. 'We'd done everything right. The performance was almost as good as against Brazil, and this time we'd got the goals. That had been the only question mark against us until then. The game was won. Done with. Over. England 2–0 up with twenty minutes to go could not be beaten.

'We'd been proving for years that our defence was unbreakable. No one had put two or three goals past us since 1967.'

In the stands, where the fans at such matches rake up the old political emnities far more bitterly than the players, the forest of German flags hung limp before the jubilant, taunting Union Jacks.

Ramsey, too, believed the field was won, believed it so firmly that again he let his suspect instinct for a substitution run away with him. Bobby Charlton had, as usual, exercised his restraining influence on Franz Beckenbauer. Martin Peters had once more asserted himself as a ghostly goalscoring threat to be forgotten at Germany's peril. Yet Ramsey warmed-up Colin Bell and Norman Hunter, strong men and true, to take their places. Sir Alf was in the act of bringing the World Cup crashing about his ears. The Germans, for the first time, were able to get close enough to Bonetti to expose a remarkable fissure in his concentration.

Even Moore's powers of calculation were defeated as it all went wrong: 'We were two up. We might have been three up because one cross went a foot past a post with Franny Lee standing watching because he thought it was going in.

'Alf has taken stick for those substitutions but in the heat of the moment it seemed reasonable. You figured he was thinking it worth sparing Bobby Charlton the latest twenty minutes because the semi-final was only three days away. Bobby was no youngster and it might have looked bad if such a key player had seemed jaded after playing on unnecessarily in that heat. Norman seemed ideal for making sure we locked them out. Colin Bell was strong, powerful, just the man to run a beaten team into the ground.

'But when you thought about it, Bobby was one of the fittest men in the squad. Always had been. Loved to play and could play all day in an oven if you asked him. You could tell Bobby didn't want to go off and as soon as he walked away it was like a ton weight had been lifted off Beckenbauer. They hadn't had a kick at the ball for seventy minutes but suddenly Franz starts coming at us for the first time. They also made a substitution of their own, bringing on Grabowski. And right off he was turning Terry Cooper at left back. From home and dry one minute, we're in all sorts of trouble the next.'

Grabowski, of course, was torturing a tired man. Ramsey had still not found any wingers and his 4–4–2 formation demanded a commitment from Cooper and right back Keith Newton to make run upon murderous run through the heat into space on the flanks. Cooper was still labouring back as Beckenbauer, on one of his first forward runs, was forced out to that side of the penalty area by Mullery. Beckenbauer's shot made the first moderate demand on Bonetti to justify his hours of personal dedication and preparation.

When all the debates about substitutions were over and you

asked Bobby Moore to answer the mystery of this defeat, he did not relish pointing the finger at the likeable and highly talented Bonetti. But point the finger he did: 'As Mullers pushed Franz out to the corner of the 18-yard box there was no cover from the left. But I still felt happy about the position. It's not a good angle to shoot from and when Franz struck the ball it was nothing special. Peter has gone on record as saying that the goal was not his fault, that is was a good shot, that he couldn't do much about it. Now I'm not a specialist goalkeeper but I do know a good shot from an ordinary shot and that wasn't anything like one of Beckenbauer's better shots. The ball went under Peter into the middle of the goal. If Peter was going to be honest with himself he had to be disappointed. I know how bad the rest of us felt. Psychologically it was a desperate goal to concede. If Franz had gone past a couple of people and smashed it into the roof of the net you'd have put up your hands and said what a great goal and got on with the game.

'But it wasn't like that. It was the sort of goal which cut into your confidence from the back. It became a big psychological barrier for us to overcome and it gave the Germans hope. From that moment it was one way traffic towards our goal. A total turnabout.'

Tactically as well as psychologically England were in trouble. The various substitutions all seemed to be conspiring against Ramsey. Grabowski's instant mastery of Cooper caught Hunter between two crises. The problem at left back was serious enough to stop him pushing forward and defying Beckenbauer with physique where Charlton had stifled him with skill and reputation. Yet he could not drop too deep. So he was trapped, doing little more than fill space on the left hand side just in front of the defence.

Again the Germans scored a late, late goal to take England to extra time in a major World Cup match. This time Germany's beloved Uwe Seeler was the scorer. Again it was a goal full of blame in Moore's dismayed eyes: 'There was an iffy clearance and not everybody got out quickly enough and Seeler was left deep at the back but still onside. So they lobbed the ball back in. Only hopefully. Really it was too far. On any ordinary day any player in the world would have given it up. But not in a match like that. Uwe did a feat, straining to get his head to the ball. He admitted he had no intention of scoring. He was just trying to keep the ball in play. Yet it flopped over Bonetti into the net. Peter's concentration might have been adrift.'

That suspicion stemmed from the team's appreciation of Bonetti's personal qualities as a genuine family man. Tina Moore, like the wives of Hurst and Peters was already a seasoned traveller, having supported her husband in various corners of the globe. Bobby knew Tina had quickly put the Bogota business behind her and would readily cope with any of the myriad problems and distractions which can present themselves during a long stay in a foreign continent. Mexico, however, was Frances Bonetti's first travelling adventure of its kind without the constant companionship and nightly attendance of her husband. Bonetti may well have been somewhat distracted by concern for his wife's wellbeing. It was the very problem Ramsey had feared might arise from the presence of the players' wives in the wings of the World Cup arena.

Ninety minutes earlier it would have been hard to find a more confident group of people anywhere on earth than the England football team. At the start of extra time all those permutations of doubt were whirling through their minds. There was never the slightest chance that they would go back out to win the match a second time, the way they had at Wembley four years earlier.

Moore's memories of the killer blow were no happier: 'We were doing all we could to stop it but somehow you knew it would come. Peter and Brian Labone were beaten by a ball going backwards and forwards over their heads in the goalmouth. Gerd Müller poked it in. The old story with Müller. He hadn't done a thing all game but he got the winner. Kept on doing it after that until they won the World Cup in 1974.

'I don't remember walking to the dressing room. Just being there. Nobody said anything. Certainly not Bonetti. No point. It was his last cap. Just silence. Looking at each other. Little Ballie stood there with tears in his eyes.'

Outside it was the turn of the English supporters to suffer the jibes. Yet West Germany proved to have defeated themselves as well as England. The physical demands of extra time cost them dearly three days later. In an astonishing semi-final against Italy, another team which seldom gave away goals, they were again required to play an extra half hour and this time lost 4–3.

Moore stayed to see the tournament through. He went to watch the final in Mexico City's monumental Aztec Stadium convinced that Italy would, in their turn, be physically spent. 'I felt Brazil only had to turn up to win the cup. Yet after an hour it was one goal each and I thought hell, they might get beaten. But I'd also gone there thinking it should be England playing Brazil and believing England might have won. I was sure they would have been worried about us because we'd come so close in Guadalajara. Every game against them I felt we could beat them and I couldn't understand how we'd failed to do it in half a dozen attempts.'

As a spectator, he found the reason during the last half hour of the 1970 World Cup Final: 'It looked like Brazil would get caught out but suddenly they found that little bit extra. Just as they had against us down the years. Boom, boom, boom. They rifled in three more goals.

'That was the wonder of them and the trouble with them. Always something special in reserve. Pele was a lot to do with that. Most people have their own special memory of him: In that Final there was the first goal when he curled himself up around a difficult cross and made scoring look easy. Earlier in the tournament there had been the dummy to let the ball run one side of the goalkeeper while he went round the other. That was brilliant even though he screwed the final shot across the face of the goal. Against Uruguay he had picked up a loose clearance in midfield and shot just over the bar, with their goalkeeper stranded around the penalty spot. So close to achieving his lifetime ambition of scoring from inside his own half. Even as a pro with a vantage point in the stand you wondered at first what he was doing. Then you were lost in admiration for the man's vision and appreciation of a situation.'

Moore took those memories with him on a soothing sunshine holiday in Acapulco. There, with a delicious sense of irony, his wife presented him with a gold identity bracelet. As he toyed with that memento Bobby began asking himself for the first time: 'How could Alf have left me in Bogota?'

16

The Doctrine According to Sir Alf

It was at first no more than a wisp of disappointment which drifted across the shimmering skyline of Bobby Moore's holiday. It did nothing to impede the sun's healing progress through the balmy days in Acapulco. It never once clouded the waters of the personal pool in which England's beaten champion periodically cooled his scorched limbs.

Yet it nagged his consciousness about the manager who had been knighted by the Queen for success built upon unquestioned loyalty to his men.

Loyalty was Sir Alf Ramsey's byword. The fierce devotion of manager to players and players to manager had proved to be England's most enduring quality. The lads believed good old Alf would always support them. So they might be off form, so they might be beaten, but the lads would never knowingly give good old Alf anything less than their best on the pitch.

Loyalty was Ramsey's most powerful weapon and he had used it to greatest effect in charging Bobby Moore with the captaincy. The world of football at once identified certain similarities of nature as solid reasons for the choice. Both men confronted responsibility with an impeccable, impenetrable mask. Both appeared cold. Both seemed calculating. Both certainly wanted to win.

Ramsey said of Moore: 'Bobby is an extension of myself on the field.' Moore said of Ramsey: 'Alf chose me because I projected on the field the qualities he impressed on the players off the pitch.

We were both calm, methodical, deliberate and kept our cool. We both ached for success.'

The destiny of both men had been linked from the day of Ramsey's first match as England manager, in Paris in '63, when he had turned his back on defeat to take the seat next to Moore on the team coach. They were interdependent and it was more than coincidence that their international careers both ended, some ten years later, after Ramsey chose to break their link for the first time in an important match.

So how had Ramsey found it in his heart to leave Moore to his fate in Bogota?

The availability of Dr Andrew Stephen and Denis Follows, the need to be with the squad, the irrational attempt to stave off publicity were all excuses. Yet the more Bobby weighed them against his own predicament, the less he could accept them as valid reasons: 'If there was a man I believed was as important to me as Alf said I was to him, then there's no way I could have walked on to that plane without him.'

The thought jarred on Bobby's image of Alf, an image which had been hardening ever since that bus ride in Paris. 'He started asking me questions then about the way things were done with England. And he didn't stop even though there was a man on the plane home who I thought should have been playing for England, could still have been captain and would have answered all the questions.

'Johnny Haynes had gone over to watch the match in Paris with a group of fans and they were on our plane coming home. We'd lost 5–2 and the punters were shouting down the plane "can't leave him out now, Alf," and "all right, John, must be back for the next one". It was as embarrassing for John as it was for Alf but it seemed to make sense.'

Moore's potential, however, excited Ramsey more than even Haynes' reputation. Alf pursued their dialogue through successive meetings, tried him as captain in Czechoslovakia and had him established in the job within a year. Even the drinking escapade prior to the 1964 visit to Portugal was turned to advantage.

The press did not begin to suspect a showdown until after Moore and his friends had redeemed themselves with a 4–3 win

in Lisbon and the summer tour had moved on to New York.
When the captain was left out of the England side which beat the
U.S.A. 10–0, questions were asked, whispers of a drinking spree
overheard and some newspapers published the understandable
but mistaken conclusion that an indiscretion in America had
forced a rift between Ramsey and Moore.

In reality Ramsey had promised the supporting members of
the England cast at least one appearance as reward for backing
up the stars on tour. The soft game in New York was the obvious
consolation for the reserves. Moore returned for Little World
Cup games against Brazil, Portugal and Argentina. After a close-
season for due consideration. Ramsey was ready to offer Moore
a permanent partnership. The deal was cemented in an hotel in
Belfast in October 1964, on the eve of a 4–3 victory over Northern
Ireland.

'Alf just asked me to join him for a few minutes,' said Bobby,
'and we talked about being ready to commit ourselves to the
objective of winning the World Cup in 1966. We sorted out our
priorities on and off the pitch and agreed we would back each
other up. Alf made it clear he expected the captain as well as the
manager to conduct himself in a responsible manner and that
was that. No problem as far as I was concerned. On we go.

'All the lads felt already that he was a players' man. We were
attracted to his loyalty. He shared our desire for success. Really,
that's all any players ever want. Success. If you win things and
get your rewards for them, you're happy. Alf's first thought was
for his players so there was never any problem about getting the
players to do what was asked of them.

'What more can you want from a manager than being successful? What more can a manager want from a player? We both
had the same incentives so we had a deal.'

Almost unconsciously Moore was forging the very relationship
with Ramsey which he had resisted with his club manager, Ron
Greenwood. It was less obtrusive, yet closely akin to the liaison
between Greenwood and Johnny Byrne. Even now, Moore was
not certain of the full extent to which he influenced team selection
but he did know that his counsel was sought and frequently acted
upon. It was a tribute to the discretion of both men that the rest
of the players never once suspected, let alone resented, their

captain's part in deciding their places in the team. Careless talk could easily have cost games.

'Looking back,' said Moore, 'Alf started drawing me into it that day in Paris. From then on he asked as many questions about players as about anything else.'

Sometimes the questions were about Bobby's friends and the answers measured the strength of Moore's ruthless control over his emotions. Although it was not his final word, there was no doubt that Moore was aware of the decisions to omit Alan Ball from two early matches in the 1966 World Cup Finals and then, harder still, not to recall Jimmy Greaves, the closest of all his footballing friends, for the Final itself.

If he needed an excuse for hardening his heart it was provided by the philosophy he shared with many successful men in Soccer: 'When did a team of nice guys ever win anything?'

Ramsey was of a similar persuasion, partly, no doubt, because he hailed from a similar background. Both were born and bred on the working-class borders of Essex and East London and after the World Cup had been won in '66 Moore, Ramsey and Martin Peters, all sons of the borough of Barking, were called to the town hall to be honoured by the Mayor.

Moore recalled: 'Alf was no better nor worse than Martin and myself. He was born just next door in Dagenham. That's why he was always at his happiest in the company of his players, his own people. Left alone with us he could relax, share in the jokes. He always bought the drinks. When he was at Ipswich that was the be-all and end-all for him. Then it was England. The trouble with being England team manager is that you are separated from your players so long and so often, planning to get them together, that when you are with them you have to use and savour every second. When he was knighted nothing changed. The players were delighted for him but some of them felt a bit strange when they met him again for the first time after he became Sir Alf. Someone said: "What do we call you now?" he replied: 'I'm still Alf, aren't I?".'

So England played on to 1970 in a proletarian harmony. Even in the hours after their impossible defeat by West Germany, Ramsey still appeared to be putting the players before even himself. Moore said: 'He never said a great deal about what went wrong. He just went round trying to console this player and that player. He was more worried about consoling people than finding reasons.'

So it was left until poolside in Acapulco for Moore to define his own, initially vague, sense of disillusionment. Whatever the reason, Alf *had* left him in Bogota and Bobby decided: 'Despite what the outside world thought, I would never regard myself as being the same as Alf. Not at all alike. The only Alf I knew was the football manager. We were together maybe a total of a month or two out of every year, in different spells of a few days here, a week in this country or that country. That didn't mean I knew the person. Alf never drew me into his social company.

'It became quite clear to me that Alf and I were different personalities outside our working relationship. Apart from football, Alf would never talk in depth about anything at all. In company the conversation might flit across the usual small talk about cars and holidays but would invariably settle on football. Socially, I like people who are interested in what you do but can also relax you and take your mind off your own line of business once in a while.

'Alf had just two worlds, his players and his home. And they were kept strictly apart.'

Nevertheless, Moore was close enough to Ramsey often enough to study the manager the press dubbed Old Stoneface. His conclusions were remarkable and their simplicity suggests they touched on the truth of a man who remained an enigma throughout his lengthy period in the full glare of publicity: 'For years everyone was busy trying to pin down the real Alf Ramsey. They look at that great photograph of everyone else on the bench leaping up into the air when England scored in the World Cup Final and there's Alf stopping Harold Shepherdson from running onto the pitch to congratulate us. Just sitting there. And they say that's Alf behind his mask, being conscious of his position. Behaving correctly. Suppressing his emotion. They say he wasn't like that when he used to go to the greyhound racing track with the lads in the old days and they wonder what he's really like.

'Well, I say that the serious, responsible Alf is the real Alf. Without trying to or meaning to, he fooled everyone. It was in the old days that he wasn't being himself. I've talked to some of the old players he used to knock about with and they'll tell you that although he used to go to the dogs or the pub, it wasn't really his scene. He went because his one or two pals were going but he stood back a bit. They remember him changing, drifting away from them. Well I'd bet my mortgage that one day he was on the train home and he thought: "I don't need all that, it's not me." He took elocution lessons and out came the real Alf who everyone found so baffling.'

One memorable television interview, conducted for the BBC by my literate *Daily Mail* colleague Ian Wooldridge, offered supporting evidence.

Sir Alf and Lady Vicky revealed that in the event of a marital tiff they would always, in the end, 'shake hands and make up.'

Yes – shake hands.

Not that Ramsey was devoid of feeling. If Moore was right in his judgement then I am one of the many journalists who, in ignorance of his sensitivity, must have cut Sir Alf to the quick.

'Unless you knew him closely,' said Moore, 'you would not have noticed when he was hurt. He had great control of his emotions and never showed it outwardly when he was under stress. He would just carry on. Yet you sensed he was hurt. Alf would be deeply upset if a member of the press expressed a damaging opinion, especially if the writer had no way of knowing the full story. He took all criticism of England very personally and very deeply.'

Many of the attendant press corps felt that if Ramsey suffered through their ignorance of detail, it was Ramsey's own fault for withholding information. Moore said: 'I'm sure he felt he was co-operating as fully as possible. His priority was for England to win matches. He felt the English press should want England to win and should understand if sometimes he couldn't organise the day to suit them, or was unable to release certain information which might have created problems for him and us.'

As Moore was sitting by his Mexican swimming pool and beginning to question Ramsey in his own mind, so the press criticism of England's manager was intensifying. They pinned the blame for losing the World Cup on his substitutions against West Germany. They jumped down his throat when he arrived home saying England had nothing to learn from the 1970 Brazilians.

Even Moore was startled by Ramsey's exaggerated chauvinism: 'Alf explained later that he meant to say there was nothing new about the Brazilians that we didn't know already. But even that was strange. You've always got something to learn in this game. From anyone. Maybe even from the waiters kicking about on the beach if you're sitting watching them. You've got to be open-minded enough to benefit from the changes in the game.

'Alf also had plenty to learn from the Brazilians about public relations. The truth is that Alf didn't particularly like foreigners and he was very wary of Mexico. So we went in with our own meat and other foodstuffs and even shipped over our own team coach to drive about in. The locals wanted to know what was wrong with Mexican food and what was wrong with the buses they were supplying for all the teams in the Finals. So they hated us from the start. The Brazilians did it the other way round. They arrived early and sat on hotel balconies waving to the crowds, signing autographs, singing and smiling. *Then* they moved into hiding and smuggled in all their own foodstuffs.

'Alf was more honest and straightforward than that and did not foresee how things would backfire on him. One of his strengths, really, was his overwhelming belief in England. He honestly believed we had the best players in the world and all we had to do was go out and prove it. In some ways there was nothing wrong with that. In Mexico, Bobby Charlton and myself went to visit the Brazilian camp. There was a pool surrounded by rooms and it was siesta time when we arrived. Quiet and empty. One of their players saw we were there and suddenly they all came chattering out of their doors. We'd gone there to ask them about the marvellous techniques in their football and we ended up bombarded with questions about our physical preparations. They were the people everyone looked upon as the best players in the world. Yet they wanted to learn from us.

'Alf was more insular. His strength was his organisation. He performed that remarkable feat at Ipswich, going from the Third Division to the First Division Championship in successive seasons, simply by getting the best out of the players at his disposal. That was the way he carried on with England.'

Malcolm Allison, then the standard bearer for the thrusting young technocrats of Soccer coaching, was among Ramsey's critics. He said: 'Alf is a good manager of a bad team but a bad manager of a good team.'

Moore said: 'I understand what Malcolm meant but I only agree in part. Alf could set up a team of players to be difficult to beat. But I don't ever remember him discouraging players from expressing their skill.'

Nevertheless, Allison's criticism represented one of the many furies at Ramsey's heels as England inched into decline. In the end not even his knighthood nor the record of his golden years could spare him the sack by the Football Association for failing to qualify for the 1974 World Cup Finals.

Ramsey had already discarded Moore in his doomed attempt to overcome Poland in the qualifying group. Bobby greeted his manager's consequent demise as inevitable: 'Football has a habit of running in ten-year cycles and when you come to the end of that period it takes a very flexible and adaptable man to move out of the pattern which has been successful for him. The cycle turned against Alf. Everyone in the world knew what he and his teams were doing. It was predictable but Alf still believed it was right. There comes a time for reviving spirit and interest by doing things a little differently.

'Alf was inflexible and I knew there would have to be a change of manager. The problem seemed to me to be finding the right way of doing it. That was where the F.A. let Alf down. Maybe they should have done it as soon as he failed to qualify for the World Cup. Not let it dwindle on for a couple more matches.

'Maybe they were a bit in awe of Alf and never really got on with the job. They let him pick a squad to go on a summer tour in Europe, which was a funny thing to do if they didn't want him to be the manager any longer.

'It was right for both parties, for Alf and for England, to make a change. But neither side seemed to see the position clearly. I understand they finally gave Alf the chance to resign but he refused. He said he wanted to go on to the World Cup in Argentina in 1978. That would have been one enormous challenge for him because they still hate him there for calling them animals in

'66 and they still believe the only reason they ever lost to England was because Rattin was sent off.

'Alf had taken stick for that insult. He had been hurt by that criticism but even by '74 he still couldn't see what he'd done wrong. The pressures on him would have been greater than ever. He couldn't see how very difficult it would be for him in Argentina. So they had to give him his cards. It was a messy way to end an era.'

Moore at once sent a telegram of condolence and encouragement to Ramsey. Later he sent a letter which read: 'I am not so much sorry that you have left the job but for the manner in which it happened. We had great times together. You made it great for the players. Best wishes in the future.'

It was simple and truthful. That May, Ramsey emerged from hiding from the media he detested and replied to Moore in kind. His letter: 'My wife is of the same opinion as yourself . . . a blessing in disguise.

'I will conclude by thanking you for all you have contributed to English football and myself. No one could have done more.'

A long, reflective year after he received Ramsey's letter, Moore was summering in South Africa, financing another exotic holiday by making guest appearances for Hellenic, the Cape Town club, which was being managed by his old sparring partner from West Ham, Johnny Byrne.

One slow evening, like good old friends, they stood together on the long brow of Signal Hill, sharing a can of lager and feasting their eyes on a huge sunset which transformed the sea into an ocean of rippling flame.

'You know something, Mooro. The players may have been lucky to have Alf but he was even luckier to have one or two of you.'

'How do you mean?'

'Tactics. Fine points. Corner kicks and the other set pieces. He'd ask your opinion and always defer to you. I can hear his team talk now. The same old team talk.'

'Yeah, Budgie, so can I. You know I could give Alf's team talk to any side right now. A bit about the opposition's pattern of play, a few of their strengths and weaknesses. Not much but enough to do his duty. Then on to: "They're more worried about us than we are about them. You're the best players in the world. The fittest. The strongest. Go out and win it.".'

'Let's face it, Bob. He didn't hold a candle to Greenwood on knowledge of the game. Not in the same street. Between them they'd have made a good manager. Ron's knowledge and Alf's way with the players.'

Moore pondered a marriage of his two managers. The huge, darkening sun dipped behind velvet folds of night on the horizon.

'Not bad,' he said. 'But not a patch on you and me, old son. Not a patch on you and me.'

17

Read All About It

Neither Sir Alf nor Ron Greenwood will be overjoyed to read that their prize pupil came to consider himself to be their master.

Yet no man easily acquires such absolute belief in himself as Bobby Moore revealed that musky evening in South Africa. Each layer of self-confidence had been tempered in the heat of crisis. And in 1970, a year which was in many ways the axis of his life, the tests of character came hard on each other's heels.

The leaden feet of Colombian justice dragged from one development to another long after the World Cup was lost. Then a fresh drama checked Moore on the brink of a new English football season.

It was August and the time for sweating away the indulgences of the summer was almost over. Long days spent pounding the practice field had flattened the most stubborn of West Ham's stomachs and that tell-tale sheen of fitness was back on Moore's skin. The final polish was applied in light training on the morning of the day West Ham were due in Bournemouth to sharpen their skills in a friendly match.

At 11 a.m. the coach was warming its engine in the car park when the telephone rang in Greenwood's office. The local police were in possession of a letter posted in Birmingham to the London *Evening Standard*.

Yes, it was anonymous, like most such correspondence. But no, this time it did not look like the work of a crank. This time it was a warning, not a threat. Tina Moore was about to be kidnapped, perhaps with one or both of Bobby's children. The ransom would be £10,000.

The team coach awaited the arrival of the police and gave Bobby time to read the letter: 'Before I picked up that piece of paper I believed it would be just another nutcase. You get them all the time. But this one was different. The writer said he couldn't give his name because he was wanted by the police on another charge. But he'd heard the kidnap plot through his underworld contacts and felt we'd had enough troubles and wanted to tip us off. He was posting his letter on the way out of the country. It was sensible and legible and I knew at once I couldn't go to Bournemouth.'

As the rest of the team set off for the south coast, Moore was hurried to his Chigwell home by Bert Wickstead, a detective who was promoted later to heavier dramas with Scotland Yard's murder squad. Wickstead posted a 24-hour watch at the front, the rear and inside the house. For the second time that year Moore was living under police guard.

This time it was for his own protection and this time it was not only Bobby but also his wife and children who could not set foot outside the house without a bodyguard. 'Everytime I went training one of the guys came with me. Whenever Tina went shopping she had a policeman to carry her basket. The kids had detectives to take them down the road to the sweet shop. For the first forty eight hours it seemed very strange having a procession of policemen coming through your own home. There were nine of them a day. But again they became part of the family. You start making tea for six without thinking. They're playing football with the kids in the garden, they play cards with you and watch television with you and drink your lager. One of the night duty lads took to sleeping in a hammock and in the early hours you'd hear him fall out, crashing to the floor, screaming and cursing. They always answered the door. When I answered the phone, they picked up the extension simultaneously.'

They kept it all secret for the first five days, the period the police deemed to be the most dangerous. There was not a whisper to the press until after Bobby had played the first League match of the season.

For that occasion, on 15 August 1970, West Ham were required

to make the short journey across north east London to Tottenham
Hotspur. They made the trip without their captain: 'The police
forbade me to travel down to West Ham and then over to Spurs
on the team coach. So we all went across in my car. Me and three
bodyguards driving into the Tottenham car park. During the
game one stayed with the car, another sat in the dressing room
and the third fellow was out on the track round the pitch. Then
we went for a drink with the rest of the team and they loved it.
Best job they'd had in a long time.'

At home in Chigwell, they came to terms with the problems of
feeding a small private police force, most of whom had enormous
appetites. On top of that, while the police were stopping someone
making off with one of the family, they went and kidnapped the
nanny. One of the detectives married 18-year-old Pauline inside
the year, just as the Moores were facing another alarm.

Bobby had left the house at lunchtime for a Saturday afternoon
match at West Ham when the telephone rang and Tina answered.

'Mrs. Moore?'

'Yes.'

'I just want to tell you that your husband is going to be shot
during the match today.'

Again the tone of the communique was flat, unexcited, unlike
the usual babbling of the cranks who force star footballers, like
most public personalities, to keep changing their ex-directory
phone numbers and only ever answer 'Hello'.

Quickly, Tina dialled the ground only to be told that the match
had already started. At once, she rang the police and again a
squad car was sent hurrying to West Ham. By the time they
arrived, Bobby was already leading the team into the second half.
He played out the game, unaware of the uniformed and plain
clothes men fanning out round the pitch. But at the final whistle
he was suddenly surrounded by police in the middle of the pitch.

Bobby looked round them and said: 'Look lads, I've probably
played better but I wasn't that bad. Surely Ron Greenwood's not
having me arrested.'

He had been bustled to the dressing room before he was told:
'Sorry about that, but your wife received a phone call saying you
were going to be shot from the stands.'

'Oh,' said Bobby. 'Well if he tried it he must be a worse shot than I am. Who's coming to protect me at the Black Lion?' The police settled for seeing Moore safely away from the ground once the crowd had dispersed. These incidents left their mark. Bobby was relieved to know the children had come home safely from an outing. For a long time he would never dream of permitting Roberta or Dean to play in the park like other children. They didn't go out of the house without their parents knowing their movements exactly. They were allowed to visit other children's houses but only if a grown up was present to keep an eye on them. Every time a new au pair arrived she was told about the kidnap threat to make her realise that the children must never stray away from the house or garden. It was confining for the children but better than the unseen alternative.

Moore accepted that fame brought penalties as well as rewards. He reminded himself that for every problem there was a pleasure, like going to Buckingham Palace in the New Year of 1967 to receive his O.B.E.

That was one of his more treasured experiences: 'There were about 150 people there to get their awards that morning and I don't think one of us knew any of the others. You're all shown into this grand ante-room and told what to do when you file into the hall. You come in from one side, stand in front of the Queen, bow your head, take two or three paces forwards and she pins the medal on you. Two or three paces back, bow your head and file off the other side.'

It was less than a year since Bobby had collected the 1966 World Cup from Her Majesty. This time his hands were scrupulously clean and he remembered the conversation, word for word.

'Well done on winning the World Cup. I saw the game and enjoyed it very much. It was wonderful for us.'

'Thank you very much indeed.'

Not quite up to the standard of debate at the Oxford Union, perhaps, but Moore was suitably impressed: 'The Queen is a stunning woman. When she smiles she really does light up. It can't be easy to light up for 150 people a morning and remember the right remark for each one of them. I mean, what if she congratulated some professor on winning the World Cup Final?'

There should have been no worries on that count For Bobby stood out not only as the youngest and fittest man in the company but as one of the few wearing an ordinary lounge suit. He recalled: 'All my life really I've liked to dress as casually as any occasion will allow. That's always been my style and the Palace requested you to wear morning suit or dark lounge suit. So I just put on my best suit. When I got there, though, the vast majority were in morning dress and I regretted not wearing a morning suit. I felt not quite right.'

Improperly dressed or not, Bobby posed happily for the newspaper photographers waiting eagerly outside the Palace gates.

That in itself was an event. For, like most leading sportsmen, Bobby Moore lived uneasily with the media. As a body, footballers resent the intrusion into their private lives, react to adverse criticism by doubting the right and the technical knowledge of the journalist to sit in judgement, lose respect for any writer who misplaces or exaggerates praise and withdraw trust at the drop of a comma.

As one who spends his working life walking that tightrope, I can be no more objective than Moore was himself about the problems of co-operation and communication between professional players and professional writers.

Simply, he expected the right in these pages to express his subjective view of a conflict which has for too long been damaging the game.

Perhaps sadly, it was not the inspired Scottish rhetoric of the *Observer*'s Hugh McIlvanney which stuck most clearly in Bobby's mental cuttings book, nor the late Geoffrey Green's lilting appreciations in *The Times*. What then? No, not my own contributions to the *Daily Mail*. Not even the ghosted columns of his own views in the *Daily Mirror* which once, years ago, were a labour of love for Nigel Clarke.

Rather, Moore remembered the words which wounded his pride or aggravated his problems.

'Certain people,' he said, 'never qualified for co-operation from me. Rather than row with them I chose to give them nothing without being rude. Sometimes I was amazed when writers who slagged you off, wrote unkind things which really hurt, had the cheek to walk up to you as if nothing had happened. I didn't want to know them. But I wouldn't give them the satisfaction of knowing I was upset. I just fobbed them off. They never had the chance with me of going back to their editors with a story that the England captain lost his temper with them or refused to talk to them.'

One football correspondent was as close as any journalist to West Ham for several years yet incurred Moore's displeasure 'for being the first to blow up the Blackpool affair'. Moore said: 'Seeing something like that hit the headlines was to me unbelievable. Then there were so many contrasting stories in different papers. Quotes from the hall porter that we were supposed to have come in at three in the morning with hostesses and drinking champagne.

'It put a strain on my marriage. At the time Tina was due to take Roberta on a skiing holiday and I drove them up to Luton airport. All the cameras were there. They could chase me as much as they liked but I didn't think it was fair to hound my wife and daughter.'

One columnist was on this subtle blacklist 'mostly for digging up whatever facts he could on some financial difficulties of mine without speaking to me. I only talked to the man at the time Fulham were having that cup run to Wembley as a personal favour to our manager, Alec Stock.'

Another widely-respected sports writer was marked down for minimal co-operation 'for gloating over my mistake in the World Cup match in Poland.'

Moore's attitude to the national press owed something to the suspicion of journalists which was latent in his West Ham club manager Greenwood and blatant in his England manager Ramsey.

Some of Moore's pet hates were rooted in 1966 'when none of the press believed we could win the World Cup until after we'd beaten Argentina but then they all started waving Union Jacks'.

Others concerned his front page exploits 'when people came on strong with the headlines without trying to understand my feelings and very often without knowing the true facts'.

All that illustrated the inevitable conflict of interests between footballers and football writers. The men on Moore's proscribed list all did their jobs to the immense satisfaction of their newspapers.

One or two of them contributed to an improvement in the

standards of sports journalism which is evident to most of us in what is still called Fleet Street and to which even Moore admitted.

Ironically, the apprentice Bobby Moore might even have gone into the print himself: 'It was the best paid trade open to me even at the time I got the opportunity to become a footballer.' And among the trophies he coveted most was the Footballer of the Year award bestowed on him by the writers association, and an exquisite Capi de Monte clock presented to him in Turin in 1973 by those of us who reported his record-setting 107th international appearance.

'Both those gestures,' he said, 'brought a lump to my throat.'

It had been with very different feelings that Moore had observed the press chronicling and criticising England's grudging decline from the heights of Mexico to that milestone in Turin.

18

The Descent of Superman

In their last four years, Ramsey's England were men running on the steep and shifting slopes of a giant sand dune, at times driving themselves unsparingly to hold their ground, yet doomed, finally, to slump exhausted into the enveloping pit of failure.

By the end of that scorching summer in Mexico, England were still within touching distance of the World Cup summit. At first their decline was almost imperceptible. Goals gradually became harder to come by, especially at home, but the first real shift of ground beneath their feet was delayed until April, 1972. Then West Germany returned to Wembley with a new star and, with a sickening lurch, the blond Gunther Netzer dumped England out of the European Championship.

Still, it was the 1974 World Cup which really mattered, wasn't it? And the draw was kind for the qualifying groups. We always beat Wales when we really wanted, didn't we? And who were Poland when it came to world championship football?

Sir Alf seemed impervious to football's winds of change, even though the sand was flying in our faces as the other great nations of Europe and South America kicked off in pursuit of Brazil's more adventurous tactical lead.

Bobby Moore and his contemporaries managed to sustain Ramsey's illusion through the first match of the new World Cup challenge, riding Colin Bell's goal to 1–0 victory over Wales in Cardiff on November 15, 1972. Two months later, England were so shocked by John Toshack's goal near the start of the return match that all they could muster was a pot-shot equaliser by

Norman Hunter. One point was lost. Questions about Ramsey's negative strategy began to be asked more intently but Poland lost in Wales in March 1973, England scythed through the other British teams in the Home Championship and that first jangle of alarm was drowned by the clamour of expectation.

Moore admitted that even England's most experienced men were guilty of undervaluing the significance of the home draw surrendered to Wales. 'At the time we were just delighted with Norman's great goal. We knew we should have beaten Wales but, as always, we'd struggled for goals at Wembley because yet another team had come to defend. So we weren't all that concerned about dropping a point. We didn't realise the importance until later.'

Moore was one of many nursing a dangerous belief in the invincibility of England. For in Katowice, a grey and forbidding city of mining and industrial workers, the Poles were getting ready.

It is to Katowice, a place far removed from the comparative culture and comforts of Warsaw, that the Poles always take the toughest of the matches they feel they have to win. It is a city where you acquire a taste for smoke, where you can almost reach out and touch the hostility of the natives to any visiting Soccer team which threatens to sour the odd ninety minutes of relief from their interminable working lives.

Ramsey tried to give his players a fresh feel of the Iron Curtain atmosphere by playing a friendly in Czechoslovakia in the May of '73. He succeeded only in giving himself a fright. For it took a late, late shot from Allan Clarke to save England a draw in Prague.

On June 6, confronted by 100,000 glowering inmates of Katowice's granite Chorzow stadium, Sir Alf reverted to type. The manager turned to experience and cold English steel, dropping potential match-winner Mike Channon in favour of reliable match-saver Peter Storey and charging Moore with getting his defensive formation out alive. Instead of finishing with a draw England ended the match without Alan Ball and with question marks appearing against the names of Ramsey and Moore.

The match was still in its infancy as Poland answered a roar for English blood which seemed to move the air within the walls of Chorzow. They won a free kick out by the left corner flag and speared it low towards the neat post of Peter Shilton's goal. To the eyes of the world in the press box and on the television rostrum, it looked as if Gadocha achieved the vital deflection. Moore now confesses to a virtual own goal: 'The ball came in low and fast and their No. 7 and me went for it, him looking for a deflection and me trying to block it. But he didn't make contact. In fact I barely got to the ball but I did get a touch. It spun into the ground and flew up inside the near post off Shilton's shoulder.'

Still, there was plenty of time left. England inched their way into the game and at half time Ramsey said: 'Gentlemen, if we keep plugging away we'll get some sort of result. A draw at least.'

Moore, of all people, punctured that theory in the first moments of the second half with a solitary, sickening error for which the price was soon to be the end of his international career: 'My confidence was still running high and right from the restart I demanded the ball off Roy McFarland. I had plenty of time but that guy closed me down very quickly, you know, what's the fellow's name, oh yes ... Lubanski. No matter where you are, a good player carries on playing the game by his usual instincts. I did what I always do in those situations. It's not my way to stick the ball in the grandstand. I looked up to see where I wanted the ball to go and I pulled it across him with my right foot to go wide into space. It was something I'd done a million times before, something I did a million times since and something I kept on doing until I packed in. And I always did it successfully ... except that once. Lubanski just got a touch to the ball and it spun behind me. Perfect for him. The momentum of his run carried him past me and then he proved himself a great striker. He stuck it in perfect, just inside the post as Peter Shilton came out. Everything about it was right for them and wrong for us. It was a bad goal at a terrible time. No one reacts well to giving a goal away just after half time. It put them two up and knocked the stuffing out of us.'

Poland's gamble on the fitness of the brilliant Lubanski, their outstanding player of his time, had paid off even though he collapsed under his recurring knee injury only minutes later. McFarland tackled him at the end of another long run and this time Lubanski did not get up. There was an unconscious minute's silence from the great crowd as an ambulance came around the running track, swallowed up their hero and sped to the hospital. Moore recalled: 'Watching the way he went down and seeing him go off in the ambulance I thought at the time that goal would be his last kick in a World Cup. I felt a twinge of pity for him because he was a fine player and a nice guy. But then I didn't know it would be my last kick as well.'

There became a desperation about England's efforts. Martin Peters was embroiled with Cmikiewicz, Poland's hard-man in midfield, their answer to Peter Storey. Alan Ball thought Peters was about to be attacked, went to his team mate's defence and was ordered off by the referee, who thought he was assaulting the Pole. Ten men were never enough to recover two goals lost by a full England team.

Ramsey reminded himself that the home game was yet to come, walked into the dressing room and said: 'Right. We're going back to the hotel. We'll have a few drinks together.'

Then he tapped Moore on the shoulder and said: 'That means you, especially.'

That was Ramsey's only reference to the biggest mistake of Moore's footballing life.

As was their habit, Moore and Ball were sharing a hotel room. They sat, depressed, on the end of their beds and Ball said: 'Well, Mooro, whatever happens we're going to make the headlines tomorrow, one way or t'other.'

Other players came knocking on the door, seeking the relief of sharing the depression with the team's leading characters.

At 11 p.m. Ramsey walked into the room, reminding the players they faced an early morning flight to Moscow and starting to suggest they got to bed. He was still there, with his captain, five hours later.

'We had a couple of beers in the room,' said Moore, 'and Alf started insisting on taking the blame for the first goal himself. He said it was his fault that he'd failed to warn us about the way they took free kicks from out wide. We argued black and blue that it wasn't his fault and although it hadn't really felt like an own goal I told him it was down to my last touch. A few of us sat there until about four o'clock trying to talk it all out of our systems.'

That World Cup tie was in fact the first match of England's summer tour and British Airways sent a charter plane next morning to take the party on to Russia. The crew brought the morning newspapers with them, which gave the players their opportunity to let off steam.

In times of distress, footballers are prone to finding someone else to blame. Sometimes they point the finger at their team mates, often it is the manager, occasionally the conditions, the referee, the crowd. When, as was the case with Ramsey's England, they are tied by mutual loyalties and expected to overcome adversity, they blame the press. And there was plenty of critical fuel to pour on those flames in that morning's editions of the daily papers.

A cloudy mixture of hurt and anger came over Ramsey's face as the headline on my report in the *Daily Mail* sank in: 'Ramsey betrays England.' Storey, at least for the duration of that emotive flight, took as a personal slight my criticism of Ramsey's tactical decision to play him as a ball-winner in midfield instead of Channon as a goalscorer in attack. Ball singled out the late Desmond Hackett of the *Daily Express* for abuse during the remainder of the tour. A whole group of players were even laughing and applauding as immigration police at Moscow Airport ordered the popular Frank Clough of the *Sun* back on to the empty charter plane home to England because his Russian visa was out of order.

It took Moore, who accepted without demur his rather large share of the blame and criticism, to restore some semblance of diplomatic relations between the players and the press, even though, as he said: 'Russia was hardly the place to go for light relief.'

Bobby's particular problem, insomnia, was aggravated by the weather. June 1973 was particularly hot and humid in Moscow and while The Metropole Hotel appeared to be a rather delightful English anachronism overlooking the splendour of Red Square, it was certainly not air-conditioned.

'It was no place to sleep for any of us,' said Moore. 'Let alone me. On the second night of it I got sick of tossing and turning and walking around the room and standing by the window. So in the early hours I took a stroll. It was cooler outside and I found a park bench, put some newspapers over myself and actually got to sleep. They were Russian newspapers. I wasn't reading the English papers after my ricket in Katowice.'

Bobby awoke to see the sun shining and two members of the F.A.'s Senior International Committee expressing their surprise as the figure they took to be a tramp came out from under the newspapers to reveal himself as England's captain.

If that incident in Moscow helped ease the tension, then another suggested to the journalists that they were dealing with footballers of rather undeveloped intellect. It is more charitable to interpret as group loyalty to their manager the refusal of the England football team to attend a last-night command performance of *Sleeping Beauty* at the Bolshoi. In preference to that majestic night at the ballet, Ramsey arranged for his party to attend the screening of an old Alf Garnett film at the British Embassy Club.

The mind boggled. Frankly, so did Moore's: 'One or two of us wanted to take the unique opportunity of going to the Bolshoi but we stuck by the majority decision.'

Bobby paid that debt to his own sense of occasion almost three years later by attending one of the farewell performances of Margot Fonteyn and Rudolph Nureyev at the Royal Opera House, Covent Garden.

England at least rose to their own occasion the day after missing the Bolshoi. Bell had flown home because his wife was unwell in pregnancy and Ramsey had to leave out Ball because he would be suspended from the return match against Poland, the next critical objective. Still, the USSR were beaten 2–1 in the Lenin Stadium by virtue of a goal by Martin Chivers and a luckless own goal by Khurtsilava, the Bobby Moore of Russia's defence. So England took flight in better temper for the brighter lights of Turin and the match on June 14, in which Moore would establish a record of 107 full international appearances.

Ramsey had the decency to announce Moore's inclusion as captain ahead of his normal team declaration, giving Bobby time to give interviews with his familiar dignity.

The players and the press made their respective presentations of Capi de Monte treasures and Bobby went out to face Italy for the first time in his career: 'It was very odd that in all those years and all those games I'd never played against this great footballing nation. I think because we had no tradition against Italy the occasion wasn't noticed by them. There was no presentation from the Italian F.A. They didn't even have the decency to lose.'

One of the goals, scored by local Juventus idol Pietro Anastasi, flew in through Moore's legs on the goal line. Suddenly Ramsey was talking darkly about gaps on the left side of England's defence, between Bobby and Emlyn Hughes.

It was the first hint of a fracture in the bond of loyalty between Alf and his established players and this time when Moore and Ball were in our group which sat up drinking all night, their manager was not with them. Moore and Ball were still holding court in the hotel foyer at 6.15 a.m. when the England amateur football team, who were also on tour, came down for the start of a long journey by road to their next engagement. Bobby saw them on to the coach with the gift of a crate of champagne and went to his room to pack for the last flight of his final England tour.

After the forced gaiety on the plane, Bobby got home to Chigwell and unwrapped his mementoes: 'I felt quite choked up about those presentations and I retained a great deal of affection for them. I knew it hadn't been a good tour. For the first time I felt fairly sickened by it all. Normally I'd always done well abroad. I'd enjoyed the different environment, the travel, getting the right amount of rest, the training, the spirit among the lads. But this time I knew I hadn't played well and all the disappointment over Poland made me depressed.

'I tried to decide if I was slipping, losing anything from my game. The odd thing was I figured I was playing well against Poland until Lubanski punished that mistake. I told myself that I couldn't go on for ever, even though in my heart I didn't want it to end. But then again I didn't feel I was on the slide. All my life I'd sweated on the letter arriving from the F.A. and then on the team being announced. But at that point I didn't see why I shouldn't still play for England.

'I asked myself if I was still helping the players around me as well as doing my own job. Perhaps I wasn't doing so much sorting out of situations that weren't really down to me. Maybe

I was less positive in committing myself to help someone else in case I couldn't recover. That would have exposed us to worse problems.

'Had Alf picked me out of sentiment? It had been suggested he only played Bobby Charlton at the end so that he could break Billy Wright's record of caps. I didn't want people thinking that about me. But I wasn't ready for the knacker's yard yet.'

The doubts whirled through Moore's mind for three months. Then, in September, England were due to play Austria at Wembley in a friendly preparation for the last, decisive qualifying battle with Poland. Moore noted that Ball was in the squad even though he was not eligible to play, and was encouraged to realise that Ramsey still included all the players he hoped he would need in the World Cup Finals in West Germany the following summer.

To Bobby's dismay, the blow came in much the same way as the start of his fruitful liaison with Alf. After a morning's training at the British Aircraft Corporation sports ground at Stevenage, Ramsey singled out Moore to sit next to on the coach journey back to the team's headquarters, the Homestead Court Hotel at Welwyn Garden City.

'Bobby, I've got a disappointment for you.'

Moore knew it then, choked back the bile of dismay rising at the back of his throat.

Ramsey hurried on, embarrassed: 'I'm not playing you. I know how much you want to play. I can assure you it's nothing to do with what happened in Poland. But Norman Hunter has been tremendously loyal and I've seen him play very well two or three times already this season and Leeds are in a tremendous run and Norman has been tremendous and there's his loyalty and the manner in which he's playing at the moment is – er – well, tremendous and, you see, I've got to get a settled side for the next game against Poland which is so important and I have to try one or two things which will be best for the team ...'

He tailed away.

Bobby thought: 'Settled side? Try things? When did he ever have a settled side without me? And when did he ever try things without asking me?' He asked Ramsey: 'Does this mean I'm no further use to you?'

No answer.

'Look, Alf. If I'm a liability and an embarrassment and you can't use me any more then say so. I'd rather know and we can call it quits.'

Ramsey: 'No, no. If we qualify I will need you. I expect to qualify and I'll need you to captain the squad in Munich.'

'All right. That's fair enough. I can't ask for any more. I'll battle to get back in the side.'

He remembered his respect for Hunter, sought him out at the first opportunity and said: 'Good luck, Norman. You've waited a long time and you deserve it.'

The England performance against Austria rendered that battle to get back into the side redundant. Martin Peters captained them on a seven goal spree. Moore: 'Many people thought I would be recalled against Poland for the sort of challenge I'd always risen to in the past. The Poles beat Wales the day we were playing Austria so we had to win against Poland and everyone seemed to think he couldn't leave me out.

'But after those seven goals went in it began to dawn on me that he couldn't change the side.'

Moore joined the playing members of the squad in their post-match celebrations, sharing in the lagers, taking the perfumed night air of La Valbonne club and steeling himself to miss the big one. Not even Bobby, in his personal disappointment, doubted that in this form England would overcome Poland without him.

The Poles were due at Wembley on October 16. Ramsey walked up to Moore in training the day before and said simply: 'Norman's in.'

As usual on the eve of a big match, the England party took in the early evening show at a local cinema. For once it was not a Western. They saw Jane Fonda playing a prostitute in *Klute* and some newspapers were moved to debate whether such a sexually stimulating movie would waste some of the players' nervous energy.

Again Ramsey spoke to Moore on the coach back to the hotel. 'When we get there I'm afraid there's bound to be a lot of fuss with the press and T.V. because you're not playing. I don't want it to happen to you but there's nothing I can do about it so you'll just have to face up to it.'

Moore's self-imposed dignity withstood the strain of television and radio interviews and a host of phone calls from newspapermen. But when I spoke to him he said: 'Everyone keeps asking me how I feel about it, Jeff. How the hell do they think I feel?'

Whereupon I had to ask him how he felt.

The answer was unprintable in a daily newspaper.

Twenty-four hours later the whole of England felt even worse. Bobby Moore, a most distinguished addition to the substitutes' bench, had to sit, watch and suffer with the rest of us.

The earlier results had simplified the issue. England had to win and were confident they would do so, Poland needed a draw and half-expected to lose.

Moore remembered the game more sharply than many in which he played: 'It was a nightmare. Even I couldn't believe it when Norman gave them a goal with the identical mistake I made in Poland. It was right in front of the bench. Again it was after half time. They cleared the ball down the line and nine times out of ten Norman would have clattered their player and the ball into the fence. But he tried to pull it back inside his man, same as me, and lost it, same as me. Roy McFarland was left with two men and Domarski was played clear through on his own. Even then Peter Shilton might have got it but he was a fraction late going down and the ball brushed the underside of his arm on its way in.

'One down. It was a joke. We were paralysing them. The T.V. lot were trying to work out whether their goalkeeper, that Tomaszewski, was a genius or a clown as Brian Clough said. He was like a cat on hot bricks, making some great saves but sometimes rushing so far out of position that our crosses were dropping between him and his goal. Never seen anything like it. Shots were hitting their posts and hitting bodies on their goal line and our lads couldn't have given any more effort than they did. We poured down on them.'

Moore sensed the need for fresh legs and a change of the attacking pattern. With fifteen minutes left there was a break for treatment to an injured player and Moore bent forward on the touchline to reason with the immovable Ramsey: 'It's getting desperate, Alf. Don't you think it would be a good idea to get a left-sided player on?'

Alf: 'I've pushed Norman forward.'

Allan Clarke recovered the lost goal with a penalty. Wembley's 100,000 knew it was not enough and tried to lift England to victory on a wave of sound. By now all England was looking for substitutes. Still none were forthcoming from Ramsey.

Down below the Royal Box, out of earshot of the watching world, Moore pressed Ramsey again, still privately, more urgently.

'Stick a left-sided forward on, Alf. We might get 'em down that side.'

Ramsey said it again: 'I've pushed Norman forward. I don't think we can do any more. How long to go?'

He had lost track of the time. Someone said: 'Five minutes.'

Ramsey: 'Too late now.'

Moore: 'It's never too late. Get Kevin Hector on for two minutes and see what he can do. Come on. Come on. Just get him out there.'

Ramsey nodded, transfixed, his world collapsing before his eyes. He sent on Derby's Kevin Hector for the shortest international career on record, just ninety seconds left in which to win his first and only cap.

Moore remembered: 'Once Alf agreed I was tearing at Kevin's track suit trousers. Someone else was trying to get his top off. You could feel the seconds ticking away. Racing the clock. We almost threw him on the pitch. And in that ninety seconds he nearly got Alf another knighthood. Alf ended up taking stick for forgetting the time and sending on a substitute so late. Yet Kevin knocked a ball only inches past a post, just before the final whistle. He might have put us in the Finals with his only touch of the ball for England.

'I think Kevin might have saved us if Alf had acted sooner. It was obvious we needed a left-sided player to go through them. Emlyn Hughes was doing his best from left back but as usual he was cutting the ball back onto his trusty old right foot and losing the angles and the chances.

Then it was over. The eyes of the Poles were glassy and staring at each other in disbelief. Wembley slumped into mourning. It was the beginning of the end for the entire Ramsey regime. Sir Alf rose, numb, and walked towards the dressing room. England's best had not been good enough. Moore echoed the sentiments of most observers of that freakish night's football as he walked alongside the manager across the familiar turf and said: 'I'm terribly sorry for you but it just wasn't meant to be.'

Ramsey said nothing much. Neither then nor in the dressing room. Perhaps pondering his fate.

It was quieter and emptier in La Valbonne that night. Hunter sped for the haven of home, crucified by his error on the one night on which he had taken Moore's place by right, only to be asked by his son: 'Daddy, is it right you lost us the World Cup?'

Moore knew exactly how Hunter felt.

Poland went on to the World Cup Finals and justified that result, playing attacking football to get within one match of the Final itself before losing to West Germany, the host nation. Yet Moore insisted: 'They were a long way from being a good side at Wembley that night. It was overcoming England which gave them all their belief in themselves and encouraged certain players to go on and prove themselves. England might still have done well in '74. Holland were the outstanding side in the world but they lost the Final partly because of Germany's fanatical support and partly because they hated the Germans so much that they wanted to take the mickey after their early goal instead of just pressing on to win.'

The Poles left Wembley with all that drama ahead of them. England had to return within a month, oddly enough to play Italy in another friendly. That outstanding fixture was one of many circumstances which conspired to give Moore a bonus cap, his 108th, and permit him to finish his England career at Wembley. Hunter was in the squad again but was handicapped by an injury which simplified Ramsey's selection. Moore led England out for the last time, but again no one told Italy they were supposed to lose. Where England had squandered chances against the Poles, this time they failed even to turn pressure into opportunities and once more the Italians caught them on the break to win 1–0.

The evening was memorable only as Moore's farewell, even though there was no announcement to that effect. He said: 'It was nice to be back but I knew at the time, although nobody told me, that it was the last England game. I wouldn't play again.

'In many ways I'd been lucky. I'd started young and kept fairly free of injuries. We'd had good runs in two of my three World Cups, which meant extra games. I thought about that night against Italy ... 108 caps ... difficult for anyone to pass me. Franz Beckenbauer ought to have done it with Germany but I doubted if anyone would ever do it for England. The game was getting harder. I knew people would think I'd had enough. Even if I was still the best man for the job, they would be looking for new players because for the first time England had failed to qualify for the World Cup Finals. They would be building for four years on. So there was no need for old Mooro. But it was nice to finish at Wembley.'

Sure enough, Moore was missing when Ramsey, thrashing about in a desperate attempt to prolong his term of office, named a new, young squad to go to Portugal in February, 1974. All for nothing. The Football Association, having already decided, finally plucked up the courage to sack their silent knight.

A golden age of English football was at a tarnished end.

19

Why the Man Called Chelsea Went to Fulham

So much of West Ham had been woven into the fabric of the England team that, in retrospect, it would have been surprising had Bobby Moore's club not fallen into decay in tandem with his country.

Like England, West Ham had been missing out on the trophies since the middle Sixties. Like England in that European Championship match against West Germany, the gradual erosion of West Ham's great team was given a savage, accelerating twist by a major cup-tie in 1972.

In the club's case the tie was a League Cup semi-final. The opponents were Stoke City and not even a rare glimpse of Moore's versatility was enough to take West Ham back to Wembley through a contest which occupied these two clubs for seven hours spread over four matches.

The first two games were the scheduled home-and-away legs of the semi-final and West Ham had begun well by winning 2–1 at Stoke. The Midlands club drew level at Upton Park, however, to push the second match into extra time and on to the first of its many dramas.

The teams were still deadlocked in the last minute of extra time when West Ham were given a penalty which brought two of England's World Cup heroes face to face. Geoff Hurst faced Gordon Banks in a one-shot showdown at twelve paces.

And lost.

Stoke's master goalkeeper defied West Ham's murderous goal-scorer and Moore set his jaw towards a replay: 'As Geoff placed the ball I felt certain we would go to Wembley. That's what a penalty ought to mean in the last minute of a semi-final. Geoff went for power and blasted away at the roof of the net. Gordon flung up his right arm in a reflex action and the ball flew over the top. Everyone acclaimed a great save and it was a marvellous piece of reaction by Gordon. But really, for my money, it was a sickening miss.'

West Ham and Stoke went to Sheffield Wednesday's Hillsborough ground, went into extra time again and still could not conjure up a decisive goal. So, on January 26, the scene shifted to Old Trafford, home of Manchester United, a grand stage for the finale.

It was one of those intense football nights when the pitch is slicked with water to favour the most skilled attackers and the crowds mass in the shadows of stands and terrace, drawn like moths to floodlights focused on that glittering green rectangle.

West Ham were in smooth control until Bobby Ferguson, their goalkeeper, plunged down among the flying feet, took a kick on the head and for once failed to rise. The crowd sighed its relief when Rob Jenkins, the trainer, at last got him to his feet. It was clear that Ferguson, lurching about his goalmouth and staggering into goalposts, was barely conscious.

Clyde Best, the Burmudian centre forward, was the player briefed to take over in goal in just such emergencies. Moore looked towards the tall, dark man: 'All right Clyde?'

The occasion was too much for Best. He made a nervous gesture and looked away, saying: 'No man. Not me.'

Moore surveyed a team of averted eyes. He thought about the two other occasions in which he had taken over in goal, first in a reserve match against Crystal Palace, then during a first team game with Chelsea. At least he had never let in a goal. 'I'll go in.'

Within minutes he was facing a penalty: 'I'd hardly handled the ball when it happened. John McDowell underhit a back pass and committed a desperate foul to try and make up for the mistake. Mike Bernard stepped up to take the penalty and it must have got to him that he ought to beat someone like me who wasn't a proper goalkeeper. I took a guess and dived to my right and the ball came that way and I went to push it round the post. But it was such a bad penalty that it was closer in to me than I expected and I was all tucked up when I made the save and could only palm it down. Mike followed up to smash in the rebound.

'Again I was sick. For the first time I had that foul feeling of picking the ball out of the back of the net. The other couple of times I'd quite enjoyed the fun of a spell in goal. But this time there was too much at stake. I was in goal for fifteen minutes and they were the longest fifteen minutes of my life. Billy Bonds equalised while we were still down to ten men but all the time I wanted to get out into the real match and do something about winning it. That goalmouth seemed the loneliest place in the world. Goalkeepers must get accustomed to it but I felt like a prisoner caged in by the edge of the penalty box.'

Down the tunnel, West Ham were working with a frenzy to get Ferguson back into the match. The goalkeeper was propped against a wall as they threw footballs at him. For ten minutes they just bounced off his uncoordinated, rag-doll body. For a few minutes more he could not count the fingers thrust inches from his face. Then they sent him back out, teetering into goal to allow Bobby to return to the fray. Almost at once he failed to see a long shot from Peter Dobing. Two-one down.

'Again we managed to equalise,' said Moore, 'but the psychological burden was too great. We were too conscious of trying to protect Fergy, so Terry Conroy got a winner near the end. All I could think about going down the tunnel was the penalty Geoff had missed, not the one I almost saved.

'That was the beginning of the end of an era. A lot of players had already left and that summer Geoff went to Stoke. That would never have happened if he'd put his penalty past them. West Ham would then have gone to Wembley to meet Chelsea and we would very likely have been in Europe the following season. Instead the team was breaking up.

'We'd already lost Budgie Byrne, Ron Boyce, John Bond and Peter Brabrook. Martin Peters had gone to Tottenham in exchange for Jimmy Greaves and then Jimmy had packed in the game. You can't keep on losing players of that calibre. Two or three of them were world class and there aren't many of them around. You couldn't replace them just like that, however promising the youngsters. Then Geoff went off to Stoke and they had to get on with rebuilding.'

Increasingly, Ron Greenwood was turning to his assistant to perform that task. John Lyall had been a hard, uncompromising wing half before injury had curtailed his playing career. Greenwood had schooled him through the club offices and reserve teams as his own successor. Moore: 'You could see Ron finding it harder to bridge the age gap between himself and the players. In the good days he'd got to know the lads by playing with them in the five-a-sides, larking about in the baths and showers, chatting in the changing rooms.

'That's not easy as you get older and it was obvious John would be given more and more control. That was all right by me because I liked John and he added some of his toughness as a player to the team. But it seemed to me that I was part of the past, not the future.'

That feeling grew as two unsuccessful years slipped by. Moore pressed in vain to be allowed to join Brian Clough at Derby County. His dispute with Greenwood flickered on through England's troubles into the New Year of 1974. Then, in a third round F.A. Cup tie against ambitious little Hereford United, the worst injury of Moore's career intervened. Bobby twisted his knee ligaments, limped on for another twenty-five minutes which aggravated the damage, and was out for eight weeks. The barely-known Mick McGiven took over the celebrated No. 6 shirt and, as if to prove Moore's point that his time was up at West Ham, a series of good performances took them clear of relegation trouble.

'Ron had agreed at the start of the season,' said Moore, 'that they would let me go on a free transfer at the end of the season. Everyone knew that if a good player could get away for nothing, he had a better chance of securing a good contract for himself. Well, West Ham were out of relegation trouble and they'd found a replacement for me. So I was pretty pleased when Ron called me in and said I could go. But suddenly he was saying they wanted a fee for me.

'I couldn't believe it of them. That was disappointing after everything we'd been through together. They'd signed me for nothing and had years of service from me and now they were using me to help balance the books. After all, what was £25,000 to them against everything we'd achieved in my time there? I had a right go at Ron but he kept saying the board were insisting on a fee. And they wouldn't let me get to speak to Reg Pratt, the chairman. So I was stuck with a price on my head.

'What made me angrier was that I knew they had to let me go if they really were going to build a new team. Whether they cared to admit it or not the team was Bobby Moore-conscious. They took their lead from me and looked to give me the ball to start everything from the back. I was a complex to them and if some of the other lads were going to blossom out and express themselves I had to get out of the way. But West Ham wanted their pound of flesh.'

The word hummed along Soccer's grapevine that Bobby Moore was going cheap, an England captain for £25,000. Stoke and Leicester were among the First Division clubs to show interest but the positive moves all came from the Second Division. Norwich made a bid to reunite Moore with their manager, John Bond. Portsmouth chairman John Deacon saw Moore as the cornerstone of his rebuilding programme. Both offered Bobby good contracts and both were prepared to let him live in London, train at West Ham and travel to join them on match days.

'That would have been necessary because of my businesses,' he said, 'but I knew in my heart it would be better to break the ties with West Ham completely. For fifteen years I'd been putting the car on automatic pilot and it had taken me to West Ham. I needed a total change of environment, surroundings, atmosphere. Something fresh to get me going again.'

Throughout the negotiations, Moore nursed the hope that the fresh challenge would come from Crystal Palace and his old instructor in the defensive arts, Malcolm Allison. 'I could have sworn Palace would come in for me. I felt Malcolm would have wanted me and I'd seen their chairman, Ray Bloye, on holiday in Portugal the previous summer when he'd talked round the subject of me going to play for them if it ever proved possible.

'That was what I really wanted. I'd played fifteen years for my pride, motivating myself, rarely getting any praise. I believed Malcolm could give me the lift and the appreciation I needed to go on playing well, raise my game again. I wanted Malcolm to tell me where I went wrong and to pat me on the back when I did well. No matter how long you're in the game you need that just like you do when you're a schoolboy.

'I wanted to play for Malcolm so much that I'd decided in my mind that if Palace were a bit tight for money I would take £5,000 less on my contract to go there instead of any of the other clubs. Truly. But Palace didn't come in.'

Fulham did. Their manager, Alec Stock, had been an acquaintance of Bobby's down the years and he understood enough about the man to time his move and gauge his approach to perfection.

Moore had given himself until that season's deadline day for Football League transfers, March 14, to make his decision. Stock made his bid on March 13. Stock knew that conversations with Johnny Haynes, George Cohen, Johnny Byrne and Alan Mullery had given Bobby a soft spot for Fulham. To a man, they enjoyed their football at Craven Cottage and the phone call to meet Stock and his directors was like a door opening to let light into a darkened room. Moore said he would sleep on their offer, but Stock knew he was hooked.

Next morning, Stock made sure of landing his catch by sending Mullery with Graham Hortop, the secretary, to Upton Park to complete the signing.

When Moore came out of an early, self-imposed training session, Mullery strolled up and said: 'Glad you're coming, Bob. You'll love it at Fulham. When I was leaving Tottenham I wanted another First Division club, just like you do. But when I got the opportunity to go back to Fulham I couldn't wait. The atmosphere's different class and all the lads are dying to learn from you. They'll do anything for you.'

It was the perfect boost to Moore's wavering self-confidence. Fulham's raiding party went home delighted to have Bobby's signature drying on the transfer documents. They might have had some qualms about their image had they seen Moore's birth certificate. His full name is Robert Frederick Chelsea Moore, the Chelsea being a hand-me-down from some distant and forgotten uncle on his father's side. Fulham had signed a player named after their closest neighbours and most intense rivals.

So the last of the World Cup winners left West Ham. He did so after sixteen years and an impregnable record of 642 first team matches, 544 in the First Division and 98 in an assortment of cups. And he walked away without so much as a backward glance or a twinge of regret: 'It had come to the stage at West Ham where

I couldn't do any more for them. I know from the letters I received after my move that the crowd appreciated me. But I couldn't surprise them or even satisfy them any longer. They'd seen it all before and they knew I couldn't go on forever. They wanted a new team and I needed a new challenge. It was as simple and final as that. From that day I was a Fulham player, 100 per cent.'

A bucket of cold water in the face could not have revived Bobby any more sharply. Stock, an old fox at the management game, knew what he wanted: a team with pace and style that spread a little enjoyment. He knew how to delegate. Stock had been first to spot the potential of Billy Taylor and appoint as coach the young Scotsman who then established himself as a part-time assistant to Don Revie, the new England manager.

At Moore's first team talk Stock said: 'All right fellows. Let's push it about, plenty of movement. Hmmm. Show 'em we can play. Enjoy yourselves. I'll leave the rest to you, Bill. I'm off for a few gin-and-tonics in the board room. Can't be bad at fifteen grand a year, can it? See you later on.'

In his unusual fashion Stock had created a helpful atmosphere for Taylor to go happily through the details of the match plan of the day. Bobby felt at home from the start: 'The mood was so light-hearted that it was like a ton weight being taken off your shoulders. It was very different from West Ham where it was always deeply technical, highly involved ... and sober. But I knew Alec was no fool under the chatter. Unexpectedly, in a very unusual way, he provided just the boost I was looking for.'

His enthusiasm survived a disastrous debut for Fulham. Moore's first appearance doubled the Craven Cottage crowd to 18,000 for the visit of Middlesbrough on the night of Tuesday March 19. In the midst of all that eager anticipation, Fulham were thrashed 4–0. Bobby recalled: 'They had some injury troubles at the time but the defence was fairly settled so I agreed to start off in midfield. From the off it was obvious to me that Middlesbrough were an outstanding Second Division side and would go on to win promotion and do well for Jack Charlton in the First Division. Which they did. We were hammered out of sight. Yet in a way it excited me. Middlesbrough exposed all Fulham's shortcomings in the first night and although the crowd were disappointed, I knew all that information would be invaluable if I was going to make a contribution. I started trying to help out a bit here and there. The lads were so eager to learn and it was lovely watching them mature around Mullers and me.'

Within a month Moore was facing Allison's Palace, the team he would have given £5,000 to join, and suffering 'the second great embarrassment of my career'.

He recalled: 'It was almost as bad as that early day when Johnny Quigley gave me a roasting at Nottingham Forest. It was Good Friday and Palace came to Fulham and gave us a good hiding, 3–1. I hated it because Malcolm was watching and I wanted to show him what he'd missed in not signing me. My pride was hurt so much that I went off up-field and scored one of my few goals.'

He really must have been upset because goals from Bobby Moore were as rare as caviar in Canning Town. During his 108 international matches he scored only twice for England, oddly enough within the space of twenty-four days in the significant year of 1966. Both came during the warm-up for the World Cup, the first giving England a 1–1 draw with Poland at Goodison Park on June 5 and the second contributing to a 6–1 win over Norway in Oslo on June 29.

The goal against Palace, however, was a futile gesture in the face of defeat. The chance for revenge was only four days away. The next Tuesday, Fulham went to Palace for the return Easter fixture and won 2–0, virtually dooming Allison to relegation to the Third Division. Busby and Barrett scored the goals but Moore, in his rightful defensive position for the first time for Fulham, produced the killing performance. He said: 'There were 30,000 people in Selhurst Park and I always loved a big crowd. On top of that I had a score to settle. I played from the heart and felt great. Full of myself. As I walked down the tunnel Malcolm came by and just said, "Well done." I'd killed his chances of staying in the Second Division but he showed me his respect. I'd played the way he taught me. Oddly enough I didn't see him for a while after that, too long after to say what I wanted to say to him: That's the way you told me. How did I do?'

Bobby, in fact, continued to do all right for Fulham. By the following season Moore and Mullery had imposed enough of their class and experience on the team to launch them on an F.A. Cup run which not even they dreamed possible.

To begin with, they needed replay after replay to dispose of Hull City and then Brian Clough's Nottingham Forest. Moore said: 'By the time we finished we'd played enough matches to have put us in the Final of the European Cup Winner's Cup the following season.'

Oddly, for every ounce of strength drained from the players by those marathon ties, they received a double injection of experience and team spirit. 'By the end,' said Moore, 'the atmosphere in the club was fantastic. We had built up almost overnight the community spirit which had been so important in the mid-Sixties with West Ham. Really, I suppose football teams are like grown-up schoolboys the way they like to do things with their mates. But without that togetherness we could never have got to Wembley with the quality of players we had at Fulham. We had to accept our limitations and try to play to our strengths and all those replays gave instant experience to a lot of young lads.'

The critics were convinced the run would end at Everton, who had been top of the First Division for much of that season. Yet Viv Busby scored both goals in a 2–1 win which was startling not only as a statistic but because Everton were completely outclassed.

'The odd thing was that I thought we could do well at Everton,' said Moore. 'They were very negative the way they played every game and I couldn't see them scoring many goals against us. Everyone got the jitters in the dressing room when they thought about all their big money players. Our younger lads began to worry that the job was too big for them to handle. But Alan and I went round chatting to them and when we got out there we played them off the park. Fulham were tremendous and Everton were a disgrace for a team who looked like they could win the Championship. No flair. No nothing.'

The ride home on the team coach that evening was a liquid affair and Bobby continued celebrating at B.B.C. T.V.'s *Match of the Day* studios. He fell into bed late and awoke in the morning to find his new house had been burgled.

A first glance downstairs told him that many of his caps, medals and trophies were missing and he steeled himself against the loss of some of his most beloved mementoes. After telephoning the police he went sadly to the front door to collect the milk and the Sunday papers and found his treasures in a tidy pile on the lawn.

'There had been a lot of robberies in the area,' he said, 'and it was the turn of our house. But the fellow must have been a football fan. When he realised whose house it was and what he had taken, he stacked them up for me. In a way it was touching. I thought then it must be our year to go to Wembley.'

First Fulham had to travel to a quarter final on another First Division ground, Carlisle. 'The team had hardened up by then,' said Moore, 'and we hung on and hung on until Les Barrett got us a goal out of the blue and we were through to the semi-final.'

Again the opposition was First Division, this time in the shape of Birmingham, but on neutral Hillsborough. Moore's defensive performance in the 1–1 draw earned ecstatic praise from Don Revie down to the youngest spectator. So Fulham survived for another replay. At Maine Road, Manchester they hung on and hung on once more until, just minutes from extra time, Moore's subsequent business partner John Mitchell snatched a goal from nothing.

Bobby Moore was going back to Wembley. By the most delicious, improbable irony, so were West Ham.

20

The Last of the Glory Days

The West Lodge Park Hotel at Hadley Wood is one of those watchful country houses which it is impossible to approach undetected. The crisp crunch of gravel beneath tyres and the tell-tale crackle of fallen leaves beneath the feet signal the end of a modest journey from London, past the northern extremity of the Piccadilly Underground line, to the Hertfordshire hillside which became a fashionable retreat for football teams pausing for breath on the way to Wembley.

We are there on Saturday, May 3, 1975. Bobby Moore's new team will play Bobby Moore's old team in the F.A. Cup Final and, as such, the occasion is unique. For the veteran of so many glory days, however, the exceptional has become nothing unusual and for once he is still sleeping on the dawn of a gala performance.

By contrast, Alec Stock is to lead a team up that tunnel of dreams for the first time in English football's longest managerial career. At 6.30 a.m. he is walking through the wet grass and gentle mists of a country morning, anxious to know if his show will go on.

One company of football boot manufacturers who claim to have Fulham under contract are seeking a High Court injunction on this of all days to prevent Stock's men wearing football boots manufactured by another company who claim to have Fulham under contract. In fact, as at most clubs, Fulham's players have painted the trade markings of the highest bidder on to their favourite footwear. But the more lurid of the morning headlines hint that the great game could be off and Stock's delicate nerve is more frayed than usual. Already, there has been a whiff of scandal about players selling tickets to the touts.

Nature chooses to be kind to one of her gentlemen. The sun rises behind trees whose branches spread their leaves in welcome. The dew glistens for a long moment before evaporating into crystal air and Stock feels good enough to illuminate the day with his own philosophy: 'Fulham are the first Cup Final team playing just for their pride and the glory. That's how I want it. That's how it should be. Wembley is about dreams, not contracts. The players have had their rewards for getting Fulham back on the map and into the black. They don't need another penny to make them give their all today.'

By 7.30, despite the sleeping drugs which became a faintly worrying part of most footballers' routine, the younger, more nervous players are coming in search of their cornflakes. As a star with no particular ties to any of his new team mates, Bobby has a room to himself and in fact it is quarter to ten before he wakes to a day filled with sunshine and looks out across lawns dappled bright with expectation. He arrives downstairs by 10.20, declines breakfast and helps Alan Mullery, Fulham's captain, calm the youngsters.

Bobby raises a hand to his shoulder, turns his head to stretch the muscles and says: 'Nothing to worry about today. Slept so well for once that I've got a stiff neck. What time is this match, anyway?'

The kick off is still the best part of five hours away but the Cup Final has already started. Moore and Mullery smile with their lips while their eyes scan other faces for the first signs of tension. Peter Mellor's grin is nervous so they poke fun at the husky goalkeeper's pansy-yellow shirt.

Moore, as is his superstitious habit on Wembley mornings, sets off to walk the hotel grounds. A blue silk shirt is his gesture of individuality on a day for wearing the club apparel. It is so warm that he leaves the grey jacket behind as he picks his way between the television cameras, across the cables and over the putting green towards the pond. Prophetically, he says: 'Hope Peter Mellor's okay. No good if the keeper's got the shakes.'

He strolls back into the packed foyer to find Les Strong, the injured full back, returned from representing the players at the

High Court hearing and reporting that the Cup Final will proceed
if they black out all the trade markings on all their boots. A typical
British compromise on a day steeped in British tradition. The
tension lifts and Moore and Mullery set the mood for a jokey
interview with B.B.C. television. The outside world is advised
that Fulham seem relaxed and confident and the players mock
West Ham's players when they appear on the screen in the hotel
lounge.

'Look at the state my old mob are in,' says Moore. 'So much
for the First Division.'

Out in the gabled doorway, Stock is dealing with the last
unpleasantness before settling down to enjoy his day. He tells
young John Dowie he has lost the last vacancy, that of substitute,
to the experience of Barry Lloyd.

'Not a pleasant job, that,' says Stock. 'But it's my job to do the
rough bit and knock him down and it's up to Billy Taylor and
Bobby and Alan to pick him up.'

Lunch is however much of an omelette you still feel like eating
which, as usual in Bobby's case, is very little. They pile on to the
team coach, jokes still flying for the benefit of their own nerves
and London Weekend Television cameras riding with them to
Wembley. Martin Tyler, the interviewer, has to conquer his own
taut sense of anticipation and announces: 'All right, lads. We're
going live ... now.'

Mullery shouts down the coach: 'Get the lagers out, Mooro.
What sort of a coach outing is this?'

Les Strong may be out of the match but he's still playing for
Fulham. Viv Busby, the goalscoring hope, has been too quiet for
too long. Strong says: 'Come on Viv, don't lose your bottle now.
Give Mooro his repair kit, poor old sod.'

Tight faces crack into smiles. Stock sits at the back, tense and
upright. The T.V. men cannot persuade the bubbling players to
stop waving girlie magazines at the cameras. But the closer to
Wembley the quieter the journey and the drier the mouths. One
street seems just like another and the surprised faces of High
Street shoppers are a blur. Around a corner to see the first glimpse
of Wembley's towers. They are reconstructing the approaches to
the stadium and those players making the trip for the first time
are saddened that they cannot drive up Wembley Way. The driver

picks his way around the back to the dressing room tunnel, through the throng of fans in their scarves and favours. The players wave jerky hands at Fulham fans beating, barely heard, on the sides of the coach. They plunge for the echoing quiet of Wembley's north dressing room.

Moore glances round the familiar cavern: 'Nice to be home again.'

He forgoes the traditional inspection of the pitch for more important business, gaining a psychological edge over West Ham. Bobby's former team mates arrive to find him waiting in the tunnel, ready to smile them in the back: 'Come on, Bonzo, give us a laugh ... where we going tonight, Frank ... you all right, Trevor? Truly? The old voice sounds a bit croaky.'

Moore judges that his presence among the opposition will be West Ham's biggest mental block. At their moment of arrival West Ham need Bobby like they need a broken leg. He jangles as many nerves as possible as they scuttle for their own dressing room.

The rest of Fulham come back down the tunnel. Aerosol cans of black paint are dug out of the kit baskets and passed round for the players to spray out the white flashes on their boots, laughingly complying with the High Court ruling. Seconds later the smiles are wiped from their faces. Somebody forgot the shinpads. Billy Taylor reaches into his back pocket for money and sends a police motor cyclist racing to a corner shop in Wembley to replace the missing equipment. When they arrive the pads are too big and cumbersome for the players' liking. A stadium official finds a hacksaw and Taylor feverishly cuts them down to size.

The atmosphere is steamy with nervous sweat. In a discreet corner, physiotherapist Ron Woolnough gives Stock an anti-asthma injection. Through it all, Moore and Mullery are moving quietly from team mate to team mate with calming words of advice and encouragement.

Moore tells Busby: 'They're the First Division side. They're the favourites. Let them worry about us.' He is dressed in shirt, boots, socks and athletic underpants. Everything but his shorts. As usual, they will go on last. Partly superstition, partly because the greasy embrocation is drying on his legs and he is as meticulous as ever about his appearance.

Taylor, the coach, appears confident but confesses a private concern: 'The build-up has drained some of them. It doesn't matter what you do, stay at home or go to a hotel, let T.V. in or keep them out, the pressure will get to a few of them. You know which ones it will be but you still can't do much about it.'

The battle plan has been discussed and decided days ago. The last team talk is short. Stock tells his mandatory joke: 'See this old suit? Had it sixteen years. Haven't been able to buy a new one. Remember the old fellow and go out and do it.'

Taylor jogs a few tactical memories and exhorts them: 'We haven't come all this way to fail now. Let's go out and play our football.'

Stock says: 'Remember lads, enjoy yourselves. This is it.'

Moore replies: 'And you remember, Alec, tall and proud up the tunnel. Stride out there and show 'em we mean business.'

Up that tunnel to face the world. Bobby knows that roar. Not so much a wall of noise for him, more a warm welcome. West Ham can still hear Moore firing jokes at them. The players warm up, coaxing the nervous stiffness from their legs. The officials settle on the touchline benches. No space between the crammed Fulham and West Ham shoulders. No malice, either. Alec Stock and Ron Greenwood embrace. Billy Taylor and John Lyall time the kick-off.

Strong, the full back Moore thought might one day play for England but whose injury ties him to that bench, wipes away the first of many Fulham tears this day. Then he settles among men who might be watching any game, anywhere. That bench is a professional vantage point on a carnival day. Down here the pace seems more deliberate, the physical contact firmer, the marking so tight that you think Wembley's wide open spaces must be in the car park.

The audience of 100,000 hardly know the game has started but Moore's psychological warfare is working and he and Mullery are already in control. They set up a chance for John Lacy. He heads just wide and on the bench Stock and Taylor slowly relax fists clenched in premature celebration of a goal. Greenwood and Lyall put it out of their minds. If a 6ft 3in centre-half comes up in attack you can only try to stop him, not always succeed.

West Ham are more worried about the balance of their team.

Lyall shouts to Holland: 'Get out right, Patsy. Go long and check out. Run him.'

Strong's injury has forced Fulham to move the right-footed John Fraser to left back and West Ham go to work on a man playing out of position. Holland, then Brooking, now Bonds, all come to test Fraser. Each time Moore is on hand, advising and encouraging. Fraser's temperament holds as firm as his tackle. Moore and Mullery are masters of the first half. The opening roars give way to respectful applause for two craftsmen. Even Lyall and Greenwood nod their heads in approval.

Fulham want to capitalise on their command. Taylor calls for more effort from Les Barrett, who looks like he might win the match from outside left. Stock berates Alan Slough for running too much with the ball, interrupting the flow of the team's passing movements. Kevin Lock, Moore's young successor at West Ham, has grown out of early nervousness and is holding them up. But only Trevor Brooking is worrying them. Once he cleverly plays Bonds in for a volley and Strong says under his breath: 'Christ, he can play.' Moore heads for the dressing room at half time demanding more action from the forwards to make it count. Taylor tells them: 'They're more worried about us than we are about them. Keep playing. It'll come.' Moore agrees. They are mistaken.

Across the tunnel, West Ham are deciding to switch their pressure to the right of Fulham's defence, on to John Cutbush who has come in to Fraser's place. Almost at once, Cutbush gives the ball away to Holland, Jennings shoots, Mellor palms the ball away and Alan Taylor slaps it back through his legs.

Silence from Stock and Taylor. All the West Ham bench are on their feet except Lyall and Greenwood. They hold a private brains trust into the incident, Greenwood with eyes screwed up, Lyall chewing and smoking. That is West Ham's way.

Five minutes later, a worse error. Mellor drops Paddon's shot and Taylor picks up the pieces once more and puts them in the roof of the net. Moore thinks: 'Bloody goalkeepers.'

This time Greenwood lets himself go. He puts one congratulating hand on Lyall's shoulder. You could almost believe they smiled.

For Fulham the dream is over. Moore and Mullery flog them

in to reprisals. Mitchell is foiled by Day a second time. Lyall senses West Ham are flagging. 'Come on, Patsy, run. Trevor, run. Get hold of them, Frank.' Bonds is seizing up and Frank Lampard is now captain in all but name. Moore suspects that but for Lampard they still might crack and curses out of respect for the man he believes has developed into West Ham's most consistent player.

Just for the moment, Lampard seems to be playing Fulham on his own. Taylor mutters on the bench: 'Get us extra time. They're dying. We'll kill them in extra time.' But when you're two down at Wembley, you know you've lost the moment the police come up the tunnel and fan out around the pitch. Moore sees them emerge, like undertakers, and experience tells him they are into the last eight minutes. There is time for one last gesture. He draws the infuriating Lampard deep into one corner, flicks the ball over his head, pulls it down and strokes it smoothly away. A masterly touch in the face of defeat. Then it's over. West Ham lift the Cup, Moore is barely conscious of climbing the steps to receive his medal. Back in the dressing room he refuses a drink, waving away the cup of champagne and saying: 'It's a new experience, losing. You live and learn.'

Stock tries to lift drooping heads, singing: 'If I could live my life again ... I'd come to Wembley every year.'

Someone says: 'Hell, two mistakes. And that Taylor only kicked the ball twice.' Moore sees Mellor smile nervously, bites on his tongue and walks sternly to the showers. The goalkeeper says: 'Well, someone's got to be the fall guy at Wembley. I wish I hadn't watched Bob Wilson's preview on the television. He was on about how goalkeepers could lose finals. John Lacy told me to go in the bathroom instead of watching but I said it couldn't happen to me.'

Moore comes out of the showers as the overflow of reporters and cameramen clustered round West Ham's door wash through the losers' dressing room. The attendants are sweeping up the debris of plasters, tie-ups, mud and plastic cups. A bottle of champagne stands half empty on the square white table, against a stark white wall in that bare white room. It is the only bottle taken from its crate.

Bobby is last out of the dressing room. The others walk up the tunnel, across a corner of the pitch and into the entrance beneath the Royal Box. They turn into the bar. But Moore pays a courtesy call on the West Ham dressing room then walks directly on to the team coach. Had they won he would have staked claim to one end of the bar and held court for his admirers. Like most winning sportsmen, he is not the best loser. On the coach he signs programmes pushed by loyal fans through the narrow air-conditioning slits beneath the plate windows. One by one the others come aboard and the coach bounces away. At thirty-four, Moore knows the odds are against him ever returning as a player. For most footballers, one appearance would be the realisation of a dream. For Bobby, Wembley has become a way of life.

He does not look back. Instead he starts opening the mountain of good-luck telegrams. It helps pass the journey to the West End hotel where Fulham's Cup Final night banquet will be held regardless. As the coach pulls to a halt outside the Dorchester, Bobby is met by his wife and two children, all dressed in Fulham's black and white and biting their lips to keep back the tears. Roberta and Dean rush to give Daddy a hug before the au pair takes them home to Chigwell.

That night, no more than one hundred yards along Park Lane at the Grosvenor House, West Ham have the Cup. But at Fulham's function they are mostly happy again and proud to have gone to Wembley. Bobby pays lip service to the celebrations.

James Mason, the actor, is staying at the hotel and begs entry to the banquet. He picks his way through the wake, seeks out Moore and says: 'As one artist to another, I would like to shake your hand.'

Moore relishes the compliment but is only partially shaken from his depression. Neither James Mason nor the lagers can improve his hidden mood.

It is well into the small hours before he goes upstairs to his room, sits on the foot of the bed, velvet dinner jacket over one shoulder, bow tie hanging loose down his shirt front.

Slowly, he fishes in a pocket, takes out a small box, opens it, looks blankly at his loser's medal and says to no one in particular: 'I'm glad I didn't get many of these.'

21

England, My England

Even by insomniac standards he had a bad night. Five stars above the hotel entrance may well be a guarantee of creature comfort, but they do nothing to still a fidgeting brain. There was little rest, in the warm darkness of his suite at the Dorchester.

He thought about his father back in Barking, no longer able to take active interest in his career because of a stroke which was also applying crippling pressures to the loving bond between both parents.

He tangled with the problems that only money can bring.

And he worried like any ordinary footballer about what would become of him the day his legs could no longer keep pace with the players of the future.

Bobby had given up counting sheep long ago. Instead, that night, he started flicking players through his mind. Great men, pictured for an instant on grand occasions. Footballers with strength of character, subtlety of mind and sleight of foot. Men with whom he had felt honoured to play. By the time he was standing at his window, watching the damp emerald of Hyde Park shimmering a welcome to the rising sun, he had selected the team he would have been proudest to captain in the name of England.

The choice was restricted to men with whom he had shared a football pitch. The team would have lined up in this formation:

1
Gordon Banks
(Leicester & Stoke)

2	5	6	3
Paul Madeley	Roy McFarland	Bobby Moore (Capt.)	Ray Wilson
(Leeds)	(Derby)	(West Ham)	(Huddersfield & Everton)

8	4	11
Johnny Haynes	Alan Mullery	Bobby Charlton
(Fulham)	(Tottenham)	(Manchester United)

7	9	10
Tom Finney	Geoff Hurst	Jimmy Greaves
(Preston)	(West Ham)	(Chelsea & Tottenham)

Substitute: Martin Peters
(West Ham & Tottenham)

Many of the arguments triggered by that selection, raged through Bobby's mind. Finally, the last key to 'my England team to beat the world' was found in a half-forgotten virtually meaningless match played by a Football Association XI on a tour of Australia and New Zealand in 1961. Moore was gaining experience as a twenty-year-old member of an English party who were ambassadors rather than competitors. The gentle, exhibition nature of the football tempted the great Tom Finney to come out of retirement. The term 'great' is not misapplied, as Moore's memory of that occasion bore witness.

'Tom had been one of the giants of the game when I was a boy and had hung up his boots at Preston eighteen months before. As a brash young lad I couldn't understand all the fuss about bringing the old chap out of retirement on that tour. Then we kicked-off. It was as if Tom had never been away. That lovely, easy control of the ball, the appreciation of the game, the finishing, much of the change of pace, it just unfolded in front of me. I'd never played with a winger like that and I never would. I was amazed by Tom Finney. He remains the last great England winger and without him I wouldn't have been able to pick a 4–3–3 formation.

'A stack of wingers were tried in my time: Peter Thompson,

John Connelly, Terry Paine, Bryan Douglas. All good players but
all failed at England level. Finding Finney in my memory makes
my team work. To partner him up front I'd have had to play
Greaves. Simply, one of the best goalscorers of all time. Even
better than Gary Lineker.

'To start with, I'd have tried supporting them with Hurst's
running. But if they hadn't blended I would have replaced Geoff
with Bobby Smith. Him and Greavesy were magic together at
Spurs and I remember them playing together for England in
Czechoslovakia in '63. Magic. Jimmy got two, Bobby one and
Bobby Charlton got another in a 4–2 win. When you watched
Smith from the stands you tended to think he was just a brute
who put the fear of hell up the defenders and goalkeeper. But
when you played with him you realised how much skill and
vision he had to offer. Geoff would have to do well to keep him
out.

'Behind them, the key to the midfield is Alan Mullery. A lot of
people opposed the way Alf Ramsey picked ball-winners, tack-
lers, in midfield. But without an anchor man you can't pick the
class of Haynes and Bobby Charlton. Teams are all about blend
and Alan was the best of three candidates for that role because
he could also offer you more constructive qualities than Nobby
Stiles and Peter Storey.

'Around Mullers you have Haynes, the perfect passer and the
perfectionist, and Charlton. Now Bobby could be inconsistent
and exasperating but he was one of our few truly world class
players and was a bigger force in the game in midfield than on
the wing, where he started.

'I know that picking those three would have Alan Ball hammering my door down. Ballie's a pal of mine and he did a great
job for England, Everton and Arsenal. He was so intense about
the game that he'll take this to heart. But he could only get in this
team if we were playing it tighter with four midfield men and
one less forward. If it's a choice between him and Tom Finney,
then Ballie's out.

'Jack Charlton wouldn't be too happy about Roy McFarland
playing centre-half. But although Jack was exceptional in the air
and a good character to have in your team, Roy was a much more
complete player, not only tough but capable of helping the team

play a lot more football out of defence. At the end of the day I suppose Big Jack and I still agreed to differ about the way he liked to whack the ball away.

'Picking the left back wasn't easy. Leeds converted Terry Cooper from a winger and by the time he came into the England team he was a tremendous attacking full back. But before him Ray Wilson was no slouch going forward and he was world class at defending, which is where your judgement of full backs has to start. So Ray's in, with Paul Madeley as his partner. Paul was not only one of the most versatile players but also one of the quickest, strongest and most intelligent. He was a player you always wanted in your side and he comes to the rescue at No. 2 because we've had a terrible shortage of class right backs.

'For goalkeeper, it's enough to say there's only been one Gordon Banks. Not even Peter Shilton should argue with that. And Martin Peters is perfect for substitute because he was a class performer who played in every position during his career, and played well in all of them.'

So only five of the 1966 World Cup Final team made Bobby's selection. More pointedly only two players, Madeley and McFarland, survived the transition from the old England of Ramsey to the next England of Don Revie. That stood even then as a question mark against England's future which grew longer with every decade which passed without World Cup success. Moore said: 'When Revie took over he found himself in the same position as Ramsey, at the start of a ten-year cycle. It's like that with football teams. One lot grow old and you have to start again. Looking back, a lot of our team of the Sixties were a long way from being world class players when we started but we grew out of experience. The problem for the future was that the players' skills were deteriorating and their potential was not so exciting. The more you looked at each one the more you worried.

'Perhaps because me and Norman Hunter were in the way, Colin Todd took a long time developing at Derby and once he came through I understand he turned down the chance to reach out and grab the captaincy. So where was his ambition? Trevor Francis looked to have all the ability in the world when he burst into the limelight at Birmingham but it took him forever to break through into the England team. If he was going to be another

Bobby Charlton he should have been playing international football as young as Bobby Charlton.

'Then there was Kevin Beattie at Ipswich. Ballie came back from one England trip telling me: "I've found one for you, you'd love this boy. A real character and tremendous player." Then the next thing you knew he was failing to turn up for an under-23 match because of the pressures. Pressures? Who had more pressures than me? Yet if Don Revie had wanted me to play as an over-age player in the under-23's, to guide the youngsters along a bit, I'd have been there at seven in the morning. If I had been his manager, I would have worried all my life that Beattie was going to let me down when it mattered, bang in the middle of a World Cup Final or something. He was a brilliant player but it was nonsense to talk about him as another Duncan Edwards. With his physical assets he ought to have been a Rock of Gibraltar, yet you couldn't rely on him. Even so, it was sad when injury cut short his career.

'Kevin Keegan was another exciting player who raised a question mark against himself. Because he wasn't picked for one match he went running home to Liverpool. If you're going to be a great player you've got to take the kicks in the teeth. You are in top football for one thing, success. If you just want an easy existence then run away to mum and stay there.

'Keegan was forgiven that sort of behaviour because of a shortage of top class players in England. Meanwhile, you found yourself still hoping that Colin Bell could fulfill his potential. Watching Colin play for Manchester City you figured he ought to become the white Pele. Two good feet, good in the air, unbelievable stamina and power. Could run anyone into the ground and then kill them off with a hell of a shot. Yet he so rarely came out of his shell for England to show his regular club form.

'So if Colin wasn't going to run the game for you at that time, who was? You know Alan Hudson could have conquered the world but there was no guarantee he was going to conquer his temperament. It was only in goal that we were all right. Ray Clemence, Peter Shilton, Phil Parkes. We were still the best nation in the world for keepers. But the more I went to watch England the more I was looking for someone to win the game for me. At the highest level, just being good is not good enough.

'Until Gazza came along – and how long will he last? – when have we even looked like producing a footballer to compare with Pele, Johan Cruyff or Diego Maradona? Pele was the best ever and the best in the world for a very long time. Cruyff proved himself the best for a period with Holland, Ajax and Barcelona. Maradona, love his ability or hate him for all his troubles and his "Hand of God" goal against England in the '86 World Cup, succeeded to the throne and it was harder for him because the game and the circumstances around it became much more destructive. He overcame the kind of pressures which look like bringing down Paul Gascoigne before he fulfills himself.

'Gary Lineker developed into a great goalscorer and Bryan Robson matured into a real man's captain and a tremendous midfield player for Manchester United and his country. But still England won nothing after 1966 and never really looked like doing so after 1970.

'In all that time, one little Northern Irishman was up there with the immortals, but the English game seemed to have a ruinous effect on him as well.

'George Best ran away in his own way.'

That judgement was based partly on an extraordinary first hand experience. Bobby, Tina and George crossed paths in Johannesburg in the summer of 1974. At a party given in his honour Best flirted with Tina: 'If you ever get a divorce, let me know.'

Little did he know.

Bobby said: 'I wasn't angry. I just felt he should still have been proving himself on the football pitch.'

That is where Moore judged men. The teams he most admired were as strong in character as they were rich in class. Brazil in '58, '62 and '70. The European Cup-winning teams of Real Madrid, Bayern Munich and Ajax. At home, the Spurs League and Cup double-winning side of the early Sixties, the consistent Leeds United of the late Sixties and early Seventies and Liverpool in their European Cup pomp in the Eighties.

The real clue to Moore's fears for English football lay in his preference for the sheer exhilarating class of Real and Spurs over the brilliant Dutch strategists of Ajax and the arch professionals at Leeds.

He said: 'I accept the game has become more difficult to play in, because the preparation of each team has become more and more thorough. A lot more thought goes into the organisation of a side now. But with the exception of one or two entertaining and skilful teams we have got to face the fact that football has deteriorated as a crowd-pleasing spectacle.

'Basically, there is a chronic shortage of top class players. The changing environment is at the root of that. I don't remember television being a big deal in our lives when I first started playing football. All me and my mates used to do was go out in the streets and kick a ball about. The first holiday I ever had was a couple of days with a relative in Hainault, which I thought must be miles away but was really just a bit nearer the Essex countryside.

'I first noticed the difference in my own kids. Roberta and Dean would start playing with other children but within a few minutes they were huddled round the old colour T.V. Even when they could tear themselves away, there were so many more distractions. For me it was football or nothing. For them there were swimming classes, riding lessons, anything they wanted. Where I grew up, roller skates were few and far between, a real status symbol. Dean was still a child when he moved on from bicycles to mini-cars.

'Then those who do become players don't work at the game. Again it's a question of distractions. When I was a young pro there was the billiard hall, which didn't particularly appeal to me but which ruined a few players' lives. There was the cinema which you couldn't go to five days a week. There was sitting in a cafe, which soon wore thin. Or there was going home, which was boring. So we went back every afternoon and worked on our ball skills. The top players would be there as well, taking real pleasure from simply kicking a football even though they were only earning £20 a week. That was how West Ham became something of an academy of football. It produced future managers from players who loved the game.

'Now it's as much as some players can do to fit training into their business and social lives. That's okay once you've mastered the craft. But the young lads are getting too much, too soon, too easy. Then most of them find themselves under managers who are governed by fear, the fear of defeat, the fear of losing their jobs.

'The Arsenal team which did the double in '71 established the pattern by which success became the sole yardstick for judging the game. A lot of people I knew were Arsenal fans and at the start of the season they could hardly bring themselves to watch the sort of negative football their team was playing. But by the end of the season they were all rolling up because Arsenal were going for the League Championship and the F.A. Cup. Yet it was still the same boring football. The trouble was it was no good the other managers playing bright stuff and getting beat. They were also getting the bullet after uprooting their families to take the job in the first place. Increasingly I came to wonder about the quality of managers. I learned a great deal from Ron Greenwood and I would like to have played for Malcolm Allison but other than them there were probably only two managers I would really have given anything to work under. Despite all the criticism of him after he walked out on England, I'm sure it would have been an education to play for Don Revie at Leeds. Like Bill Shankly at Liverpool he was so consistently successful. Greenwood, Allison, Revie, Shankly, they all made the business something more than mere survival, which is all it has become for too many managers.

'The pressure on the managers comes from bad directors and administrators. Too many of the men in the board rooms treat the whole business as a hobby. Too many of the men at the F.A. can't live up to their responsibilities for the welfare of the game. Look at the International Committee. For a good many of the early years I spent as England captain, I was addressed as Ron by certain committee men because they thought I was Ron Flowers, who also happened to have fair hair and played at wing half. It hasn't got much better.

'A lot of club directors are totally out of touch yet they come down occasionally from on high and expect the dressing room to go all quiet and respectful and all the players to call them Mister Chairman, or Sir, or Mr. John. What a joke, when they don't even know their job. When Jimmy Hill got appointed managing director of Coventry City it was a step in the right direction, and Terry Venables went further by taking over Spurs. Football is a big business and should be run by men who know the game.'

The class barriers in football, which are still enthusiastically manned by many boards of directors, were blamed by Moore for the shortage of opportunities for the talented showmen among the ranks of the players.

'Because those directors can't stand losing matches,' he said, 'managers are wary of the ball players who don't work as hard as the team men. They know that if they pick a new Peter Osgood, Rodney Marsh, Stan Bowles, Charlie George or Glenn Hoddle, they are taking a gamble on the result. So they play the percentages and shy away from the type of player who can entertain the crowd. They feel that the best way to get success is by stopping other people playing and by nicking the odd goal.

'One or two managers have been trying to change the system more recently. Good. Because it's ludicrous to try to change great individual players into robots. You wouldn't have caught me complaining if Jimmy Greaves did nothing else in my team except score two or three goals a week.

'My whole game was built around doing the simple things quickly and efficiently, playing to my strengths and only pulling out something extraordinary if that was the only avenue left open to me. No doubt the right attitude to coaching is to get people doing the right thing at the right time. But I would always have wanted one player in my team capable of doing the unusual and the unexpected. An Ossie. A Rodney. A Stan Bowles. A Gazza. Any half-way decent team should be able to cater for one luxury player. Look at Trevor Brooking – a fabulous luxury for West Ham to have in their team. If his name had been Netzer or Gerson or Rivera we would all have been crying out for an English player like him. But because he was English we complained that he didn't run about enough or tackle hard enough.

'As long as a luxury player is doing his thing – getting goals or laying them on – it's one of the duties of a manager to live with his own sense of frustration that the player could be doing more. If I'd been manager of Martin Chivers at Tottenham I would have been tearing my hair out watching him stroll about. But I'd have done it quietly. Because players like that really believe they are giving one hundred per cent. And without a player like that to score goals for them, Tottenham would have been relegated on about three successive seasons. The same judgements and values still apply.'

Bobby's concern for football was rooted in the suspicion that there are more bad managers than good, just as there is a majority of poor players, and that weak referees also outnumber the efficient. He said: 'We should have tried professional referees years ago. They should be fitter, sharper and more involved with the players and coaches so they know what is going on in football and recognise what's going wrong. For most of my career players and referees only seemed to annoy each other and it's got worse. This is a professional game in which the referee's job should be on the line against his efficiency, the same as everyone else.'

Above all, Moore despaired of the administrators: 'The emphasis should be on producing a game which the players can enjoy because they are encouraged to express their skills. That would automatically entertain the public and keep them coming through the turnstiles. Instead of worrying themselves silly about trivialities and their own private jealousies, the men at the F.A. and League should be looking for more ways of improving the game.

'By and large I'm not in favour of tampering too much with the laws. I once went to Canada with Gordon Banks and Jack Charlton for an experimental game which had, among other things, goals ten feet high. That might not sound much for a fit man who can jump. But even Gordon Banks was not the same goalkeeper in a ten-foot high goal. The score was about 9–7 even though we only played twenty-five minutes each way. Now that's a joke. Goals should be precious because their rarity value is what makes them so thrilling. But there are many ways of encouraging a better mood and a better style in the game.

'Banning players from passing back to their goalkeeper was a start. At a stroke FIFA rewarded the skilfull players. It made defenders try to play their way out of trouble and punished the men who lack the skill to do something creative in a difficult position.

'How about improving the mood of the game by borrowing a rule from Rugby Union? There is so much nastiness, embarrassment and wasted time in our games while referees try to force defenders to retreat the regulation ten yards from a free kick. In Rugby, if the defending players are not ten yards away by the time the kick is ready to be taken, the ball is moved ten yards nearer the goal. If you still don't move, another ten yards. In

Soccer, a harmless free kick on the halfway line could quickly become a scoring chance from the edge of the box. That would stop players arguing with referees.

'Why be afraid to try anything that might improve the game?'

These expressions of anxiety about the state of Soccer and proposals for its improvement were made out of a deep and abiding affection for the game and are part of Moore's legacy.

Football was, after all, the vehicle for conveying Bobby Moore to fame and fortune, albeit a somewhat smaller and less secure fortune than his life style might have suggested or his public might have imagined.

22

The First Days of Reckoning

Jack Turner used to have a room midway along the office corridor at Upton Park and the sign on the door said 'Property Manager'.

Nobody was quite sure what that meant, except that Turner could be responsible for nothing or everything at West Ham United according to how the mood took them. In Ted Fenton's time, the Property Manager found himself dealing with every problem which was either too trivial or too delicate to involve the team manager.

Turner was solid and square, of physique and character. In his sober grey suits, slim ties and shoes polished to reflection the young footballers found him a comforting figure, full of sound advice and calm reassurance. Most mornings they could be found queueing at that door for an answer to their troubles. Jack Turner could be relied upon to fix a mortgage, complete a tax return, even offer fatherly advice on the most intimate domestic problems. But the part he liked best was helping out with the scouting.

One raw winter day in 1955 found him on a wide-open touchline alongside Flanders Road, East Ham, gloved hands jammed deep into coat pockets, eyes watering in the wind, answering Fenton's request to 'go and watch a kiddy called Moore who's been recommended.' When that cup-tie was over, Leyton Boys had drawn 3–3 with East Ham and Turner went home to write neatly in his report: 'Whilst he would not set the world alight, this boy certainly impressed me with his tenacity and industry.' He proved to be a better judge of character than he was a prophet. Still, there was something about that fair-haired, fifteen-year-old

wing half which roused Turner's curiosity and he went to watch
the replay, a game won by one of Moore's rare goals. This time
he pressed Wally St. Pier, West Ham's chief scout, to make a
personal check. Bobby Moore was earmarked for the West Ham
ground staff.

So began a partnership which bridged the generation gap and
was to earn them both a small fortune, with the emphasis, as it
transpired, on small.

Not that there was any cake to cut at the start. Bobby's starting
wage was £6 15*s*. 0*d*. and from where he came from he counted
himself lucky: 'It wasn't a bad wage for a school-leaver. On top
of that you could get a bonus of £1 or £2 for playing for the
reserves in the Football Combination. And when you played
away they would give you five shillings tea money. To the boys
that seemed the best bit of all. Maybe because you could win on
the deal. If you stopped for a sandwich and a bottle of pop on
the way to somewhere like Newbury, you could make a three
bob profit. That was invaluable. You'd give fifty bob to your mum
and set so much aside for your fares and your Saturday night
out. Your wages were spoken for and that tea money was the
little bit of extra in your pocket. Sometimes you could persuade
them to give you three games a week with the reserves and the
youth team and that meant three lots of five bobs. Handsome.

'And all the time the work you had to do made you all the more
determined to make the grade and turn pro. Today's apprentice
professionals just do the same as the senior pros, train and play.
Perhaps that's why too many of the young lads are undisciplined
and not enough of them are hungry footballers. We didn't have
any breath to spare for answering back.

'First thing Monday mornings we would start sweeping the
terraces and cleaning out the stands. We'd break off from that in
time to get the dressing rooms and the kit ready for the pros
when they came in for training. You'd do some running and ball
work yourself for the rest of the morning, then clear everyone's
kit away and go back to sweeping the terraces, maybe cleaning
the toilets, painting the back of the stand. Anything that needed
doing.

'To get to your little match on Saturday you'd have to get
through Friday. There'd be the usual chores with the kit and the

Above left: close friends ... Bobby Moore and Jimmy Greaves (*Daily Mail*); above right: beating George Best; right: an impromptu training session in Acapulco (*Syndication International*).

Exchanging shirts and mutual respect with Pele. Bobby's favourite photograph, showing the true spirit of football after Brazil beat England in the 1970 World Cup in Mexico (*Syndication International*).

The end of the World Cup dream in 1970. Bobby and Sir Alf leave the pitch after being knocked out by West Germany.

With good friend and rival Franz Beckenbauer.

Heading west ... In the summer of 1976 Bobby played for San Antonio Thunder in the American N.A.S.L. (*Colorsport*).

Sign here . . . Bobby witnesses my wedding to Maria. Mexico City, February 20, 1987.

Happy travels with Stephanie in Positano, Italy.

Outside the Amber Fort in Jaipur, Bobby stopped for a rest and was charmed by a small boy who respectfully waited until he had awoken before asking for his hero's autograph.

Ordering supper at Agra Railway Station.

A restful moment at the Kamchipuram Ghats.

Roberta and Bobby, summer 1986
(*Chris Craymer*).

Stephanie and Bobby, summer 1992
(*Syndication International*).

With Dean, Sara and granddaughter Poppy, August 1991.

Above: Roberta and Stephanie at West Ham when special tribute was paid to East London's great hero. Below: Bobby's many fans paid moving homage (*Daily Mail*).

boots for training. Then you'd set about getting the pitch in shape for the first team game. When you had a pitch like West Ham's used to be, with such bad drainage, that meant three or four of us spending three hours pushing and pulling the heavy roller. Flattening it out. Backwards and forwards until you couldn't wait to go back to the dressing rooms and start polishing the taps on the baths and the showers. You'd stagger home at six and be up and out by nine next morning ready for an eleven o'clock kick off. When you look back at that it's laughable to think today's footballers are called full-time professionals when all they do is train a couple of hours a day.'

Those hours spent slogging at the heavy roller stored up the muscle power, willpower and, indirectly, the earning power upon which Bobby was to call at the high points of his career. More immediately, he was rewarded by his first professional contract. In April 1958, shortly after his 17th birthday, he signed for £12 a week, the maximum wage for his age at that time.

As a young man, he took no more than a distant interest in the struggle by Jimmy Hill's players' union to secure the abolition of the Football League's maximum wage. But by 1961, when that iniquity was swept aside, Bobby's single-minded concentration on securing a first team place at West Ham and launching his international career with a string of appearances for England's under-23s had put him in a powerful bargaining position: 'I'd not been on the £20 maximum all that long and for a while I'd been happy with that. But when it became clear that the maximum wage would go, I sat down and worked out what I thought I was worth to West Ham. And I decided I was worth £30 a week.'

The figure reached by that self-evaluation became a point of principle in Moore's first financial dispute with West Ham. By sticking to that principle, he began accumulating his reputation as a hard-headed, commercial man. When the last of his team mates settled for £28 a week, Moore stood his ground alone for six weeks, a period which affected his political standpoint for the rest of his life. He had never been much interested in politics, nor filled with the ideological zeal which grips many young men. He simply decided that any individual had the right to profit from his own talent and initiative. He was twenty. By the time he came of age, this working class lad from a staunch Socialist background had grown into a committed Conservative voter who later became a frequent and welcome guest at No.10 Downing Street when Mrs. Thatcher was in power and, subsequently, at the onset of Mr. Major's tenancy.

In that fight for an extra £2 a week he learned to look after himself and first sensed the intrinsic worth of his talent: 'Looking back, it was laughable that Ron Greenwood and I should have had such an enormous disagreement over £2 a week. West Ham were quibbling over £100 a year when they would soon be wasting £100,000 on a new player. I had made up my mind that as an under-23 international and a player already being linked with other, bigger clubs, I was worth that £30. Ron offered the whole squad £28 a week and at first none of us signed the new contracts. Then one or two gave in. Then a couple more signed. Two days before the deadline the last half dozen capitulated. If you didn't take the £28 a week, they simply retained you on the old contract of £20. But I held out for another six weeks. And I won the battle for all the players who had backed down. Finally, the club decided to put everyone's wages up to £30, so they could have done with the whole business. To be fair to them, they back-dated my rise so that in the end I didn't lose any money. I think, in the end, they accepted that I had held out for what I believed was right. If they had offered me £30 a week at the start I wouldn't have started asking for £35. I would have signed at once.'

At the first possible moment Moore had hardened himself for the new procedures of contract negotiation. Then, in order to minimise his personal embarrassment in forthcoming pay battles, he sat down and thought out a personal incomes policy: 'From then on there was going to be a lot of tough talking every time the contract was renewed and a lot of clubs were getting players to accept lower wages with high appearance and bonus money.

'That was okay if a season went well. But what if you were plain unlucky? Or out with injury? And what happened in the summer if you had adjusted your life style to a good income and suddenly you were back on a low basic? So in every financial settlement I insisted on a high basic wage, never mind the ifs and buts. Then I always assessed my value to the club according to the service I had given them and what I had achieved in football during the previous couple of years.

'Too many players want paying big money on a promise of what they are going to do in the future. I never based my argument around what I might or might not do in the next four years. Let's face it, you could get run over or cop for a bad injury or simply hit a long patch of bad form. What I insisted on was a reward for what I had done in the past and recognition of my value as an asset to the club. As a man good enough to captain England I was obviously of some value to West Ham as a player and as an attraction to the crowds.

'That might sound cold and hard, but you had to have some basis from which to negotiate. I learned in that first battle with Ron Greenwood how damaging the whole business might be to a manager and a player. We were in violent disagreement over £2 a week. It was ludicrous that we would end up the afternoon resenting each other yet next morning we would have to get out on the training pitch and try to get the best out of each other.

'The system always has been wrong in this country. Clubs expect a manager to come in from the seven-a-side, splash about in the bath with the lads, then put on a collar and tie and become a businessman. It's obvious that we should operate on the same lines as the Continentals, with a working director handling the finances. The game moved some of the way but not far enough. The team manager should be freed from all the bust-ups with players over contracts and when it comes to transfers he would just tell the financial man which player he would like to sign and let him get on with fixing the deal.

'For years it was just as ridiculous that the rules forbade a player to instruct an agent or representative to negotiate on his behalf. That was a throwback to the dark old days when they didn't think the players ought to earn much money, anyway. Everyone thinks players are money mad, but the fact is I have never known one professional footballer who enjoyed arguing for his money. Not one little bit. I would gladly have left my salary negotiations in Jack Turner's hands.'

As it was, Turner was falling from grace at West Ham under Greenwood's management and he began to interest himself in

Bobby's earnings outside the game. The first man to toy with that potential had been Bagenal Harvey, the London-based agent to a veritable *Who's Who* of sporting, journalistic and television personalities. The first of the breed, Harvey rushed in with a two year contract when Moore returned from his first World Cup, in Chile in 1962, and started well by securing a £450 payment for a Brylcream poster advertisement. But almost at once the flow dried up and Moore asked Turner to arrange his release from the contract.

Turner had already helped establish Bobby in a sports goods shop, making available a small house directly opposite the main entrance to West Ham's ground which he had been using as a warehouse for an unsuccessful venture into football boot manufacturing. When Bagenal Harvey agreed to waive his hold on Moore, Turner immediately launched Bobby Moore Ltd.

The sports shop was already progressing well. With the lure of Bobby's frequent attendance behind the counter, the fans flocked in. Consistently, for a few years, it made Bobby as much as he was earning from his football, doubling a salary which was itself constantly increasing as his reputation grew.

Turner, meanwhile, was after bigger money. Under the umbrella of Bobby Moore Ltd., he pushed his man's name at the media, the major companies, the advertising agencies. His first coup was a weekly column with *Titbits*. It paid £80 a week over a 26-week run. After paying £15 a week to his ghostwriter, Roy Peskett, Bobby was left with £65 profit, from half an hour's chat. He was earning £35 a week playing football.

By 1964 he had pushed his West Ham salary above £60, even though many of his colleagues in the team which beat Preston in the F.A. Cup Final were earning less than £30 a week.

The first real boom took another two years to materialise. Then Moore captained England to victory in the World Cup Final and suddenly money seemed to be growing on goalposts. Bobby returned to Greenwood's office to resume discussions which had been temporarily suspended by that dramatic signing of a one-month contract in the England hotel on the morning of their first World Cup match. He knew he was talking from an unprecedented position of strength: 'I was well aware that they couldn't afford to let me go to Tottenham or anywhere else after winning the World Cup. I also knew I was worth a great deal to them as England captain.

Moore remembered the nub of the conversation quite clearly.

Greenwood began: 'How can you give your best for West Ham if you really want to leave us?'

Moore: 'I've only thought about leaving in order to better myself. We've gone into a depression here but I won't dispute that we might be able to achieve things again. Let's concentrate on negotiating the right sort of figure.'

'What figure are we talking about?'

'Let's settle on £150 a week.'

'That's almost double your old contract. I don't know about that.'

'If you match my demand I'll sign a six-year contract to prove my loyalty to West Ham.'

'The club will have to think it over.'

West Ham agreed within a week and Moore signed a three-year contract with West Ham holding the option to retain him for a further three years after that. He said: 'It made me the highest paid player at West Ham at the time. But it wouldn't have worried me if I'd found out that Geoff Hurst and Martin Peters had come back from the World Cup and got better deals than me.

'I never discussed my money with anyone else and all that concerned me was getting what I felt to be a fair deal. I don't suppose I was the best paid player in the country. There were a lot of stories about big money being earned by Bobby Charlton, Denis Law and George Best at Manchester United. But they were getting 60,000 people for games at Old Trafford and I felt that on West Ham's gate of around 30,000 my money was fair. Also I was able to stay close to my business interests and didn't have to move away from my side of London, my own environment.'

Moore and Turner also realised that although England's £1,000-a-man bonus for winning the World Cup was a relative pittance, it was only the first drop in an ocean of opportunity. The Golden Age had dawned. Footballers were not only social darlings but also sure-fire sellers of everything from cars to cornflakes and the faces of those World Cup winners beamed out from nearly every packet in every household.

Bobby Moore Ltd. became a seven-day-a-week, 18-hours-a-day business. The newspapers became as clamorous for columns as the magazines and his signed articles for the *Daily Mirror* and *Shoot*, the football weekly, were grossing £160 a week plus expenses.

The ad-men fought to have Bobby Moore smile into the camera and endorse their clients' product. By the time of the next World Cup, in 1970, Kellogg's were paying him £3,000 for a single corn-flakes commercial.

Then and there, almost a quarter of a century ago, the boom hit its peak. Bobby Moore Ltd. was grossing £22,000 a year, even though Turner was instructed to turn down offers which might tarnish the solid image of his star. In fact, partly to help reinforce that image, Moore did not charge for an anti-smoking commercial for the government.

Through it all, Turner was strictly Mr Ten Per Cent. He said: 'Other agents expected fifteen or twenty per cent but I believed Bobby was something special and it was better to have ten per cent of a lot than twenty per cent of nothing at all. And apart from all that, I loved the involvement. I could have made a lot more money for myself in other walks of business. But I was happy.'

A house not far from Moore's in stockbroker Chigwell was an aid to that contentment. Nevertheless, Bobby trusted Turner. He was always loyal until the evidence proved otherwise. The first time Moore felt that Turner let him down concerned the loss of his entire collection of newspaper cuttings to that date. That record of his life was bundled into a sack one evening and left, carelessly, in a corner of Turner's offices in Manor Park. The cleaner threw out the sack with the rubbish next morning. A more emotional man might have wept at such a loss.

Others began to fail him more grievously.

In the boom years, the acquaintances came thick and fast with their propositions for jumping on the Bobby Moore bandwagon. Hatton Garden jeweller Peter Younger begged permission to launch Bobby Moore Jewellery in 1968. Net proceeds: Nil.

That same year, clothing retailer David Walker set up Bobby Moore Shirts and Ties as a London outlet for goods being mar-keted in the north of England by Manchester City footballer Mike

Summerbee. 'It might have worked,' said Bobby, 'if they could have produced enough gear to satisfy the orders on the books.' Net proceeds: a dozen monogrammed silk shirts and ties.

Again in 1968, Moore involved himself in a more substantial venture with Freddie Harrison, a manufacturer of suede and leather wear for ladies, and Morris Keston, fanatical supporter of Tottenham in general and football in particular, as well as a successful gown manufacturer.

They decided to attack the suede and leather market for men. They formed Harrison-Moore Ltd., and this time Bobby invested £5,000 as well as his name. Net proceeds: minus £5,000.

To start, they used a factory in East London, then opened a West End showroom in Percy Street. Keston withdrew because of personal differences with Harrison. They expanded into a larger factory at Wickford in Essex but when the government met a power crisis by declaring a three-day working week, they were forced to close down and sub-contract their work to outside manufacturers. Harrison purchased a small factory in Cyprus which had only just settled to producing a regular flow of quality goods when the Turks invaded the island. They again contracted their work outside the company. They re-opened operations in Cyprus at the end of 1975 but Harrison went bankrupt in March 1976, having already passed on his share of the company to his brother.

Still, Moore hoped Harrison-Moore Ltd. could be a strong plank of his economy at the end of his playing days: 'Every penny I might have taken out was ploughed back into the business.'

At first the problems with Harrison-Moore Ltd. seemed incidental. Even the football itself became lucrative. Moore returned from the 1970 World Cup in Mexico to make arrangements for his testimonial match, a privilege for which every footballer used to become due after ten years with one club. Celtic provided the opposition to West Ham at Upton Park. Esso secured some publicity for themselves by sponsoring the event and 26,000 people came through the turnstiles. By the time Bobby left to host a reception at The Sportsman Club, he was assured of a tax-free benefit payment of almost £20,000.

That may seem a trifle in the Nineties and the sum did not compare with the £40,000 testimonials of Denis Law and Bobby

Charlton at Manchester United and Billy Bremner and Norman Hunter at Leeds United. But it was a killing by southern standards at that time.

Two years later he negotiated yet another new contract with West Ham. 'To be fair,' he said, 'they had improved on my £150 a week during the period of my six-year contract. Without much prompting from me they accepted that times changed and came up with rises accordingly.'

In 1972, however, he pushed his basic wage well clear of the £200 a week milestone by agreeing a contract 'comfortably in excess of £10,000 a year.'

After another two years he harvested the proceeds of his transfer to Fulham. At that time another of Moore's acquaintances, Bill Larkin the roasted peanut manufacturer, organised a whipround among businessmen fans of West Ham to keep Bobby at Upton Park. Between them they promised to cover the £30,000 extra which Bobby could expect to earn from a three-year contract with Fulham. However touching, it was an impractical gesture and the transfer proceeded.

By 1974, Moore was in need of an injection of extra capital: 'You get used to a certain standard of living.'

His life style had progressed apace. The humble semi in Ilford had been bought for £3,600 and sold for £6,500. The mock Tudor residence in Chigwell cost £11,500 and brought in £41,000. Morlands, the new mansion, came to £80,000 worth of luxury, purpose-built to satisfy Mrs. Moore's tastes.

The move to Fulham coincided with the sale of the West Ham sports shop to one of Tina's cousins: 'There didn't seem much point keeping it on since I was leaving the club.'

Besides, by then he was up to his neck in a much grander enterprise which for a time threatened him with bankruptcy and proved to be a highly costly self-indulgence.

The nightmare had a name: Woolston Hall. It identified a charming manor house set in a cleft of Essex countryside between Chigwell and Abridge. It seemed perfect for a country club. Del Simmonds thought so. A car dealer and yet another of the fraternity of Chigwell businessmen, Simmonds was on friendly terms with two star names who could front the operation, his golfing partner Sean Connery and his favourite footballer, Bobby

Moore. He could also count on financial aid from Lou Wade, his and Bobby's mutual friend, Wade's businessman son Michael and a seventh partner, East End publican Kenny Bird.

Together they agreed the project was a winner. Jack Turner opposed Moore's involvement but Bobby and more relevantly Tina were taken with the glamorous nature and apparent potential of a country club. Bobby said: 'It seemed perfect for the area and the deal seemed tremendous. We had the house valued at £$\frac{1}{2}$ million and the total cost of the project was only £250,000. There were twenty-six acres of land only twelve miles from London and we all knew we lived in a rich area where you had to queue up to get a table in the local restaurants. What we didn't know, between us, was the slightest thing about catering or organising a club of this kind.'

That did not deter Moore from investing £5,000 cash and encouraging the confidence of the group's backers, the Dunbar Bank in Pall Mall, by becoming a director and freely giving the use of his name. Even before the refurbishing work was completed, Bird, the publican, had withdrawn from the project. Before the club could open there was an underworld attempt to burn down Woolston Hall and a shotgun was fired at Simmonds' home from a passing car. The five remaining partners duly accepted Simmonds' resignation.

They pressed on with the opening of their exclusive £100-a-membership country club which embraced a restaurant, discotheque, cocktail and lounge bars, sauna, golf driving range, swimming pool and tennis courts.

'The great problem,' Moore acknowledged later, 'was that with the exception of the restaurant, discotheque and bars, we spent a fortune on facilities which did not bring in a penny piece. And we had bought the best of everything, from the teaspoons upwards.'

The debts mounted. Moore's agents took on increased guarantees at the bank. They changed the style of the Woolston Hall operation, sacrificing exclusivity for a more popular appeal. They cut prices. They increased the share issue. In vain. The club had opened for business in August 1972. By early 1974 they decided to cut their losses and sell out. They were left with an outstanding debt of £100,000.

The following year, Moore found himself in the embarrassing position of being the only partner sued under an alleged guarantee for that six-figure sum. The subsequent lengthy litigation added to the burden for which minimal help from his so-called friends was forthcoming.

By the standards of many of the world's leading sportsmen, the entire sum of money involved might have been an acceptable amount to risk in business. Jack Nicklaus, Gary Player, Muhammad Ali, Jackie Stewart, Lew Hoad, all could have withstood that sort of racket without long-term grief. So could Pele and Johan Cruyff. But unlike his Latin American and Continental contemporaries, Moore was no millionaire. He was in financial crisis.

Bobby was in more optimistic mood by his 35th birthday on April 12, 1976. The problems had given him a new sense of purpose and direction. For a long time he had been fidgeting with the thought of giving up football completely when he retired as a player. He said: 'I had been lucky enough to be around for the first good years for professional footballers in this country.'

The sudden, sour taste of commerce came as a sharp reminder of his appetite for big time soccer. Suddenly he realised he would like his playing career all over again: 'Maybe I had proved myself the best at my business for twelve years non-stop and I didn't have to go on proving that forever. But I wish I could have gone on playing forever.'

As if on cue, rich American clubs, headed by San Antonio, materialised with offers tempting Moore to join Pele and other distinguished names in giving the world game a fresh and exciting impetus in the hitherto unconverted United States. The money and the challenge were ideal and again he felt the spurt of adrenalin through his veins.

Beyond that he began to hunger for a chance to show what he could do in management: 'I had never thought much about running my own team but that prospect excited me as well.'

Seemingly right on schedule, like most events in his hitherto well-ordered career, Bobby's character had been unbending in time to accommodate the extrovert sporting mentality of America and the more varied demands of management.

A twinkling wit and warmth of nature had been allowed to

surface slowly through the dignified image he deemed suitable for an England captain.

Whether his future lay with the eager Americans or with the suspicious brethren of English managers, he was ready to come among them a richer, rounder, more open personality with all the more to offer for his latter, sobering experiences. Not that any of those expanding qualities had weakened his basic stiffness of resolve nor dulled that hard edge of competitive spirit.

Ron Greenwood had observed when it all began that Bobby Moore was a very ambitious young man. He still was.

Unfortunately the game he loved, the game to which he had devoted the prime years of his manhood, the English game to which he had given its finest hour, was not sufficiently grateful to cooperate.

23

Going West

America the beautiful was beckoning, so at first it seemed more a pleasure than a necessity to keep playing on.

All right, he was thirty-five.

But by virtue of his self-imposed regime of staying in training every close season that imposing physique had been subjected to none of the ravages of forced recovery which confronts and corrodes so many footballers upon their return from holiday, however brief. Spending time at the beach with Mooro involved declining his well-meant daily invitation to 'put on a rubber wet suit and let's go running through sand and lose a stone before lunch'.

Yes, the offers to take over every team from Arsenal to Workington did seem slow in coming. But with a reputation like his to take care of him everyone was certain it was not even a matter of time but a question of when he wanted.

'I'm told they'll be snatching my hand off in due course,' he said. Then, with his usual delayed drop when exercising his humour rather than his torso, he added: 'And they still won't find a bracelet.'

Okay, U.S.A. here we come.

Playing in the North American Soccer League, burgeoning as it was in the summer of '76, promised to be no more demanding for this particularly dedicated athlete than his customary vacation work-out programme. The U.S. clubs – with their jazzy names, exotic cheerleaders and snazzy outfits – were busy recruiting the cream of the immediate past generation of international players and Moore, especially since he was still an active professional in the English league, could take his pick from the numerous clubs bidding to compete with New York's signing of Pele.

With a little help from his family he chose San Antonio Thunder. The exotic Tex-Mex atmosphere, the shimmer of a high-rise city in the sunny south, the river meandering through its centre as the picturesque meeting place for the bar and cafe society, the dry heat generating a healthy outdoor life for Roberta and Dean and the warmth of the people all contributed to the appeal. So did San Antonio's Texan location, only a few hour's drive from the colourful Mexican border but well off the beaten track for British tourists. The Moore family, an English rarity in that neck of the prairie, were treated like royalty.

Bobby was able to play 24 games without undue exertion and actually scored a goal for the Thunder that long, hot and pleasantly diverting summer. He also found himself playing not only for a foreign club but for another country. As if to complete a most ironic equation, his last international match transpired to be not for his beloved England but against them.

Team America was created from a melting pot of overseas stars mixed with a handful of U.S. citizens who had acquired a passable grasp of how the rest of the world's game was played. Their purpose was to give the Americans someone to cheer in their Bicentennial Soccer Tournament, even though no one gave this amalgamation of knowing veterans and willing novices much chance against the other components of the four-nation event, Brazil, Italy and England.

Nevertheless, Pele was in the line up. With his old friend Bobby – who else? – as captain they gave a reasonable account of themselves. They recovered from an inaugural 4–0 roasting by Italy to restrict Brazil, the eventual winners of the tournament, to half that score. Then, fittingly for Moore, the last match was against England.

It was a humid 75 degrees in Philadelphia on the evening of May 31, 1976, but even as some of the older legs gave out Bobby marshalled his slender forces with sufficient resource to again restrict the margin to two goals, this time 3–1 with Kevin Keegan scoring twice for England.

That evening the past and present captains of England agreed
that Soccer had a future in America, although it would be almost
20 years until the allocation of the 1994 World Cup Finals to the
United States acknowledged that the grass roots of the game
were flourishing there despite the intervening collapse of the
N.A.S.L.

Bobby saw a future there for himself. At his own request he
had added coaching duties to his playing commitment to San
Antonio and as the Thunder considered moving its franchise to
Hawaii – 'with all due respects a little more appealing than a
transfer from Wolverhampton to Middlesbrough' – they offered
him the managership.

Fulham, however, still held his permanent contract and they
wanted him back for one last hurrah of their own. The Moores
returned to England in August with Bobby prepared to put a
typically neat end to his playing career.

The long, cold winter of the Second Division was more rigorous
than the Indian summer in San Antonio but even in his thirty-
sixth year his professionalism shone through. As Fulham
manager Alec Stock put it: 'Bobby Moore was royalty ... but he
was always first in for training.'

On Saturday May 7, 1977, he staged his farewell performance
in London. As if to record that No. 6 of his for posterity, Fulham
scored precisely that number of goals against Leyton Orient,
conceding only one in reply. Then, with a turn and a wave to
acknowledge his standing ovation, he was down the tunnel and
into the bar above The Cottage.

That was his 999th game in senior football and such a tidy mind
could never have rested had he left it there. So he volunteered to
play at Blackburn Rovers the following Saturday in Fulham's last
match of the season. It was an occasion which took its place in
history not for the home team's 1–0 win but as Bobby Moore's
1,000th first class appearance.

Geoffrey Green, the late doyen of football writers, summed up
his genius in *The Times*: 'By his masterly reading of the game,
his uncanny anticipation, his temperament, his coolness under
pressure and his ability to turn defence into counter-attack by the
accuracy of the long pass, Bobby Moore dominated all.'

However, as one door closed the others, at least those of any significance, remained surprisingly reluctant to open. There were tentative overtures from America and Arabia but he had his heart set on a football job in England. Three months elapsed without a hint of a realistic offer to make the short walk from the dressing room to the manager's office. He said: 'This is a frustrating period in my life. I'm open to offers as a manager or a coach. That's what I want to do and that's where I feel I have something to offer. But I can't sit and wait forever. I must start earning again.'

To that end he turned what was by then a somewhat wary eye to the outside world of commerce. He had been a principal loser in a system of cross guarantees between friends he had trusted, not all of them wisely, for the ill-fated country club venture in Chigwell. The leather goods business had gone under. And as well as an army of admirers he seemed to have attracted a personal arsonist. The fire at the country club had been followed by an equally inexplicable blaze at the Old Black Bull public house in Stratford Broadway the night before it was due to re-open under Bobby's direction as Mooro's.

Undeterred, a loyal friend, businessman Jimmy Quill, offered him further partnerships in pubs in East London and Essex. Those, as well as his earning power for personal appearances and some sporadic involvement in football, restored the cash flow, as did the backing of Corals, the bookmakers, for The Bobby Moore Soccer Schools. If the senior clubs did not want him to educate their footballers, he might as well start passing on some of his immense knowledge to the kids.

The most amusing diversion came when he starred alongside Michael Caine and his fellow actors as well as Pele and his fellow footballers in the feature film *Escape to Victory*. The plot was a rather implausible one about World War II prisoners using a football match against their German captors as cover for a break to freedom. The unusual amalgam of sporting and screen celebrities, however, guaranteed a profit at the box office. And the chaps had fun in the making of it.

The movie was shot on location in Hungary and Bobby enjoyed several weeks discovering the many delights of Budapest – the historic steam baths beneath the classical Gellert Hotel, the gypsy restaurants, the old quarter of the city, the island spars in mid-river – in friendly company.

They were feted wherever they went in a country equally steeped in football tradition and eager for contact with glamorous western Europeans. Bobby said: 'In some ways it was like being on tour with England, except that we could go out on the town, see the sights and get to know more of the place than just the hotel and the stadium.'

Later, as he became increasingly frustrated by intermittent and unfulfilling employment in the lower reaches of the game, he joined our ranks of journalists. As a man who had scuffled with the *Sun*, he had to smile at himself in 1986 when he took up a three-year position with the *Sunday Sport*, the more inventive, most lurid and, certainly as far as pictures of young ladies is concerned, the most transparent of all the tabloid prints.

It was some other newspapers which erred when he was rushed to University College Hospital on October 9 of that year. They reported that Moore had suffered a heart attack while at his editor's desk. In fact, he had contracted a temporary medical condition which induced hyperventilation while he was visiting his daughter Roberta at the West London offices where she worked. He was discharged after examination and the alarm had no connection with the far more serious illness which was to assail him five years later.

John Mitchell, once a promising full-back whom Bobby had helped and guided at Fulham, sought to repay those favours. A young man acquiring as good an eye for entrepreneurial opportunities as he once had for openings on the pitch, Mitchell set up a sports marketing and promotion company called Challenge.

The name alone would have been irresistible to Moore even had he not known his prospective partner so well. At first business expanded rapidly, into a group, but then Challenge went the way of so many others as the boom of the Eighties subsided into the recession of the Nineties ... into liquidation.

The pair salvaged one potentially viable arm of the group and Mitchell–Moore Associates was still trading at the time of Bobby's death. Meanwhile, Bobby had exchanged the word processor for the microphone, leaving the *Sunday Sport* to join Capital Radio in 1990.

His work as a commentator gave him such involvement with football and so much satisfaction that he insisted on continuing as long as possible. All the way, as his idol Frank Sinatra sang, to Wembley just one week before he died.

All manner of theories were expounded for what was perceived as Moore's failure in commerce. But in truth he was neither a fool in business nor a naive judge of character. On occasion he may have been let down, but for the most part the people with whom he entered a partnership were victims either of circumstance or misfortune.

If he had faults as a businessman they were an excess of honesty and generosity. He considered it right and proper to invest in most ventures he joined, thereby risking and losing some of his own capital. He frequently declined to accept his due fees if he found he was putting himself out for a good friend or a needy cause.

Honesty and generosity, however, were not virtues he would have abandoned for profit and they were repaid by a good life. Even so, one mystery remained to the very end: why did the game he loved so deeply and understood so profoundly turn its back on the great Bobby Moore?

24

Our Forgotten Genius

Reg Dwight always loved his football. He grew up watching Watford in the nether regions of the Football League and shared the dream of all those standing on the terraces at Vicarage Road – that one day their homely club would be up there with Arsenal and Liverpool, Tottenham and Manchester United.

That is the illogical belief which sustains the huge supporting cast of English football, the repertory clubs out there in the shadow of the theatrical dramas played out on the big city stages, through winter upon winter of defeat and discontent. But little Reg dreamed on and the longer he did so the more his fantasy embraced the notion that it would be he who would make it come true.

When his personal ambitions took him to London, to Tin Pan Alley as a messenger boy, he was thrilled to find himself in an office next to one frequently occupied by Terry Venables. Then a celebrated Chelsea and England footballer, Venables was co-writing books as one of the first of many ventures ancilliary to his playing of the game, a kaleidoscope of activities which proved to be a preparation for his take-over of Tottenham Hotspur.

Reg always volunteered to fetch the tea and biscuits whenever Tel was in the office, especially if he was being visited by friends and fellow internationals such as George Graham and John Hollins. Then he could hang around and listen to all the football chatter and imagine the day when he, too, would be a star.

Little did they know.

*

It was too early in the morning after one of those long nights with Bobby Moore when everyone else had gone to bed and too many bottles full of memories had been uncorked.

The ringing of the telephone was like a knife through the brain.

'Good morning. Not too early am I?'

'What time is it?'

'Quarter to seven.'

'Who is it?'

'Elton ... Elton John.'

'How many Eltons are there?'

'Don't know. But there's only one Bobby Moore.'

'Don't tell me. Not after last night. What about him?'

'Does he really want to be a manager?'

"Course he does.'

'Then I'd love him at Watford. Can you fix a meeting?'

'Why not?'

'Quick as possible. Please.'

'Day after tomorrow?'

'Yes, yes. You sure that'll be alright for Bobby?'

'I'll get him there.'

It was hangover Monday but lunchtime Wednesday could not come soon enough for the tea-boy who had climbed the rock and roll ladder to a pinnacle of fame loftier than that scaled by the footballers he idolised.

Elton John, née Reg Dwight, had bought control of the club which was his first love. His appetite for the game, ravenous already, had been whetted further by a friendship with England manager Don Revie which had brought invitations to travel with the national team.

On several of those trips he went to the hotel piano and sang for the players, not unlike the old stars of wartime entertaining the troops. Sometimes he lingered at the bar. He and I got on well and on occasion we ended up chatting about Bobby Moore and what might be next for the figurehead of English football.

Then Watford needed a manager.

It was the second week of May in the sunny springtime of 1977, the midweek between the home-and-away appearances for Fulham which commemorated Moore's farewell from the English game. We lunched in the discreet elegance of the restaurant at the Howard Hotel, a marbled retreat from Fleet Street on the Thames embankment. It was part of my function to effect introductions and deal with the bill. The lengthy period in between was full of good conversation, fine food and positive intentions.

They liked each other instantly and both recognised the immense market potential of a working partnership between them, an arrangement which would transform Watford's image. Elton said he was convinced that his money and Moore's know-how would lift them into the First Division and establish them there, towards the forefront of the game. Bobby was more than willing to try, for an initial three-year contract worth a minimum £15,000 a year. This would be above average in the Seventies but not extortionate and they shook hands on the deal, each as enthusiastically committed as the other.

As Elton left, Moore said: 'It really is exciting. I've been thinking about a big club in the First Division but this is a challenge and with a man like this so involved there's a tremendous chance of achieving something worthwhile.'

It seemed like a *fait accompli*. Elton had invited Bobby to lunch the following Monday, with their financial advisors, to finalise and sign the contract. Since each had expressed a liking for Oriental food he went so far as to nominate the restaurant as well as the time. One o'clock at Ken Lo's temple of exotic cuisine in the West End, Memories of China.

They never met again.

Another of Elton's dawn phone calls came that Monday morning. Would Bobby object to postponing the lunch for a day or two while he went through the polite formality of informing his fellow directors? Since courtesy came as second nature to Mr. Moore, of course not.

Then nothing.

Nothing until, a few weeks later, Mr John announced the appointment of Watford's new manager. Whether under duress from those directors to make a more orthodox appointment, as he intimated, or by his own instinct, which did seem more likely since it was his money, the Rocket Man had found his own Pinball Wizard.

Graham Taylor, the frenzy of whose long-ball game had worked minor wonders for Lincoln City in the lower tributaries of the game, became the man who would light the blue touchpaper under the potential with which Elton was investing Watford.

Whether he had been a victim of downright discourtesy or simply a message which never got through, Moore retained his dignity. He put newspapermen off the scent of controversy by saying: 'Elton John did make some promises to me but if he believes he has found a better manager for Watford then I can do no more than wish them the best of luck.'

Neither was there to be much arguing later.

Taylor created a buoyant family atmosphere at Vicarage Road and capitalised upon it to help fuel Watford's rise to the First Division, into Europe for the only time in their history as the 1983 League Championship runners up and on to the 1984 F.A. Cup Final, albeit as 2–0 losers to Everton.

Thus Taylor gave Elton and Watford their taste of glory while laying the foundations for his own departure for Aston Villa and subsequent elevation to the managership of England. But there was one shadow over his success. The physical, cavalry charge football based on percentages and statistics rather than skill and intelligence which Taylor helped pioneer became the subject of increasingly critical attention from those who believed there had to be more to football than results at all costs.

Moore was a subscriber to the ideal which Pele described as 'the beautiful game'. As the Wimbledons and Sheffields followed Watford's simplistic example, he felt compelled to voice concern.

Taylor, like many a devotee of dogma, could not understand the objections. He concluded that criticism from purists like Moore were rooted in personal resentment or private antagonism. He cited the way Elton John had appointed him instead of Bobby. He could not have been more wrong.

Bobby said: 'Graham did a magnificent job at Watford. Maybe I could have achieved something similar with Elton but there's no saying so for sure. The style he chose to employ there was his affair and it was not so extreme as some of those who copied Watford. The problem was that the more successful those methods became the greater the danger of every club following suit and taking the skill and the pleasure out of the game.

'It is a professional view, not a personal one, to say that what-

ever might have happened had I gone to Watford the team would
not have played in that style.'

Taylor, later with England, began to compromise. He sought
to marry the philosophy of what became known as 'direct football' with the more refined demands of the international game. It
was not an easy alliance but it did acknowledge a shift in public
opinion against the guileless repetition of the indiscriminate long
ball. In that, for certain, he differed from Moore. Behind his
unemotional facade Bobby was a passionate idealist. He would
never have compromised his beliefs. In fact, never did. Even
though he sensed that may have counted against him in the
pragmatic minds of many a football club chairman. Even though
frustration required him to accept employment beneath his
stature.

The rest of the world still loved him. Always would.

In the autumn of 1977, at Pele's personal behest, he flew from
the humdrum disappointment of Watford to the glamour of New
York. There he was a guest of honour at his great rival's farewell
match for the Cosmos. At his retirement dinner in Manhattan
that evening, Pele referred warmly to 'the English gentleman
who is my friend'. The spontaneous applause rendered it
unnecessary for him to mention Moore's name.

The following summer he flew back across the Atlantic to play
seven matches for the Seattle Sounders, an American experience
he was still fit enough to repeat at the age of forty-two as a favour
to a friend at Carolina Lightning.

In the spring of '78 he banked £24,000 for taking the shorter
flight to Jutland at weekends only, to guide the Danish Third
Division side Herning through ten matches. As the novelty wore
off and the crowds around their roped-off pitch dwindled to the
regular few hundred for Scandinavian football at that lowly level,
Moore released the club from the financial embarrassment of
their contract.

If it had to be small beer, it might as well be of English brew.

On December 12, 1979, at the approach of a third Christmas
out of employment although not bereft of funds, he agreed to
join Oxford City in the Berger Isthmian League. If this was the
equivalent of Pavarotti singing at the Hackney Empire or Faldo
playing clock on Blackpool sea front, then so be it.

At least the money was good. Oxford chairman Tony Posser, the owner of a chain of local newspapers, announced his coup by saying: 'If Mr. Moore is half as good a manager as he is a negotiator he will do extremely well.' Bobby did his best. But even at that it could never be more than a non-League holding operation. Within 12 months they terminated their three-year contract by mutual consent.

Five months of 1983 spent in Hong Kong coaching Eastern Athletic did little for his curriculum vitae. Still, when he came home in August, there was one offer on the table in Essex. If not exactly paradise regained, after six years of waiting, of silence, of closed doors, it was too good an offer to refuse.

'Why Southend United?' asked the world.

'I want a job in football,' answered Bobby.

And, Third Division or not, The Shrimpers were members of the Football League.

Moore was mildly flattered when Southend gave him the role of chief executive as well as manager but it turned out to be a poisoned chalice when a local entrepreneur found his financial problems linked to those of the club. Southend were threatened with bankruptcy as well as relegation to the Fourth Division.

The parallel problems were confronted by Bobby with his usual humour. As we watched one game together he remarked: 'I've got a centre-half who must be scared stiff of heights because he won't go up to head the ball. And we've got so many bailiffs knocking at the door that every night I go round collecting all the televisions, lock them in my office and keep the keys in my pocket.'

It couldn't last. In May 1986 he handed back the keys. And that, incredibly, was his last direct involvement with the game.

'I've no idea why no big club has offered me a job,' he said. 'You'll have to ask them.' None of those questioned could provide a satisfactory answer. There were vague mutterings about his apparent aloofness making it difficult for him to communicate with lesser players. Yet as a teenager at West Ham he had been among the youngest to qualify for the Football Association's full coaching badge. And after asking him to polish the education of his youth team players at Crystal Palace for a time, Terry Venables said: 'Bobby was brilliant. He received a tremendous response from those lads and all of them were improved by the experience.'

One West Ham director, a member of the old board which gave way subsequently to more enlightened men keen to honour the finest player in their history with a memorial, saw fit to 'most vehemently deny' a speculative report that they had approached Moore to return to the club.

They should have been so lucky.

It seemed the English game had decided that its greatest player would not make even a reasonable coach. It was absurd. Moore had never been a natural player. His game was built on intelligence and application. He was one of the finest match readers who ever lived. He was a profound judge of a player. He knew more about defending than most men know about their wives. If ever there was a footballer with the makings of a manager, it was this one.

What he needed was to manage where he had played, at the zenith of the game. But while his friend and exact German contemporary Franz Beckenbauer was given just that opportunity and so became the first footballer to win the World Cup as player, captain and manager, the Football Association remained as resolute in its rejection of England's living legend as his old club.

In August 1977 Moore wrote the only job application of his life. It was for the England managership after Don Revie had defected to the desert. Six good men and true were interviewed, Brian Clough among them. If the F.A. sent a reply to the hero of '66, it never arrived. Now, for the F.A. and for English football at large, it is too late. That treasure trove of knowledge has been allowed to go to waste.

The England job went to Ron Greenwood and Moore approved. The philosophical differences between the two men had come to a sharp head of disagreement years earlier but their mutual respect was undiminished. After Greenwood's England were knocked out of the 1982 World Cup Finals in Spain, on goal difference but without losing, Bobby said: 'Ron was unlucky that two of his outstanding players (Kevin Keegan and Trevor Brooking) were unfit. He was made for international football and he always wanted to test his knowledge of the game against the best. I was delighted for him that his chance came to be involved in the World Cup.'

The next time they met, at an awards ceremony at London's Waldorf Hotel early in 1986, they fell into animated, affectionate conversation. Ultimately, Greenwood's idealism prevailed over Ramsey's practicality in Moore's matured vision of football.

Not very long before his illness took hold we paid one of our occasional visits to my club, the R.A.C. in Pall Mall. There he liked to relax in the Turkish bath and reflect on life after football. That day he was in the mood to evaluate what had happened to his game: 'I watch the matches now and I see so much aggression and violence. Teams and players have always wanted to win but they have known how to lose. In England now there is a desperation which is threatening to destroy the game's spirit.

'The faces of the players are contorted with rage. They snarl and scowl at each other. There is no pleasure. Even when they celebrate they look angry. Where is the joy of playing? They have forgotten how to smile. There are exceptions. Some of the major clubs keep trying to play good football and they have their disciples down the divisions. But for so many managers the emphasis is on effort and intimidation. We need to put the skill back in football and take out some of the fight.'

As the clouds of steam swirled about us we engaged in football's eternal debate. Name your all-time world XI. Only one England player of the modern era came into consideration. Not Gazza but Gary. 'Lineker is a role model for the game,' said Bobby. 'And he's a tremendous goalscorer. But not quite, I'm afraid, in the same class as Pele.'

With apologies to Charlton and Finney, Greaves and Wilson, only two Englishmen made his dream team, Gordon Banks – 'the best goalkeeper ever' – and himself. With a little prompting he accepted the captaincy alongside Beckenbauer at the heart of defence.

The King and the Kaizer would have been flanked by Carlos Alberto's Brazilian flair for turning defence into attack and Giacinto Facchetti's classical Italian defending. 'As the tallest man in the team,' he said, 'Facchetti would also have given us protection in the air at corners and free kicks.'

A la Greenwood rather than Ramsey, Bobby picked a four-man midfield overflowing with genius but without a recognised, ball-winning enforcer in the mode of Nobby Stiles. With Real Madrid's legendary Argentinian Alfredo di Stefano, Dutch total footballer Johan Cruyff, Argentine *enfant terrible* Diego Maradona and his old Irish sparring partner George Best, he reasoned: 'The opposition would only have the ball when they were picking it out of their net.'

And, just in case, he reminded me of how the late Bill Shankly had offered this description of Best as a corollary to the usual rhapsodising about his ball-playing brilliance: 'That little rascal is the deepest tackler in the game.'

Garrincha, the Brazilian winger with the mesmerising runs and unstoppable free kicks, would have been the partner in attack for the greatest of them all, in this 4–4–2 formation:

Banks
(England)

Carlos Alberto	Beckenbauer	Moore (cap.)	Facchetti
(Brazil)	(Germany)	(England)	(Italy)
Best	Cruyff	di Stefano	Maradona
(N. Ireland)	(Holland)	(Argentina)	(Argentina)
	Pele	Garrincha	
	(Brazil)	(Brazil)	

It is a selection to remind the Football Association gentlemen at Lancaster Gate that football is about footballers, not pen-pushers, badge-wearers and mathematicians. And it would have been a team made in heaven.

25

Love and Marriage

According to romantic legend, swooning imagination and dreamy misconception, Robert Frederick Chelsea Moore – Mooro to his friends and admirers around the world – and Susan Lesley Parlane-Moore – Stephanie to her family and colleagues with whom she travelled the world – fell in love at first flight.

He was bound for Johannesburg in June 1979 as a member of Bobby Charlton's All-Star team on a goodwill tour of South Africa. She was aboard an aircraft in her normal line of duty as an airline stewardess.

If it had all the makings of a Mills and Boon encounter with Hollywood potential then they were not aware. Not even blissfully. Although they were heading in the same direction, they were not even on the same plane.

Stephanie was tending to the needs of the first class passengers on one aircraft while Bobby was travelling, as he put it, 'in the back of the bus' aboard another. So, not so much as a glance was exchanged during the journey and they might never have met but for a little idle chatter between Stephanie's crew and another footballer travelling to join Bobby's tourists.

Bob Wilson, the Arsenal goalkeeper turned B.B.C. television football personality, was seated in business class. He whiled away part of the journey by talking with the cabin attendants. By the time they landed he had invited them all to watch the next day's exhibition match and attend the party which was to follow in the evening.

The forces of chance and destiny drawing Bobby and Stephanie together were doing so in such unlikely circumstances that the sensation of how easily she might have missed the introduction which changed her life remains vividly with Stephanie to this day. 'I had no real interest in football,' she says. 'I went along to the game only because all my colleagues were going and I didn't want to break up the group. To be honest none of the players were recognisable to me. Then I had no intention of going to the party. It had been a long trip and for me an even longer day at the stadium. I went to the coffee shop with one of the stewards, but before I could finish my snack and go to bed Bob Wilson happened to walk past again and asked why we hadn't joined everyone for a drink.'

So she went. So they fell into animated conversation, which for Bobby represented a rare departure from his customary, studied reserve in unfamiliar company.

So began one of the great love stories of our time.

It is a story of heartache and compassion, devotion and passion, difficulties conquered with dignity and happiness fulfilled to overflowing. A story in which the human spirit triumphed over the onset of mankind's most ravenous disease and prevailed, in its way at the end, even over death itself. It is a story to lift the heart and offer hope to others whose lives and loved ones are afflicted by cancer. And it is a story which would never have been told had Stephanie not set aside her deep-felt reluctance to surrender their privacy.

She has done so for the best of reasons: to encourage fellow sufferers to confront the disease by living every moment to the precious limit; to set the record straight; to pay her own tribute to the man whose memory she cherishes as 'the most beautiful human being who ever lived'.

That was the impression Bobby gave her at the beginning and it remained true until that grey dawn almost 14 years later when he squeezed her hand for the last time.

'I didn't realise who Bobby was when we were introduced,' she says. 'But I recognised at once a man whose courtesy was not a front and whose manners were not affectation. Here was a gentleman. A handsome one, that's true. But more importantly he was a gentle man, too.'

Whether they knew it or not, by the time they finished a first conversation sparkling with human electricity they were committed irrevocably to a path which neither had been seeking. As they parted for the first time Bobby made the first of what would become many commitments.

'When are you going home?' he asked.

'On the flight from Nairobi the day after tomorrow.'

'Well, we're off to Cape Town. But I'll be on that plane.'

And so he was. From Kenya. Which, considering he had only just arrived in South Africa at the start of a three-week visit, was a remarkable act of faith.

'He came walking into first class,' says Stephanie. 'I was overjoyed to see him. I don't think I realised how much he was putting himself out. I didn't know anything about football tours so I assumed he was going home. In fact he had invented some pretext to fly on to Norway ... and straight back to South Africa.'

They agreed to see each other when he returned from Charlton's missionary expedition, during the passage of which he actually got sent off for arguing in a goodwill game against a multi-racial XI – 'my mind must have been elsewhere' – and survived a crash landing with Bobby and Jack Charlton in a light aircraft – 'we were lucky'.

On his return to England, Bobby nurtured the tender shoots of their romance. He was a married man living what appeared to outside intents and purposes to be the ideal family life. Loyalty ranked high among his principles and he was not unfaithful by nature. Not until much later, to very few friends and never to Stephanie, did he reveal that some rifts were widening already in his relationship with Tina.

Stephanie says: 'For some months we kept our relationship purely platonic. Bobby asked me to lunch. We went for long walks in Richmond Park with my dogs. We talked about a life and a world outside football and beyond the social whirl. It was tranquil. We saw each other as often as possible but he was as protective of our situation then as he remained throughout our time together.

'We did go to dinner occasionally but he always went home to Chigwell. I wouldn't say that was easy but it was important to both of us. Although he never mentioned his wife I suspected that he was wrestling with his conscience. It took him a long time to come to terms with whatever sense of guilt he may have been feeling.'

The process – for he confided that he most certainly did feel guilty, especially about Roberta and Dean – was helped by the realisation of hidden depths in his character and an awakening of wider interests, both of which had been long suppressed by the all-consuming demands of football. Still it was a protracted evolution, not free from pain.

Bobby was never a womaniser. He said: 'Even when the girls were chasing young footballers my game was a few lagers with the lads at the bar. What the others got up to was up to them but it wasn't for me.' His fidelity stemmed in part from his unswerving loyalty to his few, carefully chosen close friends. Both his wives, Tina in her time and then Stephanie still more so, were cited by him as his best friends.

So a true and vibrant passion, which was to excite and illuminate their partnership to the end, was kept waiting to be released. Even after it was, Bobby needed three years to disentangle himself from the protocol and propriety of the family life to which he had been brought up by his mother.

Doris, it transpired later, proved highly if unexpectedly supportive of Bobby's right to pursue his happiness, helped him overcome the trauma with his children and encouraged him to marry Stephanie while she herself was still alive to see it happen.

But for the moment, the rights or wrongs of his situation and the worsening temper of his marriage notwithstanding, he always went home. Every night.

'It would be pointless to deny,' says Stephanie now, 'that we wanted to be together as much as we possibly could. We couldn't help ourselves. We met whenever Bobby could get away and whenever I could hurry from work.'

When Bobby took up a six-month coaching appointment in 1983 with Eastern Athletic in Hong Kong she was able to join him for holidays in that bustling, exotic colony. But the moment of decision was approaching. In all sanity it could be delayed no longer. And when it came it was not what either of them wanted.

Stephanie remembers: 'We agreed to separate. Never to see

each other again. It was awful. It lasted four months. It was the worst time of my life.

'I began having a dream which kept recurring until much later, until we were happily and completely settled down together. In it we were standing on a beach as a huge tidal wave was approaching. I was stretching out for Bobby's hand but could never quite reach him and I knew we were going to be swept away and apart forever. It was the worst possible feeling.

'The days were a nightmare, too. But then Bobby called and we started seeing each other again. Once we did we both knew there was no turning back. We never doubted each other for a moment. We felt committed but still there was no outright suggestion of our living together.

'He would telephone and I would leap at the chance of seeing him. Just as he did one afternoon and asked if I would like to go for a drive. I got into the car and he said that instead of simply going for a drive we were going to visit a couple of his pubs where he was helping with charity collections.

'It was quite late when we arrived back at my cottage in Surrey and I didn't expect him to come in. I asked him how long it would take him to get back to Chigwell at that time of night.

'He said he wasn't going back. He'd left home two days ago. He'd been staying with his old team mate Brian Dear at his pub in Southend. That was to deflect any accusations from me. His unselfishness was one reason I loved him. And now he was staying. For good.'

For good turned out to be a fortnight, at least to start with. It was 1984 and the newspapers had come knocking at the door of Stephanie's cottage to reveal their secret. Bobby was engaged in a scuffle on the doorstep with a representative of the *Sun*.

The publicity, the loss of her husband becoming public knowledge, was more than Tina could bear. Roberta telephoned her father to report that her mother was not coping with their separation. More guilt. Another genuine attempt at self sacrifice.

Heavy of heart, Bobby took the long drive from Surrey to Essex once more. Then, in the middle of the night while staying in

Calcutta, the phone by her hotel bedside roused Stephanie from her sleep. It was Bobby, asking how to work the central heating at her home.

She knew then that he had made up his mind.

The repercussions were immediate.

Bobby's reconfirmed separation became common knowledge. He had been married for 21 years and the world was curious. He offered no more than one sentence of public explanation: 'The responsibilities for this situation are entirely mine.'

It was the same after the undefended divorce hearing on January 6, 1986: 'The only person to blame is myself.'

Stephanie herself never once gleaned a scrap of information about the cracks behind the eventual facade of his first marriage.

'Bobby never talked to me about Tina,' she says. 'Not once. Not from the day we met until the day he died.'

To those who knew him well, that will not be so surprising. By such means, while Tina was moving on to Florida without so far remarrying, Bobby's infinite capacity for protecting those for whom he cared was carried to the grave. It was his generosity of spirit – a self-sacrificing quality of which Tina had sometimes despaired when the flow of the good life was interrupted by financial constraint – which Stephanie found most appealing.

It reminded her of her father, Peter Moore: 'Bobby is the only man I've ever met who is like him in his unselfishness.'

Mr. Moore senior, a namesake and eventual father-in-law to whom Bobby grew close, offered no complaint when Stephanie's mother Vera suggested their children should keep her maiden name of Parlane, nor when she changed her mind about their Christian names within hours of their baptisms.

Thus Kevin Parlane-Moore became Nicholas and Susan turned into Stephanie, along with an early change of nappies.

It mattered not. The name of real importance was the one which came last. By a coincidence which the couple regarded as too extraordinary to be anything less than a sign or omen, Stephanie had no need to change hers for convenience when she began living with Bobby.

They were the second Mr. and Mrs. Moore not only in spirit but by divine providence, if not yet in wedlock.

It mattered, neither, that Bobby surrendered all things material – the Chigwell home, its entire contents, the accumulated capital – in a divorce settlement intended to secure Tina's future and enable her to make provision for Roberta and Dean.

Stephanie says: 'He had left Tina for me. I cannot deny that. And it wasn't easy for him. But we were totally committed to each other, whatever. I had not proved that commitment the way he had, leaving a family and starting again from scratch. He came to me with not much more than the clothes he stood up in. But I knew what it had taken for him to do that and I committed myself and my home and my income and together we built a wonderful life.

'There were no real problems before the illness, then Bobby dealt with that magnificently. The difficulties with some business were outweighed by his capacity to earn his living in other areas. The reality was that throughout our time together we lived well. Far more comfortably than most people.

'Perhaps it wasn't easy at the start but we loved the cottage and when he became manager at Southend we moved to a lovely house. There were problems at the football club but our private life was idyllic.'

Bobby's life style, in fact, changed overnight. The superficial social rounds which had reached their glittering zenith in the company of prime ministers and princes in the Sixties, and which had been sustained to great extent by his celebrity, gave way to a life of intimate simplicity.

Stephanie says: 'When we first moved to Leigh-on-Sea Bobby said we would not be going out so often. He wanted to lead a quieter life with me. I would get home later than him and we would walk the dogs along the cockle beds at Southend. He would set a fire in the lounge and we would take turns to cook for each other. It was beautiful. It couldn't last because Southend United's situation was so fraught but we confirmed our relationship and our commitment there.

'When the time came to move back to London we found a delightful flat overlooking the Thames at Battersea. We entertained more. We had only to stroll across the bridge to be at the cinemas in King's Road or at a pleasant little restaurant in Chelsea to meet friends.

'I had been playing squash for a long time and Bobby had toyed with the game down the years. So we began playing together three times a week and the habit I had acquired for sporting exercise was to prove invaluable later when Bobby became ill. Because I wanted to work out with him.'

Against a perceived background of financial difficulties which they felt distinctly unobliged to rebutt, they moved to Putney Heath with its security gates and every comfort and they travelled to all the strange, distant and romantic places which had not been on Bobby's football itinerary.

'Until then,' he said, 'my life had been the game, a few drinks with the chaps, Marbella and a bit of America. You don't see much of anywhere when you travel to play big football matches.'

Bobby and Stephanie visited museums and art galleries in many European capitals and Bobby went on to share Stephanie's love of the Far East.

'Our most rewarding holidays,' she relates with much pleasure, 'were in India amid all those dazzling colours and exotic bustle and strange excitement. So were many of the happiest memories. We once drove across southern India from Madras to Cochin. It was so dry and dusty and the heat was tremendous but it was wonderful. Bobby had become accustomed to nothing but the five-star best but on this trip he insisted on only two things every night. A shower and a gin and tonic.

'One of the trips he loved most was to The Maldives where we spent hours snorkling off the reef among the most amazing sea-life in the world.

'We visited the palaces and museums of the sub-continent and when we reached the Amber Fort at Jaipur he said enough was enough. He sat down and fell asleep, propped against the wall by the front door. When I came out a child with huge eyes was standing at his feet with a scrap of an autograph book and a pencil waiting for him to wake up. Bobby was deeply touched that the boy was too respectful to disturb him.'

Once, when they were seeking a more restful vacation on the beach at Goa, the hotel manager asked Bobby if he would be gracious enough to be guest of honour at a local Cup Final. The irritation at two hours' drive in an overheated ramshackle car – 'but we do have air-conditioning madam, the windows never close' – was dissipated at once by the reverence with which the Moores were greeted by 800 people gathered with their goat herds by an open field.

'What we thought at first was an imposition on our time,' says Stephanie, 'became the absolute highlight of our holiday.'

There were so many blissful journeys together, to favoured parts of Italy, to Australia, Tahiti, Zimbabwe, the Grenadines and previously undiscovered parts of America. As a professional footballer, required not to risk injury unneccesarily, he had been to a ski resort only once before. Now they were able to enjoy the snowy delights of Colorado and the Alps. To the astonishment of some of his old pals from West Ham he was able to pursue his love of ballet – from Harlem to the Bolshoi – and he rhapsodised ever-after about the night he heard Placido Domingo sing *Il Travotore* at the Royal Opera House.

Once at dinner, while our wives were chattering about the merits of a performance of *Cinderella* at Covent Garden, he leaned across the corner of the table and confided: 'This girl has changed my life. She's made it richer and fuller. She's opened up a new world for me. Do you know how much I love her?'

The expression of emotion was surprising, not characteristic of a man accustomed to presenting an implacable image. But, yes, we knew. There's no hiding real happiness. It shows in the eyes. He adored her. And sometime you have to tell someone.

The way they lived, greedy for each other often to the exclusion of everyone else, it was as if they sensed their time might be limited.

'Looking back now,' she says, 'we packed so much into our short time that its amazing to think we were both working full time. Thank goodness we did.'

Mexico 1970 had been a pivotal experience in Bobby's life – the bracelet, Pele and all that – and he was determined to take Stephanie back with him to that vividly exciting and varied land. They went to the 1986 World Cup. Shortly after the Final the four of us spent a long, reflective day on the beach at Cancun, standing in the bath-warm waters among a profusion of exotic fish, before Bobby and Stephanie travelled on to marvel at the extraordinary Mayan ruins at Chichen-Itza and Tulum.

Bobby had found not only love but also the woman of intelligence who helped him to explore the wider horizons of his mind and spirit.

They returned to Mexico seven months later to witness our wedding, a compliment Maria and I were destined to return in more restrained but equally uplifting circumstances. The Mexico City affair was crowded and lavish, in accordance with my wife's position as a most eligible girl of high family and expensive breeding. The Moores were an elegant and welcome part of an occasion dignified by heads of state, ambassadors, ministers, the rich and the famous. And from that day on our talk invariably turned to their own prospects for marriage.

To say there was no rush is an understatement.

One day he would tease her about her reluctance, another day she would chide him. It was a gentle charade for the benefit of friends which disguised various obstacles to the formalising of their union.

'To begin with,' says Stephanie, 'Bobby's children needed time to come to terms with the situation. Their father had left their mother because of me and it required care and patience for them to understand why.

'Then, as Bobby re-established his relationship with Dean and Roberta and they began to accept me, my mother began reminding me that she regretted not having a white wedding herself and she wanted one for me. As a lady around the uncertain age of 40, I was not sure that would be entirely appropriate or dignified.

'Then came the idea that we would simply go far away to one of our weird and wonderful places. Do it. Then come back and tell everyone.'

This possibility became a regular topic for after-dinner discussion and they settled one evening, on a Buddhist ceremony at the monastery of Tangboche which was near a base camp on Mount Everest. When Stephanie informed us that it would require a two week trek from Kathmandu to Tangboche, Bobby replied, 'I'll tell you what, darling, I'll meet you all up there – I'll be coming by helicopter.'

Tangboche, it had to be said, was about as far away as they could possibly go. But they had come to Mexico so we promised we would be there. For better or worse, as they say at most religious couplings, the proposal was scuppered when Stephanie's mother suddenly told her daughter: 'Promise me one thing, don't ever take off and get married without telling me.'

They wondered if she was telephathic.

Sickness, on several fronts, finally became the catalyst. Bobby's mother had contracted cancer and wanted to see him marry Stephanie, whose own mother was becoming increasingly poorly.

Then, in the early spring of 1991, came the news Stephanie had been dreading but which Bobby had not countenanced. At her insistence they sought a second opinion on the stomach irritation which he regarded as more of a nuisance than cause for alarm.

Cancer of the colon was diagnosed and during the operation on the colon signs of secondaries in the liver were detected. It was terminal.

The fight, not for a long full life but for extra time, was beginning. So, in its most moving and dramatic dimension, was their great love story.

Major intestinal surgery at the London Clinic was only the start. As he recovered, strongly the way he would, they discussed how to deal with the inevitable.

'We decided to tell no one except the closest of the close family,' says Stephanie. 'It was one of the wisest decisions we ever made, purely because Bobby was deemed public property by some. I wanted Bobby to continue living his rich life as fully as possible.

'Even then, in our hearts and with our private knowledge, there was no justification for the pictures of gloom which everyone seemed so eager to paint. We had a beautiful home, our love and everything to live for.

'It was important that our life should continue as normally as possible. From that moment on Bobby never again made reference to me that he was terminally ill. Again his only concern was not for himself but to protect me. The doctors don't like to give you a timescale. They prefer to leave you with a corner of hope. Not once did Bobby ask "how long". So neither did I. He took up the battle.

'He recuperated miraculously. We spent every minute possible together. I didn't want to be apart from him for a second.

'Bobby would have scorned pity. He wanted to spend his time with his friends certain that they were not weighed down by any knowledge of his condition and therefore reacting unnaturally. He wanted people to go on liking him or not, wanting to spend time with him or not, employing him or not according to their natural instincts. Not because he had cancer.

'Such fierce independence he inherited from his mother. For my part I had to keep smiling. There were times I took the dog off into the woods and shed my tears. But I would tell myself that I had to be strong. I couldn't let him down. So I would return to the house cheerfully.

'He was incredible. He was living proof that it was possible to deal with cancer and cope with chemotherapy and radiotherapy and still lead a normal life. I want people to know that. It is important. He had such indomitable courage and a true love of life. He was so incredibly unselfish. It came as no surprise to me that everyone loved him.

'I was so proud of him. I loved his humour. He always used his jokes and one-liners as a defence mechanism with people but with his family he used it to help us. On the last day he was still making us laugh. Humour was a very important part of our relationship.

'I was always so very much in love with him and I loved him most of all for giving me such complete emotional security. Security is the most important gift from one human being to another. I also had a deep and abiding respect for him, especially the way he treated everyone who came into his life so fairly and decently. He had such dignity and decency and humanity.

'I was so lucky to have him for 12 years. Especially the last two. Does that seem strange? It shouldn't because in a time like that you devote yourselves to each other. It's better than having a loved one struck down by a bomb or a bus. I couldn't have handled final parting that sudden. We had time to tell each other how much we loved each other and in how many ways.

'From the day of his operation we had no arguments. Nothing else seemed remotely important enough to disturb our happiness.

'I want people to know that Bobby's last two years were happy years. Years in which he could golf and swim and do the things he enjoyed. Years full of love and life.'

They were also the years in which they became married. Radiantly.

26

The Good Fight

It was late afternoon when the telephone rang. Bobby was out and for the only time she could remember Stephanie was glad he had been delayed in the heavy traffic at Putney Bridge.

Yes, it was cancer. Yes, it would require an operation. Yes, it was urgent.

She composed herself. By the time he arrived home she was able to delay the inevitable. She said nothing about the call from Dr. Barnardo: 'I wanted him to have a good night's sleep. The morning would be time enough to break the news.'

Of course, he took it well: 'Right, what has to be done?'

April 1991 was a busy month. The 12th marked the celebration of Bobby Moore's 50th birthday and Stephanie, in conspiracy with Roberta and Dean and with help from her best friend and colleague Susie, laid secret and elaborate plans for a party at home.

Somehow, despite organising the catering herself at home, she managed to surprise him. The guest list had been carefully compiled to include all those the family could think of who had played some special part in Bobby's life and had remained in warm contact with him.

He greatly enjoyed his January visits to Jimmy Tarbuck's annual celebrity golf tournament in Spain and the popular comedian who is as funny among friends as on the stage looked in early on his way to a working engagement and made them laugh.

Big Mal and little Ballie stayed late, wallowing with Mooro in champagne and nostalgia. In between the house filled and eddied with old West Ham team mates, fellow heroes of '66, famous faces in equal number with people content to recognise each other as nothing more nor less than mutual friends of Bobby.

He enjoyed the party with all the old gusto, with that hollow-legged capacity for the lager and wine so familiar to his guests. It was a night to remember, even though none of us realised yet how important and precious that memory would become.

Of course he said it, late on when toasting his family and friends, the people he loved best: 'All is well.' Except that all was not well. What had to be done, only 12 days later, was surgery of the major kind.

Upon their return from the London Clinic's operating theatre the surgeon, Peter Hawley, advised Stephanie that the operation was a success but the prospects were not good. All the malignant growths had been removed from the colon but the first traces of cancer were evident in the liver. Bobby's condition was terminal. The consolation was that for however many years he had left he might lead an active life. And it might be years and they would be good if he worked at his rehabilitation and his attitude was right.

If dedication and positive thinking were required, Bobby Moore was their man. Stephanie knew that and drew moral strength from it. A few days later, as Bobby grew physically stronger, the position was explained to him as he requested. In detail. In all its implications. And he dealt with the psychological impact once and for all.

He said: 'I discussed every aspect with Stephanie and we decided to tell no one except Dean and Roberta and the close family and to get on and handle the situation as it had presented itself.'

She said: 'He was extraordinary. Never again, from that day until his last, did he utter one word to me about how long he might have left or even that there was no cure. He was so positive that at one point I began to wonder if he had grasped the full position. But then I realised he had been protecting me from worrying about whatever he might have been feeling. As always, he was the epitome of composure.'

Post-operative recuperation and therapy were entrusted to

Professor John Smythe, head of the Imperial Cancer Research Unit at Edinburgh's Western General Hospital. Bobby could not have been in better hands. The counselling as well as the medical care were of the highest order and Smythe steadfastly refused to give his specialist services by any other means than on the National Health Service.

The Moores were to repay his skills and his kindness by nominating the Imperial Cancer Fund as the charity to benefit from the huge public response to Bobby's death, earmarking a substantial proportion of the donations for Edinburgh.

It was to Edinburgh that they flew each fortnight for him to be monitored and treated. Says Stephanie: 'In one sense it was worrying for us, going up there every two weeks never knowing what they might tell us. But Bobby was always positive and optimistic. It was clear that the unit needed more funds and they were forever trying to improve and modernise the facilities as best they could.

'Bobby was unperturbed because he believed in Professor Smythe. One day when we arrived there was no examination room available so he offered to be examined on a table in the office, loosened his shirt and made Professor Smythe laugh by insisting on being examined right there and then.'

Because the disease was too advanced to be cured another decision was taken early. Chemotherapy in this case could not provide a miraculous remedy. But it might delay the cancer's progress and would need only to be administered in its mildest dosage.

If there was a small corner of ego in Bobby's make-up it concerned his appearance. He had no conception of himself as a handsome man but he liked not only to dress well but also to present a pleasing, clean-cut image.

Chemotherapy of this order would not necessarily be accompanied by loss of hair, weight or a healthy complexion. Bobby had maintained his daily training since retiring from professional football, and so continued, as normal, with the jogging, squash and golf which gave him so much pleasure and enjoyment.

Stephanie went with him. Everywhere. To the hospital, across the fields and into the gym: 'I was determined to support Bobby at every appointment and every X-ray. I had always enjoyed sports like squash but I didn't like jogging. So I got to like jogging. I went running with him and it became a therapeutic part of our life.'

So purposefully did Bobby rebuild his strength, fitness and outward appearance of good health that few doubted the Moore family's insistence that all fears of cancer were unfounded and he was on the road to full recovery.

'We didn't like not telling the truth,' said Bobby. 'But we had no option if we were to enjoy the rest of our life in the way we wanted.'

To almost everyone Bobby appeared to be spectacularly on the mend. He was back on the golf course, thrashing us. He was back at his Capital Gold radio microphone, alive with constructive criticism of contemporary football. Few detected how cleverly he was balancing his social life with his rehabilitation.

The lower public profile Bobby had adopted since finding Stephanie enabled him to negotiate his diary of engagements diplomatically. When my turn came to be 50, in February 1992, they came to dinner at Simpson's-in-the-Strand with fellow football personalities Terry Venables, George Graham and Bobby Keetch, French rugby union legend Jean-Pierre Rives and one or two close colleagues with all their ladies. But he asked to be excused drinks the following evening because of a pressing family commitment.

In fact, he was due in Edinburgh but no way would he have said so. Not least for fear of spoiling the party.

The most important function of all took place on Wednesday December 4, 1991.

Two weeks earlier they had been driving along King's Road when Bobby suddenly stopped the car outside Chelsea Town Hall and suggested they check the arrangements for a marriage ceremony. Another beautiful and ultimately rewarding experience was being plucked from adversity.

The registrar co-operated with their request for secrecy. Among the very few present from outside the family, my wife and myself were honoured to act as witnesses. It was a simple and moving ceremony at which Stephanie looked radiantly lovely in a white suit and Bobby, as well-suited as always, positively exuded happiness.

It was a delight to see them and to lunch afterwards in a charming private dining room at The Ritz overlooking a sun-kissed Green Park. It was a measure of how thoroughly Bobby had come to terms with his ailment that he said to me that day: 'I regard myself as a very, very lucky man.' Stephanie, likewise: 'It's me who is the fortunate one.'

Long before the fact of their union became public they were safely away on what was really one of their many honeymoons.

The opportunities to travel to faraway places provided Bobby with an abundant source of distraction. So did his radio commentary work which kept him vitally in touch with football.

It was with Capital Gold that he went to Sweden in his last summer of '92, analysing the sorry performances which led to England's early return home from the European Championship Finals, spending more rewarding time with his new wife and playing golf with new-found colleagues in the commentary and press boxes.

By keeping their secret, by sparing themselves the inevitable questions and curious intrusions, by avoiding self-pity and the sympathy of others, they were able to minimise the anxiety and continue living a good life. 'In a bitter-sweet way,' says Stephanie, 'the last two years were the very best years of our time together. It was a full, happy and normal life with its enjoyment intensified by the circumstances.

They spent his last New Year's Eve dining with Malcolm and Lyn Allison and playing with little Gina, the apple of Malcolm's paternal eye and the Moores' god-daughter.

Bobby still looked fit and well and Malcolm was surprised to see him take some tablets. 'In fact they were only vitamin pills,' says Stephanie. 'They were part of the fitness regime he kept going right up to the last few days.'

As late as January they were able to take another sunshine holiday, this time at Palm Beach in Florida: 'Bobby was very happy. He golfed. He still swam 20 lengths of the pool every day and although he sometimes looked as if he had run a marathon afterwards he enjoyed the exercise and felt better for it.'

In February, not long after their return, the first faintly visible signs of a deterioration in Bobby's condition led them to ask me to issue the first of the two statements which touched such a powerful nerve of compassion in the outside world.

As for Mr. Moore, off he went on his valedictory tour of the Royal Garden Hotel, Wembley Stadium and, although not quite making it in person but in his heart, West Ham United.

At Wembley he was touched by the warmth and sensitivity of everyone he encountered, from old friends and acquaintances to complete strangers. Still upright, still commanding deference and respect, he went to join his co-commentator Jonathan Pearce at the microphone and express his opinion of an England victory over San Marino which was a somewhat laboured match despite the 6–0 scoreline.

Stephanie says: 'Being actively involved in football as a commentator was one of his real pleasures. He was determined to continue as long as possible. I was concerned about the effort it required of him to go to Wembley that evening but Roberta and I went with him and we were so proud of how wonderfully he handled everything. Then he made us laugh by getting out of the car and directing the traffic out of the car park.'

The bond between the couple and Bobby's grown up children had grown ever stronger through the crisis and they spent the last few days and nights together in peace and affection illuminated by Bobby's shafts of wry humour. They refused the routine medical advice for him to be moved to hospital.

'Bobby left us with a lasting image of his dignity and courage,' says Stephanie. 'I want it to be known that there was no pain and that when we announced that he had died peacefully surrounded by his family, it was absolutely true.'

Not once had he asked, 'Why me?' Not once had he said, 'It's not fair'. Not once had he even complained of feeling unwell.

The tributes were lavish without exception but one or two of their authors, perhaps surprised by the unexpected depths of their own emotions, sought to conceal a faint sense of embarrassment by reminding themselves that Bobby Moore 'while a wonderful human being was not a saint'.

'In that,' said Stephanie, 'they were mistaken.'

27

We All Need a Hero

The homage was at its most profound in the East End. The whole world was mourning the loss of a hero at a time when men who could attract modest admiration were in desperately dwindling supply in all walks of public life.

But West Ham had lost one of their own. The favourite son.

First to come to the gates at Upton Park was someone with his own most prized possession, a No. 6 shirt in the famous claret and blue. He hung it on the railings and then, slowly at first but gathering the momentum of an avalanche, the shrine grew.

Men brought their scarves, the bobble hats which kept them warm on cold match nights, more shirts. Women laid flowers. Boys propped their toy mascots against the walls. It piled up and then it spread to encompass the ground in a wreath of affection and respect. Its path was picked out in handwritten poems which expressed in heartfelt, if often half-rhyming, couplets much of what the public felt about the majesty of the footballer and the dignity of the man.

It took on the appearance of Anfield whenever Liverpool, the city or the football club, has been stricken by tragedy. And, yes, as the community came to pay its tribute not only women but grown men wept.

Yet it had a character all its own. Something more hopeful. The sense of loss was relieved by an instinctive feeling that by his passing Bobby Moore had rekindled the flame of nobler values, uncommon decency, higher aspirations.

Some kept a vigil at the gates. Many made the pilgrimage

to Sunderland for West Ham's next match and applauded the
Wearsiders for their reverence through the minute's silence which
was observed, for the most part uninterrupted by hardly so much
as a cough, across the country and around the planet. The whole
world of football wore a black armband.

While Wembley pondered which part of the famous stadium
might be most fitting to bear Moore's name West Ham prepared
to dedicate their new stand to his memory.

Two rivers flowed into London, one brimming with accla-
mation for the man, the other swollen by donations to those
fighting the disease which had plucked him from our midst. East
London, especially, opened its pockets as well as its heart.

Stephanie promised to pay her first visit to a West Ham match
once she had attended to the funeral. Then, on Saturday March 6
in company with Roberta and Dean and as the guests of Peter
Storrie, a Bobby Moore fan since his boyhood on the old chicken
run terraces and now managing director, she duly fulfilled her
pledge to West Ham.

Before beating Wolves to sustain their challenge for promotion
to the Premier League, by its name alone the echelon in which all
Moore's teams ought to play by right, West Ham paid further
supplication.

The No. 6 was not worn. Who could hope to have filled it on
such a day? Instead, accompanied by Greenwood, Hurst, Peters
and other Hammers among those closest to him in his pomp, an
appropriately king-size replica of that shirt was carried to the
centre circle. It was made from flowers and again the tears flowed.

The Queen sent Stephanie a telegram of condolence in which
she also remembered Bobby captaining her country to its finest
football hour. Hardly surprising. She had, after all, handed him
the World Cup and then his O.B.E.

The flag at the Football Association headquarters in Lancaster
Gate was not the only standard which flew at half mast.

From learned professors in human behaviour to rough-hewn
graduates of the university of the London streets, our society
strove to interpret why Moore's death had struck such a universal
chord. Perhaps it was because the last hero was the first to go.

George Cohen won his own huge battle with stomach cancer,
Gordon Banks might have lost more than an eye in his motor

accident, Ray Wilson is an undertaker. But that is as close as any of the other boys of '66 had come to death.

Not only was Bobby survived by most of his contemporaries – Pele, Beckenbauer, Charlton, Eusebio and their galaxy of kindred greats – but even by those elder statesmen at whose collective knee he had learned his craft, Greenwood and Winterbottom, Allison and Ramsey.

Stephanie was 43, Roberta 28, Dean 25 and the distinguished company in which they grieved added yet more poignancy but still no rational explanation for such a widespread sense of loss.

That, finally, was forthcoming not from some occupant of high office but from a sweet old lady in Wimbledon Village. Mrs. Mary Smith wrote to Mrs. Stephanie Moore offering to donate to the relevant charity her copyright of a song written and recorded in the Sixties by her nephew Jimmy Scott.

The title said it all: *We All Need A Hero.*

Epilogue

The morning of Tuesday, March 2, 1993 dawned cold and grey, as if in mourning.

One memorial match was being planned for West Ham, perhaps another at Wembley, Westminster Abbey was readying itself for another state occasion, the subsequent service of thanksgiving for the life of Bobby Moore.

But the funeral was a private affair. A whole world of celebrities, each one cherishing a genuine affection for the man, respected the request to stay away.

The media crush of which the family had been so apprehensive was restricted to a handful of photographers, each of whom kept a decent distance down the pathway to the crematorium at Putney Vale.

The man's dignity was exerting a calming influence, still.

Some 30 members of the family were present, those who had travelled from East London having paused to reflect upon the homage at West Ham's ground. That dedicated number was augmented only by the best friend of each of Stephanie, Roberta and Dean.

His wife, daughter and son had nerved themselves for the last goodbye and their composure matched his own in such moments of emotional duress.

Dean, who had been a pillar of strength at the end, deferred to Stephanie and Roberta for the readings. The hymns *Land of All Hopefulness* and *Who Would True Valour See* were sung unfalteringly. Canon John Cox led the prayers.

A stirring rendition of *Jerusalem* cleared the throat, mercifully. It was my privilege to deliver the eulogy and it helped steady the voice to focus on the upright and unwavering manner in which he would have expected it to be spoken.

No words are ever enough, and many of those spoken that day should remain within the pristine walls of that simple chapel. Yet some of those sentiments would have been familiar to his public:

'He was a human being in all the goodness which that description is supposed to imply: unselfish ... protective ... loyal ... a gentle-man and a gentle man.'

To every man, finally, his epitaph. And when John Keats wrote his own he also served the memory of Robert Frederick Chelsea Moore:

'I have served the principle of beauty
And had the time to make my friends remember me with pride.'

Chronology

Born April 12, 1941	Robert Frederick Chelsea Moore, only son of Robert and Doris Moore, at Upney Hospital, Barking.
Educated	Barking Primary; Tom Hood School, Leyton.
1958	Turned professional for West Ham shortly after seventeenth birthday.
1962	May: Moore, 21, won his first England cap in a World Cup warm-up match in Lima against Peru. Played in all four World Cup matches in Chile, ending with the 2–1 quarter final defeat against Brazil.
	June 30: married Elizabeth Dean at the Church of St. Clemence, Ilford.
1963	October, Wembley: played for England against the Rest of the World.
1964	May: captained West Ham in their first F.A. Cup victory at Wembley against Preston North End.
	May: elected Footballer of the Year.
1965	January 24: Roberta Moore born.
	May: led West Ham to victory in European Cup Winners' final at Wembley against TSV Munich.
1966	July 30, Wembley: led England to World Cup triumph against West Germany, 4–2 after extra time.
1967	Awarded O.B.E. for services to football.
1968	March 24: Dean Moore born.
1970	May 26: Moore falsely accused of stealing bracelet in Bogota, Columbia, on eve of World Cup finals in Mexico. Remained in

Columbia after being arrested, released May 29.

Joins Sir Alf Ramsey's squad in Guadalajara, Mexico. Played against Brazil, losing 1–0. Despite Pele saying to Moore, 'see you in the final,' England lost 3–2 in the quarter finals to West Germany in Leon, after being two goals up.

1973   November: played last match for England in a friendly against Italy at Wembley – his 108th cap, a record until Peter Shilton's 125. Moore also won eight England under-23 caps and a record 18 England Youth caps. Captained England 90 times, during which period the international team lost only 13 matches.

1974   March 14: left Upton Park for Craven Cottage after 16 seasons with West Ham. During his West Ham career Moore played a record 642 first team matches, 544 in First Division and 98 in assortment of cups.

March 19: debut for Fulham against Middlesbrough, doubling Craven Cottage crowd to 18,000.

1975   May: helped Fulham reach their first F.A. Cup final in the all-cockney showdown against his old club at Wembley. West Ham won 2–0.

1976   Summer: played for San Antonio Thunder in American N.A.S.L.

June: played against England XI in Philadelphia for Team America in a bi-centenary fixture. Pele also in Team America. England won 3–1.

1977   Played his 1,000th senior match, and last for Fulham; 15 F.A. Cup appearances, 11 League Cup – 150 altogether.

1978   Played for Seattle Sounders.

1979	Manager of Oxford City (non-League). Left 1981.
1983	Coached Eastern Athletic (Hong Kong) for nearly six months.
1984	March: manager Southend United F.C. Left April, 1986.
1986	January 6: divorced by Tina Moore.
1990	Joined Capital Gold radio as match analyst, where he worked until his death.
1991	April 25: underwent operation for suspected cancer of the colon.
	December 4: married Susan (Stephanie) Lesley Parlane-Moore, at Chelsea Register Office.
1993	February 15: made public announcement of his illness.
	February 17: attended his last match at Wembley in a working capacity – England v. San Marino.
	February 24: died.
	March 2: family funeral at Putney Vale Crematorium.

Tributes to a Sporting Hero

Pele
: 'He was my friend as well as the greatest defender I ever played against. The world has lost one of its greatest football players and an honourable gentleman.'

Sir Alf Ramsey
: 'If people say England would not have won the World Cup without me as manager, I can say it would have been impossible without Bobby as captain. In so many ways he was my right-hand man, my lieutenant on the field, a cool, calculated footballer I could trust with my life.'

Ron Greenwood
: 'He epitomised everything a great footballer should be. He was a master on the pitch and an ambassador for the game off it.'

Eusebio
: 'As well as being a great man, he will always be an example for all sportsmen and sportswomen.'

Gary Lineker
: 'Bobby was a colossus. He won respect for the way he played and the manner in which he conducted himself.'

Franz Beckenbauer
: 'Bobby Moore was a real gentleman and a true friend.'

Geoff Hurst
: 'I followed him up the steps at Wembley three times. It was a privilege to have spent most of my career playing alongside him.

'He made himself a great player and the bigger the stage, the better he performed. If the world had played Mars, he would have been man of the match.'

Nobby Stiles	'He was a great captain and a great player. There was a great feeling in the team and it only seems like two minutes ago.'
Brian Clough	'Bobby did our game proud. He brought it grace and elegance. 'I wish I could have worked with him.'
David Platt	'He was a great person in every sense: a footballer of intelligence and vision, a man of dignity and stature. I admired and respected him immensely.'
Terry Venables	'I am devastated. Everything just seems meaningless compared to this. He was a brave man.'
Graham Taylor	'My enduring picture of Bobby Moore will always be of him lifting the World Cup in 1966. As a young professional player myself, that day he was captain of all of us, not just the England team.'
Billy Bonds	'The whole country will be saddened – but no more than in the East End. We talk about superstars, but he was the genuine article.'
Gerry Francis	'Bobby was the greatest England Captain of all time. People use the term nice guy a lot, but he was a genuine nice guy – a true nice guy.'
Bobby Charlton	'I am terribly shocked, even though I knew he was ill. I know that all football people in the country will miss him. he was a gentle man, he always did things with dignity and a bit of style. He was the most stylish of players.'
Gordon Banks	'We all remember him as a great player for both West Ham and England and we will all remember the happy and successful times.'

John Major   'One of the immortals of soccer. Bobby
                      will forever be remembered for leading
                      England to victory in the 1966 World Cup.
                      But he did much more than that. He
                      enhanced the sport by his example, behav-
                      iour and skill.'

Denis Law   'He was a good friend and a fine person. I
                      played against him many times for Scot-
                      land and in our club matches. It was always
                      a battle, not so much in the physical sense
                      but because Moore had such a superb brain.
                      Fifty-one is no age, is it? You feel you had
                      no chance to say goodbye.'

Index